TH
FOR P
FED U WITH DIETING

Every day many people start dieting. And every day almost as many give it up, bored with the routine of uninteresting food, irritated at the constant insult to their natural appetites, discouraged by their lack of noticeable progress.

Now, however, the situation has been dramatically changed. Dr. Irwin Stillman, co-author of the phenomenally successful THE DOCTOR'S QUICK WEIGHT LOSS DIET, shows how you can still enjoy meals—*and lose five, ten and even more pounds the first week*. More than that, he shows how without strenuous exercise, simply through the right foods, *you can take inches off* your ankles, thighs, hips, calves, buttocks, abdomen, arms and other strategic parts of your body to achieve a more beautiful figure than you ever thought possible.

You will find all this, and much more, in Dr. Stillman's great new diet book—

THE DOCTOR'S QUICK
INCHES-OFF DIET

THE DOCTOR'S QUICK INCHES-OFF DIET

By Irwin Maxwell Stillman,
M.D., D-IM
and
Samm Sinclair Baker

A DELL BOOK

Published by
DELL PUBLISHING CO., INC.
1 Dag Hammarskjold Plaza
New York, New York 10017

Dell ® TM 681510, Dell Publishing Co., Inc.

ISBN: 0-440-12043-8

Reprinted by arrangement with
Prentice-Hall, Inc.
Englewood Cliffs, New Jersey

Printed in U.S.A.
First Dell printing—July 1970
Fifth Dell printing—April 1971
Tenth Dell printing—February 1972
Fifteenth Dell printing—November 1972
Twentieth Dell printing—December 1974
Twenty-fifth Dell printing—June 1977
Twenty-sixth Dell printing—June 1978

CONTENTS

Dedicated to
your increasing beauty, health and happiness
as you take off inch
after inch
after inch. . . .

1

Rule One: Get Extra Inches and Pounds Off Quickly

"O, that this too too solid flesh would melt,
Thaw and resolve itself into a dew!"

Your unwanted overweight and bulky extra inches on "problem spots" on your body won't "melt" away nor "resolve into a dew" just by wishing it so. However, you *can* lose weight and inches so rapidly with my quick weight loss methods that it almost seems as though your flesh is melting away. This has been proved for hundreds of thousands of overweights . . . many of whom call mine the diets with *"instant rewards."*

Wishing will not make you slim, nor will balanced dieting methods where you lose a pound or so a week work with most overweights, as you have probably discovered most unhappily yourself. Nor will flabby advice such as that from a psychologist quoted in *The New York Times*: "Go to the hills, live in a cave and wear a slow wrist watch." Such suggestions may amuse you but won't reduce you.

That you *can* lose weight and stay at or near your ideal weight after that is proved by the overweights who have slimmed down with my quick weight loss recommendations, which can reduce you swiftly, pleasantly, healthfully and beautifully.

There is painful reality for many overweights in a magazine cartoon. It shows a heavy woman on a large scale in a store, the kind of scale that also tells fortunes on a card. The woman stands

1

on the scale, the pointer swings way over to indicate her excess weight, and a card falls into the slot with the single word on it: "HELP!" The help you want and need is on these pages.

Why you can succeed . . .

The key to *your* success, which has worked so well and has made the crucial difference for other overweights who had failed in the past, is that *you lose 5, 10 and more pounds a week* with my quick weight loss methods.

This is the "built-in will power" that works for you and makes your hopes for a slim, attractive figure finally come true. Instead of waiting hopelessly while you go from 140 to 139 pounds in a week, you can drop from 140 to 130 pounds, or even to 125 pounds, in one short week with my dieting methods.

The figure you admire can be your own—and not by dieting on and on, week after week and month after month for what seems like an eternity, but in a remarkably short time. How long it takes you to lose all your excess pounds depends on how over-weight you are.

Another asset of my quick weight loss methods is that you can use this successful, speedy way of reducing for the rest of your life. If you let yourself go for a week or so at a convention or cruise, or by indulging yourself, *you can take off that overweight in a week or less* by using my quick weight loss recommendations. You can do this safely, healthfully, with no harm but only good to your overweight body, as my successful dieters can testify.

Remember, these are *proved* methods, not theory or guess-work.

You benefit from my experience . . .

With the success of my preceding book, *The Doctor's Quick Weight Loss Diet,* I found myself speaking face-to-face with many thousands of men and women in television studio audiences, in bookstores, in auditoriums, all over the country. Before that I had successfully advised over 10,000 overweight patients across the desk in my office during my 45 years of medical practice.

Repeatedly I was asked questions which concerned these over-weights or members of their family or friends. The answers are in this book. I know that the information will help many. I hope and believe that my recommendations will help you finally to get rid of your own excess pounds and extra inches—no matter how many times you may have failed in the past.

Please READ this book thoroughly . . .

It is important to yourself, and it is vital to me, since your successful reducing is of great concern to me, that you read not only the details of the Inches-Off Diet and other diets here, but also this entire book. Each page can be of definite added value to you in helping to convince you thoroughly as to why you should get down to your ideal weight for health, beauty and youthful vitality.

You will learn why you should start dieting *now*, why you should then go on keeping your weight down and your dimensions trim. You will read how you can take proper precautions as on any diet, and how to overcome temptations and problems faced by many overweights. You will absorb the how's and why's and wherefore's of the ways my quick weight loss ·and inches-off methods will work for you.

The more you read, the better are the chances that you will lose weight rapidly, slim down problem spots and stay slim and trim. I tell you on page after page what I tell office patients and overweights whom I meet face to face. You will find some points, recommendations and instructions repeated again and again in various chapters. This is done purposefully. I find that it is often necessary to repeat statements and details to overweight patients in order to have them sink in so they can get the slimming results they want. Furthermore, since you may be returning to sections of the book for rereading (rather than reading straight through as with a novel), I'd rather repeat than have you overlook or bypass vital, helpful information.

In addition to the actual diet details, you will find much helpful guidance and many recommendations throughout these pages. All combine to help you live a slimmer, healthier, longer life. You will learn to turn aside common myths that keep so many overweights from reducing because they give in to false fears and empty excuses.

I have spent most of a lifetime in learning how to reduce people burdened by overweight. That is my lifelong crusade. By giving a few hours to reading and rereading all my recommendations, you can benefit through years of greater attractiveness and more healthful living.

Profit in good health as well as beauty . . .

A lot of nonsense has been written about people, women especially, wanting to be slim because fashion authorities and advertisers have set up standards of beauty to which they feel pressured to conform. This is utterly untrue. It provides just another excuse for some overweights to keep them from avoiding steps to remove the flab.

A noted medical researcher, tracing the course of what has been considered the "ideal human figure" through history, concludes that the current ideal of the *slim* figure did not evolve by chance. Nor was it due to fashion or advertising pressures. Actually, more billions have been expended by advertisers to get people to eat more, more, more of numberless brands of tempting foods rather than toward dieting and taking off weight.

The true basic reason for the desire to be slim, the scholar maintains, is that *"slenderness gradually came to be equated with good health."*

Have you any doubts personally that medical facts prove that the individual at ideal weight generally has a better chance for good health and longer life than the overweight? The medical and other statistics given later provide convincing evidence that it is much healthier to be slim.

Overweight . . . a DOUBLE problem . . .

Many people who are overweight have a double problem. When they take the pounds off effectively with my quick weight loss methods, or by any other way that works for them, some inches of bulk come off along with the loss of weight. But for a good many individuals, women particularly, certain "problem spots" remain bulkier than they like. These trouble spots are mostly the muscle-mass areas—oversize buttocks, hips, stomach (abdomen actually), shoulders, arms and wrists, legs, thighs, calves and ankles.

I have devised and perfected a simple method for reducing and taking off a good many of those *extra* inches for thousands of my patients with that problem. This is the *Inches-Off Diet,* an easy, pleasant, healthful dieting procedure which will be told to you in simple, clear detail in the chapters that follow. The Inches-Off Diet should work for you, even after you are down to your ideal weight, as it has done for those under my personal care. This method, followed exactly as advised, can slim and

These drawings from photographs show the main problem spots on the body where the Inches-Off Diet reduces and smooths out bulges for a slimmer, far more attractive figure from back, front and side views. Inches-Off Dieting can accomplish reduction of dimensions for men as well as women.

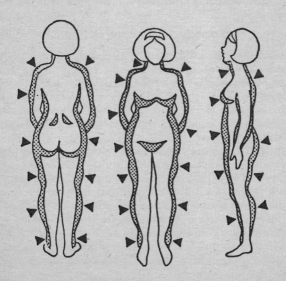

trim problem spots on your figure, smoothing out dimensions that have plagued you through all your adult years.

There is a saying, as one example of the difficulty of smoothing out extra inches that are piled on the body, that "French-fried potatoes remain in the mouth for several seconds . . . in the stomach for several hours . . . and on the hips for the rest of one's life." Many of my patients had the same idea: It would be too difficult to take off extra inches that had been piled on year after year by eating too much. That need not be the case for you anymore.

My Inches-Off Diet has worked excellently for men and women who found, as you may have, that such methods as strenuous exercising, massage, electrical devices and so on do *not* take the inches off problem spots and keep them off. That's why I created the Inches-Off Diet. This dieting, plus the specific moderate exercises I recommend later, work wonderfully together.

This cannot be emphasized too strongly or too often: While my Inches-Off dieting recommendations alone can take off the extra inches, exercising alone cannot accomplish what you want.

Trimming in two stages . .

Trimming off the extra inches from problem spots is done in two stages if you are overweight.

First, you get down to your ideal weight in a hurry by using my basic Quick Weight Loss Diet, or one of the other quick weight loss diets in this book, including the quick Inches-Off Diet—whatever you find you prefer after reading the details of each diet.

Second, after you are at your ideal weight, if you want to take extra inches off what you consider are oversize areas on your body, you go on the Inches-Off Diet as instructed in detail.

Once you discover and use my methods, overweight and oversize dimensions need never again be a problem for you. You can look forward to a more beautiful figure and a healthier, more vigorous and therefore happier life. I must make it clear that because individuals vary in the way they are built, I cannot promise everyone a figure of Miss America or Mr. America proportions.

I can assure you that the Inches-Off Diet will reduce your dimensions in the problem spots, as well as in your total weight, to the minimum possible in your individual case. If you follow the instructions given in this book, you are bound to be delighted with the results that you see in the mirror, unclothed and clothed.

At this point, you might like to take a snapshot of your unclothed figure in the mirror (or have someone take your photo) before you start dieting along with the mild exercising I recommend. Or take a photo in a scanty bathing suit. Watch how the inches vanish rapidly from week to week as the pounds come off. Take a similar snapshot of your figure when you are down to your ideal weight. Compare the before and after photos. You will be thrilled by the remarkable improvement in your figure, along with the wonderful feeling of improved attractiveness, slimness and greater vigor and gracefulness.

How much should YOU weigh?

More and more over the years I have become convinced that the "average" weight tables you usually see are too high. An enormous percentage of the population is overweight; estimates run to figures as high as 50 percent and more—far more than the percentage of people who are obviously underweight (not counting uncivilized or starvation areas).

Accordingly, when you average the weights of hundreds or thousands of adults, you come up with an "average" figure that includes so many overweights that the final "average" is more than an individual should weigh in order to attain his ultimate in good health and good looks.

The following is what I recommend to my patients now and to you as to the "ideal weight" you should strive to reach and maintain, figured according to your height. My recommended figures here are a little lower than those given in previous years.

IDEAL WEIGHT AND CALORIE TABLE

These figures provide a guide for adults and young adults, women and men.

According to your height, you will find your ideal weight here.

I suggest that you measure your height as of now, for most people tend to tell a physician that they are taller than they actually are, while they usually claim that they weigh less than the scale shows.

Alongside your height and ideal weight, you will find the number of calories you can consume daily to stay at your ideal weight once you are down to it. The correct figures for you personally may vary some, but certainly no more than 10 percent higher than the number of pounds and calories I suggest for ideal weight according to your height.

The numbers listed are based on the unclothed body for weight, and without shoes for height.

WOMEN			MEN		
Height	Weight	Calories	Height	Weight	Calories
5'0"	98	1000	5'0"	105	1300
5'1"	100	1100	5'1"	110	1350
5'2"	105	1200	5'2"	115	1400
5'3"	110	1250	5'3"	120	1450
5'4"	115	1300	5'4"	125	1500
5'5"	120	1350	5'5"	130	1550
5'6"	125	1400	5'6"	135	1600
5'7"	128	1450	5'7"	140	1650
5'8"	133	1500	5'8"	145	1700
5'9"	138	1550	5'9"	150	1750
5'10"	140	1600	5'10"	155	1800
5'11"	145	1650	5'11"	157	1820
6'0"	150	1680	6'0"	160	1850
6'1"	155	1700	6'1"	165	1900
6'2"	160	1750	6'2"	170	1950
			6'3"	173	1980
			6'4"	175	2000
			6'5"	178	2050
			6'6"	180	2100

While these weight figures, compared with "average" weight tables, may seem low to you, it may be of interest to note some other significant numbers. The average beauty contestant in a

recent USA Pageant was 5'7" in height and weighed 121 pounds
... 7 pounds less than my ideal weight figures. The winner was
5'9" in height and weighed 127 pounds ... 11 pounds less than
my ideal weight figure. One reason for this lower weight is that
models and personalities, who appear in photographs and on television, tend to look heavier through the camera's eye than they
actually are, therefore such women often prefer to be even slimmer than ideal weight.

Good health is the goal I use for these weights according to
height. In my experience, these ideal weights, which admittedly
are low according to many other tables, are the best to permit
and promote most efficient and healthful functioning of the body
and organs for a longer, more healthful lifetime for adult men
and women.

If you weigh 20 percent or more over your ideal weight as set
down here, you are not only overweight but dangerously so. In
other words, if you are a woman who is 5 feet 4 inches tall, your
ideal weight is 115 pounds. Even 10 pounds above that is a drag
on your health, so if you are 125 pounds on the scale, you should
start trimming off the extra fat now.

If you are 20 percent over, that is, over 135 pounds, you are
not only giving up a lot of good looks of which you could be
proud, but you are also risking serious illness as you burden your
body and your organs with excess fat. At 150 pounds for your
height, you are classified as "obese," and you are permitting your
health to be subjected to breakdown and your life to be shortened drastically. Is any amount of overeating worth that?

How to avoid heart attacks . . .

"Control your weight" to help avoid heart attacks . . . that's
one primary rule stressed again and again by the American Heart
Association in advising men and women. Yes, women also are increasingly subject to heart attacks, especially when overweight
and over age 45.

You, like most others, probably think of overweight just as
layers of fat on your middle, hips, buttocks, all over your body.
You know that your heart and other organs must work extra
strenuously to carry the extra burden of overweight pounds,

whether those extra pounds are fat or muscle. You may not realize that fat also gets into the blood and can clog up arteries to bring on heart attacks and death.

The frightening evidence increases each year, spotlighting the menacing effect of overweight in relation to heart disease. This is a most serious problem facing everyone since there are over a half-million heart-attack victims each year in the U.S. alone. Overweight is not the only factor in heart attacks, of course, but it is certainly a major factor.

Cholesterol deposits formed in the lining of blood vessels tend to narrow them and make the blood vessels more likely to be blocked by a clot (thrombus). Such blocking when it occurs in a heart artery results in a heart attack (coronary thrombosis). When the arteries are narrowed by the slow accumulation of fat, this is called atherosclerosis. By any names, they all spell *danger*. Since fatty deposits may start in early years, the sooner you switch to low-fat intake and remove excess weight, the better are your chances to avoid heart disease and heart attacks.

In a careful, detailed study in Norway of over 400 men who had been victims of heart attacks, half the number were placed on diets low in saturated fats and cholesterol. The other half continued eating "normally," as they had done before the attacks, which is the way most Americans eat. In the next five years there were *over twice as many deaths* among those who ate "normally," compared with those on the corrected low-fat, low-cholesterol eating.

"There is little doubt," according to the Heart Disease Control Program of the U.S. Public Health Service, "that the association between overweight and mortality is real." In other words, if you are overweight, you are more likely to die younger, by a good many *years*, than if you live a vigorous life at ideal weight.

Overweight is a menace and a drag even if you regard yourself as a "very healthy" individual. The dangers increase in cases of high blood pressure, heart disease as stated, diabetes and other major and minor illnesses and disabilities. Excess fat impedes surgery and may be a crucial factor in success and recovery from surgical procedures.

The dramatic drawings that follow reveal another fact that may come to you as a shock. These drawings of human hearts are made from actual photographs. The heart at the left is of a person of ideal weight—there is little or no visible fat on the organ. The heart at the right is of a considerably overweight individual, and you will see that it is almost completely covered by a heavy layer of fat. This confining fat burdens the organ, impedes its most efficient functioning and places the person in grave danger of serious heart troubles, attacks and worse.

Another shocking fact of life or death is that the heart of the

Simplified Diagram-Drawings from Actual Photographs of Hearts

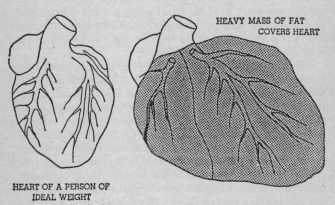

HEAVY MASS OF FAT
COVERS HEART

HEART OF A PERSON OF
IDEAL WEIGHT

HEART OF A CONSIDERABLY
OVERWEIGHT PERSON

Heart of very overweight person at right weighs *almost 3 times as much* as heart at left of a person at ideal weight. The overweight heart is covered by layers of fat. Muscle is considerably enlarged. Less blood flows to "overweight" heart.

overweight (at right) ·weighs *almost three times as much* as the heart of the individual of ideal weight!

Even if you don't care about your overweight appearance or about the discomfort of carrying around extra pounds, can you afford the risk of continuing to coat your heart and other organs with heavy, choking layers of fat? Shouldn't you take action immediately to dissolve that fat and live more healthful, more vigorous years— as well as taking inches off your figure? You can do both in a short time with my quick weight loss methods— simple, safe, healthful.

Following instructions faithfully is one of the key factors, perhaps the basic most important point, in reducing successfully. Unless followed exactly, most diets (mine or others) will fail. On my diets, I ask you to proceed according to my instructions for just one week to start. That's because I know from experience that the result, *quick weight loss,* is all the encouragement and "will power" you need to keep dieting. You know that you'll keep losing pounds and inches rapidly.

After you are down to your ideal weight, you can relax some, indulge occasionally in forbidden foods, and deviate a little from the exact rules. But I have found, and I believe you will too, that the successful dieter—once down to ideal weight—doesn't gamble away his "profits" or risk a return to a heavy, flabby, unhealthy existence, but instead follows the rules to stay slim.

Calorie count to maintain the ideal weight for your height, once you attain the desired slimness, is figured in general as 11 calories per pound of weight for women. Thus, a woman at height 5'4" is figured at 115 pounds ideal weight, times 11 calories per pound, a total of about 1300 calories a day.

For men, I figure about 11½ calories per pound of weight. By this rule, a man at height 5'10" is at ideal weight at 155 pounds, times 11½ calories per pound, a total of about 1800 calories a day.

Total calories to keep you at your ideal weight may vary somewhat from the figures in the table, but not very much. A calorie, as you probably know, is a unit of measurement of the amount of energy provided by the foods you eat. Different foods supply different amounts of what comes under the broad term of "energy." As you move, walk, exercise, get involved in any activity, such as sweeping a floor or working around a machine, you use up "units of energy," or calories.

If you take in more calories generally than you expend with your activities, the body stores up the calories in the form of fat. If your calorie intake exceeds your calorie output day after day and week after week, you pile on pounds of fat and you layer in the fat in your body's storage centers. To lose weight, you must take in fewer calories than you use up daily.

By this process, as happens in my quick weight loss diets rapidly and very efficiently, your body uses up pound after pound of stored fat, pulling it out of the storage depots by natural functioning. You lose weight in a hurry. When you are down to your ideal weight, you stay that way by balancing your calorie intake with your calorie output, according to the figures listed here. Remember that calories not only count, but they also add and multiply if you're not on guard constantly. Check your weight on the bathroom scale first thing each morning.

Of course, how much you should eat to keep your ideal weight is the simplest thing to determine. If the amounts and types of foods you eat tend to increase your weight, cut down on calories. If you are going under your ideal weight, just increase the number of calories you consume daily.

Soon you will find the balance between intake and output of calories, and you can maintain that quite naturally and comfortably without even counting the calories in each portion and meal. Remember that the more active you are the more calories you use up daily. Therefore you can eat more and still stay at ideal weight. However, activity or exercise alone won't reduce you, no matter how vigorously you work or exercise. If you are taking in more calories in food daily than you are using up, then you will put on excess pounds.

You cannot see a calorie but you certainly can see the results of piling in too many of them when you eat. You can see it in the weight figures on the bathroom scale each morning. You can see the excess in the extra inches around your stomach, hips, buttocks, thighs, shoulders, arms and legs, all over your body. If you don't watch your daily calorie intake, you are soon bound to be in the unhappy state of watching your body swell to unattractive and unhealthy proportions. A man said unhappily about his wife, "After we were married, she not only kept her figure, she doubled it!"

Do *"small, medium and large frame"* factors mean much in computing what you should weigh? Many weight tables give the numbers according to size of frame, but I have found this undesirable in my practice and in advising overweights anywhere. The average individual cannot determine whether his or her frame is anatomically "small, medium, or large."

I have learned unhappily that when you give a person a chart with three sets of ideal weight figures, according to size of frame, the result is disastrous. If she (or he) is overweight, she will invariably indulge herself by using the "large frame" figures as her guide, even though actually she has a "small frame." That is human nature. In most cases even the "large frame" figures make her an overweight. (I only allow 5 pounds extra weight for patients with big bone structure.)

Unfortunately I have seen too many cases of people running into trouble, often serious health problems, because of this one factor. They have permitted themselves to be burdened by excess fat because they are unrealisticly following the "large frame" numbers. It is not a laughing matter when the result can be a flabby figure and ill health due to excess weight.

My experience has guided me in deciding in this book to give you one set of numbers as a guide to your ideal weight rather than the usual wide range of numbers. Here again I have learned too convincingly that most people always use the *top* number rather than the lower or the one in-between. For example, when a weight table states to the woman of 5'4" that her "desirable weight range" is 112-132 pounds (I'm looking at the printed numbers in a "weight guide" in my hand), she is likely to permit herself at least 130 pounds. I consider her to be about 15 pounds above ideal weight. Her mirror will also show that she is a chubby overweight, looking years older than she should, much to her consternation if she is honest with herself.

When are you overweight? Many ingenious tests for self-analysis have been devised which are intended to help you decide whether or not you are overweight. One of these is the "pinch test," or "skinfold test." In this test, you grasp the skin of either arm midway between the elbow and shoulder with your fingers. Pull the skin away from the underlying muscle and hold between the fingers. For this test it is usually stated that if the fold of skin between your fingers is more than one-half to one inch in diameter, you should consider yourself overweight.

The pinch test is of some value to physicians in checking the amount of fat and overweight, usually with the use of special instruments. The doctor may also check skinfold thicknesses on the chin, back, chest, waist, abdomen and knee as well as the arm. He considers the age of the patient and whether woman or man, as well as a variety of other factors.

Another method that has been devised by researchers to gauge whether you are fat is this: They suggest that you measure your *height* in inches, then measure your *waistline* in inches. If there is a difference of 36 inches, they consider that "normal." A difference of 38 inches or more shows "a tendency toward leanness." A difference of 33 or less "indicates obesity." While this is a generally fair gauge, I have found it to be misleading in at least 10 percent of cases, since a person who is heavy in all places with the exception of a small waistline would be considered "normal" by this guide but "overweight" in my judgment.

To decide whether you are overweight, a look in the mirror and at my ideal weight chart will give you the answer instantly. Let the bathroom scale be your guide, according to your height and my recommended ideal weight.

How much can you vary from my ideal weights? I recommend that you permit yourself no more than 5 pounds over your ideal weight as a woman, and no more than 10 pounds over your ideal weight as a man. When you see the pounds creeping up on you, go on my Inches-Off or Quick Weight Loss diets and get back to your ideal weight rapidly. Then reduce your daily intake of calories until you stay steadily at that number.

Should men weigh more than women? You will note that at the same height, a man is permitted more pounds than a woman. There are basic overall reasons for this. A man is allowed more pounds because his skeletal structure, bones and muscles, are generally larger than a woman's of the same height. Men tend to metabolize faster, burning up food and calories more quickly and readily than women.

Elderly people, whose metabolism has gone down as much as 20 to 40 percent over the years, do not burn up food and calories as quickly as in earlier years. If you are in this category, you will have to watch your weight extra carefully in order to keep down your consumption of food and calories lest you pile on unwanted, potentially harmful pounds. I urge you to stay at the suggested ideal weight or a few pounds below.

You will probably find that you should eat fewer calories than in the ideal weight listing because you burn them up less quickly. I suggest that you have your doctor measure your height (which is usually part of the general examination) at your next checkup; make a note of it because, especially as we grow older, we are apt to think we are taller than the current measurement usually shows us to be in actuality.

It is important for most everyone to become slim and stay slim, but it is especially vital for the elderly. Ideal weight or under is an essential for the older person for the sake of maintaining and promoting maximum health, vigor and long life. Overweight pounds may put a crucial strain on the continuing well-being of the elderly person.

Don't blame "personal metabolism problems" automatically for your overweight, as so many "fatties" do very glibly and falsely. If you have any medical disorder, such as an abnormal thyroid function that may pile on the pounds no matter how little you eat, your doctor will tell you so when he examines you. The medical facts show that a minimum of 95 percent are normal in this area. Only 5 percent, that's only one out of every 20 persons, have some physiological disorder that keeps them from losing weight on low calorie intake.

If you have a disorder, by all means give your physician the opportunity to try to correct it immediately. If you go on stuffing yourself with excess food and calories and blaming some mysterious physical cause that is exclusive in your case—in spite of a medical examination that proves you are normal in this respect—then you have only yourself to blame for your overweight.

There is no point in grumbling, "I eat less than my husband and he stays slim while I keep gaining weight." Over my years of medical practice I have checked thousands of overweight patients with this type of complaint. While it is a fact that the metabolism of individuals differs, *the person who is getting fatter is consuming far more calories than needed or than she (or he) will admit.*

Don't excuse yourself because of somebody else's case. Face the fat and the facts in your own mirror. You *can* change that reflection in the mirror to a trimmer, more attractive and happier one, starting now. Every statistic proves that you are not ship-shape if you are shaped like a battleship.

See your personal physician. My recommendations should not be taken as replacing your doctor. I suggest that before you go on any diet, and at reasonable intervals thereafter, you should be checked by your physician. My advice is a supplement to his personal checkup, since I have the experience in reducing individuals that few doctors have.

As an internist greatly overweight a good many years ago, I suffered a severe heart attack. From my medical knowledge I realized that I had either to diet . . . or die. I perfected reducing methods that took more than 50 pounds off me very quickly. With my new slimness, health and vigor (which I have maintained through decade after decade), reducing overweight patients and thus saving their lives and good looks became my personal crusade.

Since my quick weight loss methods have worked for my overweight patients through the years, and for hundreds of thousands of others in the past few years, you can use them with the assurance that they will work for you.

How I talk to my patients . . .

Losing weight, I am convinced, is primarily going about it in the way that works, through quick weight loss methods. It helps to keep dieting, and to stay slim once you get down to ideal weight, to understand the all-important reasons for staying slim. This understanding helps provide motivation to get slim and stay slender and attractive. This is the way I have talked with my patients to help them succeed, and therefore the way I talk with you on these pages.

In my opinion, all women were born to be beautiful, to be as poised and graceful as possible for themselves as individuals.

The same applies to men, to make the most of their masculine good-looks potential. Charm, attractiveness and a slim figure go together. Most any man who lets himself get fat and ungainly, most any woman who lacks a graceful, lovely figure and the charm and self-assurance that usually accompany good looks, must blame himself or herself rather than anyone else. We can't all attain "perfection" but each of us can achieve his or her maximum potential of attractiveness.

You can acquire the desirable qualities of a slim, graceful figure by following my dieting instructions, and accompanying them with a little moderate exercise. You can attain your desired weight without too much self-denial, and certainly without monotonous and excessive exercise, which can do you about as much harm as good in relation to taking inches off.

Not just vanity . . .

It is not just vanity but personal pride and a constant search for greatest possible well-being that leads women particularly to want a lovely face without swelling and jowls, a slim, trim figure and slender, shapely legs. Compliments from others are always welcome and gratifying, whether from the same or the opposite sex.

It makes good sense to try to eliminate bulky buttocks and swelling hips, legs, thighs, calves, oversize shoulders and thick arms. Styles are designed to bring out the best in a figure free from unnecessary bulges. My combination of the Inches-Off Diet and a moderate amount of easy exercise daily can produce the desired more slender figure and more graceful legs, along with slimmer buttocks.

Now you can accomplish something with my methods that was not so readily possible before. "Piano legs," "cardplayer's table-like backside," other bulky figure faults should be smoothed out and even disappear when you work at it persistently. Clumsy, unappealing, heavy legs and thighs should be slimmed and many excess inches eliminated by following instructions to the letter. My methods are not difficult or time-consuming.

For every individual who inherited an unusually large frame, there are a hundred or more who brought on the bulges themselves. Your muscle masses can be reduced, bulges smoothed out and bulky lines slimmed down and replaced by graceful contours. The proper exercises can help, but always keep in mind that overexercise can be as inhibiting to having graceful legs, for example, as can excess fat or poor muscle tone due to lack of activity.

Who really knows about reducing?

It has been said that a little knowledge is a dangerous thing. Nevertheless, when it comes to the subject of reducing, most everybody seems ready to shoot off his mouth or hammer his typewriter as an authority. This bewilders those overweights who are earnestly and often desperately seeking an answer to the simple question: *"How can I take off excess pounds and inches?"*

Too many so-called reducing diets and methods are based on the observations of an individaul who is not a medical doctor, or on experiments with animals performed by nutritionists and scientists which the unknowing interpreter presents wrongly. Even when they encounter fallacies and contradictions in their recommendations and then in the unsatisfactory results, such diet "authorities," and even a few physicians, refuse to change their views. Thus, the overweight is left out on a limb and does not achieve success in reducing.

Quite the opposite, my quick weight loss and inches-off methods are based on 45 years of experience in reducing women and men of all ages, along with many overweight youngsters—and doing it *successfully.* For example, "balanced eating" recommendations to which many physicians adhere year after year are fine in theory but I discard them in practice because *they do not work.*

My aim always is to *get that weight off* for even my most frustrated overweight patients—and to do it safely, healthfully and *as quickly as possible.* The best proof that my quick reducing methods can work for you is that they have taken off millions of pounds for patients in my medical practice and for readers of my writings on the subject.

How much eating is overeating?

It is a sad fact of life that humans, unlike animals, don't eat just to keep body and soul together. Most people who are slender stop eating as soon as they feel full and comfortable. To most overweights a feeling of fullness and even of beginning to feel bloated is just an invitation to start packing in more food on top of all that's already been shoved into the abused stomach. Such "fatsos" are just as eager for the heaping second helping as if they had not eaten at all. Then, overweight and overstuffed, they grab the rich dessert as a reward for having already stuffed themselves almost beyond capacity.

Most all the excuses given by the overweight are empty, many of the alibis are ridiculous, as you'll realize from my answers "across the doctor's desk" in Chapter 11. Piling in the wrong calorie-rich foods and excessive quantities is dangerous. Don't believe claims that fat in the stomach satisfies more, results in fewer contractions and blocks the appetite and further overeating by staying in the stomach longer.

Others incorrectly blame the "appestat, habistat, glucostat" and other "whatnotstats" for overeating. The plain clear fact is that the overweight is indulging in excesses that he enjoys. He uses every possible and impossible excuse to keep from facing the truth: that he is overeating and indulging in calorie-heavy foods. For most overweights these harmful habits can be broken by my quick weight loss methods.

Fearful about malnutrition?

Most fears about dieting and a resultant malnutrition are without foundation. All my diets, all recommended for use during the reducing period to get you down to your ideal weight, contain plenty of everything the overweight needs. On most any diet, the overweight gets plenty of proteins, carbohydrates and fat for good health. If one or more of these elements are lacking in the actual food intake, the body is very adaptable, a "miracle" system that readily converts carbohydrate into fat if needed, fat into proteins, fat or proteins into carbohydrates.

Vitamin and mineral deficiency is thus very rarely present in the fat person. It can only occur if the individual stays on a strict reducing diet for a very prolonged period when he might just possibly develop a deficiency in a certain vitamin or mineral. This is easily prevented by taking a vitamin-mineral tablet daily when dieting, as I always recommend as an extra protective measure. That should be a sure antidote for the overweight who has any fears about bringing on such a deficiency due to dieting.

In the early stages of your dieting it is essential, as stated earlier, that you adhere to the instructions strictly. Once you have been on the diet for a while and are down to ideal weight and desired size, slimmed all over, you will have learned the approximate caloric values of foods. On Stay-Slim Eating you can adjust and switch foods within the caloric limits to suit yourself. If you go a few pounds over, then a few days on the Quick Weight Loss or Inches-Off diets will slim you down to ideal weight again.

Chances are, as with most of my reducing patients, that you will be able to adjust your eating habits to staying slim without even thinking about it once you have broken overeating and wrong eating habits. You will be one of those happy, slender individuals who has no feelings of being deprived of anything important in eating. You will be dieting unconsciously without realizing it, as you achieve your goal of staying slim, better-looking, healthier and more vigorous.

"Don't sit if you can stand . . ."

One of my first instructions, along with your dieting, is to get around as much as possible. Use your legs and your body actively. Don't sit if you can stand. Don't stand around looking for the most effortless way to do things. Move about—use that wonderful mechanism which is your body. It was designed for *action.*

Don't lie around sleeping for more than eight hours. By lying supine you are in effect adding extra calories and extra weight to your figure by not using up calories through motion. By being sedentary, your body tends to deteriorate into lazy, flabby flesh and ugly muscular formations. Inertia produces tiredness and fatigue—far more than the chance of getting tired from dieting properly and undertaking the right moderate exercising for only a few minutes per day. As you will learn again and again in taking inches off, flabby muscles, especially as they become enlarged from overeating and underexercising, are muscles stocked and swelled with excessive deposits of fat. Few people realize this.

I urge you to understand now, so that you will be self-convinced once and for all, that rapid weight reduction is not harmful or detrimental to your health, energy or well-being. If you are overweight, you have enough energy stored up in the fat depots of your body to keep you well supplied with this element for days, weeks and months. This has been proved in the cases of people lost or shipwrecked eating practically nothing but water for over a month, yet emerging in good health as the body fed on its own reserves.

If while dieting you think that you are getting a feeling of light-headedness or giddiness or dizziness from not eating enough, understand that this is usually a sign that you are breaking the bad habit of overeating. Like most bad habits, this is harmful self-indulgence and must be eliminated. Denying yourself such routine indulgences when dieting results in some mental frustration.

In turn, the frustration may exhibit itself as a feeling of fatigue, light-headedness or dizziness deriving from self-denial and even a sense of boredom and futility. All this will vanish in a day or two as your weight drops, your looks improve, your energy rises and your frustration about limited eating is more than compensated for by the joy of accomplishment as cumbersome pounds drop away.

Your symptoms, if any, resulting from frustration are likely to be purely psychological. They bear no relationship to the lack of sugar or other such elements in the blood. If your body and muscles are loaded with fat, the surest way to success is the quick loss way. The rapid drop of weight gives you the encouragement you need to combat the frustration that may come from changing your bad eating habits. In any case, it is usually helpful to take 2 ounces of orange juice to counteract dizziness if it occurs.

Serious problems from overweight . . .

As must be emphasized repeatedly for the overweight who resists change in his indulgent eating habits, excessive weight anywhere on your body is likely to be harmful. Few of my overweight patients understand this and give it the serious thought it deserves if good health and a slim figure are to be restored.

The problems exist in the extra weight around your muscles all over your figure, in the fat in underlying layers and tissues of the body, face and chin, in the abdomen and in organs including the intestinal area, along with other parts of the body. All the overweight adds to an unattractive, sloppy, even grotesque and older look beyond your years.

This excess weight, wherever it settles in and on your body, tends to impair not only the workings of your heart but also your blood vessels, lungs, pancreas and other organs. Overweight puts extra strain on your joints, makes you more susceptible to hernias and often produces skin problems, especially where the skin overlaps. Burdensome fat promotes shortness of breath, varicose veins and other marring leg troubles and slows the circulation of legs and thighs.

It is a fact proved by many and various dependable statistics on life, death and illness that excess weight tends to make people awkward and accident-prone. An added high mortality risk is incurred when undergoing an operation.

Please ask yourself: Is it worth subjecting yourself to all these discomforts and dangers, at the same time spoiling natural slenderness and loveliness, just for the sake of the harmful habit and dubious pleasure of overeating? The decision must be yours, but remember this: If you decide to keep on overeating, or eating the wrong calorie-rich foods, and thus remaining overweight or even increasing your dimensions, you bring your troubles on yourself.

You *can* be slimmer, healthier, more vigorous, if you will follow my simple quick weight loss and inches-off instructions.

Inches-Off—a compelling goal . . .

In my practice I have found that women with excess weight concentrated in certain spots are apt to be more determined to reduce those dimensions even than those who are heavy all over. When a woman takes off most of the excess pounds, or even gets down to her ideal weight, and is still too bulky in the buttocks, legs or arms, she is more eager than ever to slim down those problem spots. These motivated women who have succeeded wonderfully on my Inches-Off Diet are' among the most satisfied and grateful patients I've ever had.

These ladies have told me that getting the extra inches and extra flab off is one of the most delightful feelings a person can enjoy. Their pleasure in slimming down and trimming inches off, transforming a heavy, bulky figure to a slim, graceful, youthful body, is my greatest reward.

At times when losing weight successfully, a few individuals have complained that they thought their cheeks and facial contours look a little drawn. If this condition occurs at all—except with the very elderly—it is only temporary. In a short time the skin fills in and firms naturally, and the face soon looks thinner, trimmer and more youthful and attractive. Toning-up exercises, which I give later, are also helpful.

The rewards are worthwhile . . .

With the excess weight off and your figure trimmed, you are far more likely to walk erect, poised, with a springier, far more graceful posture and appearance. You can go back to pleasurable dancing. You can get more enjoyment from sports such as bowling, bicycling, horseback riding and swimming without being self-conscious about ungainly bulges. You will feel proud and be admired for your new gracefulness, ease and agility. Your tired feelings are apt to be a thing of the past. No matter what your pleasures are, you are bound to enjoy them more. Enhanced love between couples and greater sexual enjoyment are often among the rewards of removing burdensome, unbecoming pounds and inches.

For me as a physician there is a special tragedy in a potentially lovely woman (or would-be attractive man) telling me how sad and lonely she is because she feels so overweight, clumsy and unappealing. This can be wretched for the woman who is eager to get married or for the one who is losing the respect and love of her husband and even her children and friends because of excess weight.

The concept of the fat, jolly girl or man is a myth. The truth is told in the confidential confines of the doctor's office, as I have too often encountered. I've had many people, women and men, break down and weep because overweight was ruining their lives. The purpose of my writing is to help all who are seeking aid and need it now, some quite desperately.

My quick weight loss methods have helped many, as stacks of letters to me attest—unsolicited testimonials from every state in the union. I expect the same results from my Inches-Off Diet and methods that include moderate exercising. Many people who have never been able to slim down their problem spots will do so now with happy results for their attractiveness. I hope that you will be among them. And you will be if you follow my simple instructions faithfully.

2

Diets With Built-In Will Power ... Proof That YOU Can Take Inches Off

ANCIENT PROVERB: *"Great souls have wills; feeble ones have only wishes."*

It's a fact of living that most overweights are "feeble" when it comes to giving up the rich fat-producing foods they enjoy. Early in my practice I came to realize that there are not many "great souls" who have the will to follow all medical instructions exactly, particularly when it comes to denying their personal wishes. What to do about it?

The poet Robert Browning wrote about the marvelous achievements that man could attain if he not only had the "will" but also the "power and knowledge." You certainly have the "will" to reduce, otherwise you would not be reading this book. Unfortunately, like most overweights, you probably have more "won't" power than will power—that is why you may have tried a number of different dieting methods but never succeeded.

I felt in my medical practice that in helping people to reduce, it was part of my function to provide overweight patients not only with the "will" but also with the "power and knowledge." For I found at the start, and this continued to be true through my 45 years of working with overweights and others in my office, in hospitals and clinics, that the most frustrating term that keeps cropping up with the overweight is "will power." It was up to me, I decided, to provide diets with built-in will power.

The key to successful reducing . . .

I found the key to successful reducing for myself (as I have stated, I was more than 50 pounds overweight at the time of my heart attack as a young man), and for others in *quick weight loss*. The built-in will power, which I emphasize repeatedly to my patients and in my writing, is in watching those pounds drop on the scale day by day and seeing the inches vanish as the figure slims down rapidly in the mirror.

It is one thing for a doctor to reduce patients with whom he has personal contact so that he can follow their changes and progress weekly; it is another to help people take off many pounds by reading how in a book, even though I give the same instructions, in greater detail than is possible in face-to-face sessions.

By now I know that my printed directions on losing weight and inches have succeeded beyond my most hopeful expectations. Letters have poured in from those who bought and used my book, *The Doctor's Quick Weight Loss Diet*. Now, on these pages, with greater emphasis on taking extra inches off the figure, I am sure that wonderful success will be attained by dieters, since the method embodies quick weight loss also. For the overweight, the Inches-Off Diet takes the pounds and inches off rapidly. The dieter is convinced that the method is worthwhile, with the proof that it has worked for her. Then she stays with the Inches-Off Diet to remove the extra inches from problem spots.

Since nothing succeeds in convincing overweights before they start dieting like the success of others like themselves, I suggest that you read and profit from the stories of just a few of the tens of thousands who have slimmed down rapidly with my reducing methods. Here are some selections from the many un-solicited testimonials I've received from people who have reduced through instructions in my book and articles.

I wish to thank everyone who has taken the time to write.

Your letters have given me some of my proudest moments, for the greatest reward of the physician is to make the sick well (the overweight is afflicted with America's No. 1 health problem). Some of the original letters go on for pages; I have excerpted what I believe will be most useful to you. I am not using the actual names, since the overweight deserves privacy. What was accomplished is what is vital, not who did it—these are men and women like yourself, from many walks of life.

From Size 16 to 12 in a month . . .

(WOMAN): I love you! I am 34 years old but I feel like a teenager. On August 28 I tipped the scales at 162 pounds—today, September 30, I am down to 140 pounds. I have lost a total weight of 22 pounds. I have gone to the doctor and my blood count is all right but I do have a tendency to hypertension (high blood pressure), so really the overweight is bad for me. I now feel wonderful and so happy. I get depressed when I get on the scales and weigh more than I like, but now I love to look at the scales! There is a difference from size 16 to size 12, which I am now.

Your book is wonderful, it makes diet kind of fun, like a project. It comes second to my Bible. I wish I could talk to people or write or something to put across how one can lose weight and enjoy it, make a joke of it, laugh with yourself because you can't eat something. I am very fashion-conscious and the diet is worth the results! I have an expression I use, "People can go on diets, I am a people; therefore I can go on a diet." It works if you are determined.

This lady enclosed "before and after" color snapshots. "Before" shows a pleasant, moon-faced middle-aged woman. The "after" picture is of a very attractive young woman—a remarkable, uplifting transformation. I am sure that she will go on dieting and losing until she is at her ideal weight and will be a breathtaking beauty. Since she failed in the past on other diets, it is obvious that quick weight loss, dropping pounds each day, provided the will power she had lacked—"now I love to look at the scales!" The same can happen for you.

Doctor's family loses weight . . .

(Surgeon's Wife): I think your Quick Weight Loss Diet is *fabulous!* My 21-year-old son has lost 20 pounds in ten days, I have lost 11 pounds. We have not been hungry, and have felt well. When I have lost 3 more pounds I will have reached my weight loss goal. However, my son intends to lose 80 pounds. He has "thought about" going on a diet for several years but your book, with its compelling statistics and professional grounding, did the trick. We're grateful! His feeling of accomplishment and heady new sense of will power are a joy to behold.

There are several important points brought out here that I urge you to note. First, many doctors, their wives and families follow my dieting instructions; that is further proof that quick weight loss is *healthful*. A psychiatrist who had never been able to lose weight before wrote that he took off 14 pounds in two weeks by my method, "feels wonderful" and is "delighted."

Second, it's generally very successful when two or more members of a family diet together. Third, in this case as in many others, it was a big help to the dieter to read the entire book for greatest understanding and motivation. Fourth, notice that this intelligent lady emphasizes that the young man's loss of "20 pounds in ten days" gave him a joyous "feeling of accomplishment" and "new sense of will power" to keep reducing.

If you're worried about the "will power" that you have lacked in the past, follow my instructions for a trial period of a week or two and you'll probably find, like so many others, that the drop in weight and "feeling of accomplishment" form the will power you thought you never would have.

Waistline down from 38" to 32" . . .

(Man, manager of a "health education service"): Many thanks for the excellent diet. I followed it carefully for eight weeks and reduced from 214 to 173 pounds. Waistline came down from 38" to 32". Had to spend quite a bit for a new wardrobe, but it surely was worth it!

This gentleman, concerned in his work about the health education of the family and the individual, nevertheless let the pounds creep up until his own health was endangered, as is true with every overweight. Losing 41 pounds in a short period of time proved to him that he could reduce, and I'm sure he won't let the pounds add inches to his body again. For one thing, as soon as he gains a few pounds, if he does—and most of us do so at one time or another under unusual conditions—he knows how to get back to his ideal weight in a matter of days. Wouldn't the cost of "a new wardrobe" be worth it to you in order to show off an attractive new figure?

"Lost 16 pounds the first week . . ."

(WOMAN, Director, Department of Nursing Services of a fine State Hospital): I have been overweight all of my life, especially since my late teens. Under a physician's care, I have been on practically every diet imaginable and even though I stayed on them strictly I rarely lost much weight. If I was successful for a while, I would soon reach a plateau and could lose no more weight. The most drastic regime was 500 calories per day divided into two meals plus an injection daily intramuscularly. The last three months I was on that, I lost 3 pounds.

I started on the quick weight loss diet and have consistently lost weight. I am 5 feet 10 inches tall and weighed 254 on December 10. Today, the following April 19, I weigh 185 pounds and I look and feel so much better, it is really amazing.

During an educational meeting for one week last month, I went off the diet. I gained 14 pounds. As soon as I started on the diet again, I lost 16 pounds the first week. I am thrilled to be losing weight successfully for the first time in my life. I have no doubt that I will continue to lose. Half of the staff here at the hospital are also losing successfully on your diet, inspired by my success. I am certain your diets have brought new meaning and great happiness into the lives of many persons.

After reading a letter like this, by a person of such exceptional authority in the field of medical care, how can you fail to start dieting and succeeding on my quick weight loss and inches-off methods? When you can drop 16 pounds in a week, more or less depending on how much excess weight you're carrying, that provides any will power you need. I can assure you from experience that you are not necessarily "a mental weakling" (as one patient called herself) if you fail on slow weight loss. Very few individuals have the moral stamina to stay with a rigid diet when after four weeks of denial and food sacrifice, the scale shows a loss of only a few pounds or less.

Teenager lost 13 pounds in eleven days . . .

(FATHER): Our seventeen-year-old daughter has always been about 25 pounds overweight, and never succeeded in reducing although she often tried different diets. Her mother and I considered this tragic because she felt that she was clumsy and homely, which wasn't true. Because of her plumpness she wouldn't date or go to high school social events.

She tried your diet and lost 13 pounds in eleven days. She looks absolutely beautiful and has accepted an invitation to a big school dance. We bought her a dress in a size and style she could never wear before. She is a changed girl, has gained new confidence. We are all delighted, she most of all by her new transformation.

When an overweight teenager, like a heavy adult, can be "transformed" by proper dieting, one wonders that so many stick to habits of overeating and overindulgence which, in effect, tend to ruin or at least mar their lives. In the teenager, the "won't" power, the resistance to denying themselves anything, is generally strong. This factor is made even worse by indulgent parents. Most teenagers, I have found in my practice, have enough determination to give a dieting method a chance for five days or a week. If they lose pounds in a hurry, they invariably continue down to ideal weight. But if the result is only a loss of a pound or two, they are likely to go back to overeating and grabbing the wrong, calorie-rich foods with a vengeance.

Taking off "that roll of fat" . . .

(WOMAN): For years, as I entered my thirties, I have carried 20 pounds more than I should. Since I am petite, only 5 feet tall, those extra pounds weighed me down like a spare tire around my waist. Try as I might, I couldn't take off that roll of fat. A friend recommended your book, and by following your quick weight loss methods I took off 9 pounds in one week. It was unbelievable to my husband and family as well as to me. Not only is my figure much better but people tell me I look years younger. What a relief to get rid of that ugly fat!

When you take off "a spare tire" from around your waist, you are slimming down your entire body beautifully at the same time and improving your looks all over. Your face too slims down, and it all adds up beneficially to make you look "years younger." With my Inches-Off Diet, you can go on to trim heavy legs or hips, or wherever you have any special problem places that you feel still mar your figure.

Delight your doctor . . .

(WOMAN): I lost 22 pounds in May on your diet. I feel great, and my doctor was delighted. Your book is a tremendous help, and I think you are doing a wonderful service.

It is a sad fact for too many fat individuals that a good many doctors still go on offering old-fashioned "balanced dieting" methods that fail for most. I am most gratified that more and more physicians, perhaps influenced by the exceptional success and improved and continuing good health of women and men using my quick weight loss methods, are favoring such dieting more and more. You have nothing to fear from losing pounds fast, only from keeping that debilitating fat on your body and throughout your system, clogging your blood flow and coating many organs.

"Really works" . . . lost 16 pounds so far . . .

(BUSINESS EXECUTIVE, letter sent to publisher): I thought you'd be pleased to know that your diet book really works! So far, I've lost 16 pounds. My wife is keeping nice and trim and all our friends to whom we recommend it, without exception, have done likewise. You must be doing something right! As a matter of fact, I've sent copies of the book to the President and his Chief Attorney at the White House, with whom I visited the other day. When I told him of my experience with the book, he requested one for himself and one for the President, which I promptly sent him.

Of course this letter pleased me greatly, although I have no knowledge of whether either of these eminent individuals used my methods or not. Fat is no respecter of rank or affluence, especially since the well-to-do more often encounter the temptations of rich food and drink. It may be encouraging to you that a number of well-known personalities, one of the world's most glamorous women, prominent Hollywood actresses and actors to whom overweight can be ruinous from a career as well as a health viewpoint, practice my dieting methods. Should I say, "You, too, can have a Hollywood Star Figure"? No, I cannot promise everyone perfection of face and form, but you can get down to your ideal weight and minimal measurements with my quick loss methods. Of that you can be sure, as others attest.

"We checked first with two doctors . . ."

(WOMAN): I felt that I should say "thank you"—my husband and I are so grateful to you. In brief, I am 52, 5 feet 4 inches tall, have a sluggish thyroid and I had gone to 143 pounds. Incidentally, I was hungry constantly. On your diet I have gone down to 125 pounds (18 less!)—and I am not hungry all the time either.

My husband is 56, 6 feet tall and was 208 pounds. He has an ulcer, only one kidney, had high blood pressure, uric acid quite high and high cholesterol. Sounds dandy, doesn't it? We checked first with two doctors before he went on your diet, and both said it was a fine diet and safe for him. He is down to 186 pounds (22 pounds lost), and says he is feeling stronger and better than he has in years. Best of all, his blood pressure is now 140/80 (a considerable drop from his high blood pressure), the uric acid is normal, as is the cholesterol.

We sing your praises to everyone who notices the difference in us (and they all do notice).

This couple was very wise in following my recommendation to always have a checkup by a doctor before you start any dieting routine. I hope this case will convince you that overweight can contribute to serious ills, and that getting the burdensome pounds off can help alleviate many troubles and help you feel "stronger and better than in years."

"Our love-life is now great . . ."

(MAN): Last March we sat in our easy chairs watching TV and were impressed enough (with your statements on the show) to start that very day in attacking our problem of obesity. My wife is 52, 5 feet 2 inches and weighed 206 pounds. I am 54, 5 feet 7 inches and weighed 176. In only four weeks my wife lost 30 pounds and I lost 26 pounds on your dieting methods. I got down to 140 pounds where I leveled off several months ago to maintenance dieting as you suggested. I now weigh 138 and feel like 18 again.

My wife is 145 and going to continue dieting until she gets to 125 pounds. We feel great in every respect and are much happier. I used to take three different kinds of medication daily but haven't needed a pill now in four months, thanks to you. Needless to say our love-life is now great besides—need I say more!

Improved sexual activity is often a vital benefit of taking off unattractive, impeding pounds of fat. While sexual power and desire don't necessarily go with ideal weight, the experience reported by this couple is often if not always one of the benefits of trimming off excess poundage. This has happened for women and men in my practice but, I must repeat, not necessarily and not always.

"Succeeds where others fail . . ."

(WOMAN): This diet succeeds where others fail. I've tried all kinds of diets for seven years now, and my weight thought it was a yo-yo! Well, this diet is doing wonders for me. I started at 196 pounds and went down to 175 in a little over a month! It's really a miracle. There's no starving and no nervousness. You are well fed and more than satisfied. You feel good!

I have always realized that a diet might be the greatest in theory but fail in practice if it is too difficult for people to follow and stay with. Thus, my Quick Weight Loss Diet provides plenty of food so there is no "starving" and you are "well fed" and "satisfied." My Inches-Off Diet permits a wide variety of tasteful, filling, nourishing foods—yet reduces you rapidly, then takes extra inches off while eating plentifully. You'll prove this to your personal gratification.

"A much happier teenager . . ."

(MOTHER): I have an overweight seventeen-year old. I cannot begin to tell you how many diets we have tried and adhered to. None of them produced any appreciable weight loss. Your book made good sense when I read it and I gave it to my teenager to read. We began the diet. You must understand this is a girl who ate simply prodigiously! She weighed 166 pounds. In a short time she lost a number of pounds. First time she has ever lost weight and she just glows!

She won't budge off that diet for any money. Now she is quite content with much less food and not craving things to eat. She feels good and sleeps well and is looking forward to wearing a bathing suit this summer. I now have a much happier teenager, full of confidence and strengthened in determination.

A vital point in dieting success is the fact that with my Quick Weight Loss Diet your appetite diminishes soon. You *don't* go on craving the rich foods that led to your downfall. It seems especially important for the young to gain "confidence" in the power of the diet to take off weight, as happened with this young lady because the figures on the scale quickly showed her that the diet was working.

Exploding dieting myths . . .

(PHYSICIAN): I have patients who have followed your plan and have done beautifully. I think you have done a great service in exploding the "balanced reducing diet" myth.

It is a particular pleasure to receive increasing confirmation from doctors who have discarded the "balanced reducing diet" myth, which is still being given lip service by some physicians who are hardly concerned about overweight. I find that many of these sincere gentlemen who still suggest balanced dieting are really concerned about treating a specific problem—such as a bad back or broken leg or kidney trouble—and don't even bother to tell sick overweights to get rid of excess pounds, which bring on many troubles (not all troubles by any means). When you want to lose weight, use the quick weight loss method that takes pounds off in fact, not only in theory.

Tightening the chin . . .

(WOMAN): I am happy to report that we just started and my husband has already lost 6 pounds. My chin is tightening beautifully.

You should realize that quick weight loss by any method, including my Inches-Off Diet, also shows results rapidly in *more beautiful facial contours* as well as in the figure. If you claim, as some people do, that you are afraid to lose weight because "my skin will sag," you're just using an empty excuse to stay fat. Excess weight will keep the cheeks and chin puffed out, rounded and doubled because that fat is right under the skin and in between the muscles. If the skin sags from great weight loss, it will soon firm again naturally.

"Thought they could never lose . . ."

(WOMAN): I have gone on many diets but nothing ever helped me before. I started your dieting methods at 142 pounds, and today I am 125 pounds. I work in a rather large office and everyone that is overweight is on your diet. Women that thought they could never lose have lost—it's just great.

There's an important lesson here, that you shouldn't give up hope no matter how many other dieting approaches you have tried or how often you have failed before. I have told many of my patients who claimed they couldn't lose, "If you don't lose on my quick weight loss methods then you either have some medical problem (which checkup proves you have not) or you are cheating." In the cases of patients who didn't lose on my diets, close questioning revealed that they were not sticking to the instructions—they were fooling themselves and were the sufferers until they changed. However, losing pounds daily helps keep overweights on the diet.

Proud of his manly figure . . .

(MAN): We met a man aboard this cruise ship who used your dieting methods and goes around telling everyone to do the same!

He loves to hang around the swimming pool and tell others, "A few months ago I was an ugly, fat old man—now look at my figure, flat stomach, no fat anywhere."

I don't advise people who have lost weight and regained a fine, attractive, healthy figure to rub it into others who are overweight and ungainly. The admiration of others should be enough, but I can't stop you if you want to brag. The overweight usually tries to hide at the swimming pool or beach, so you can't blame him too much if he stands up and pounds his chest to spotlight his slimming triumph. Fatties among women, even more so, are apt to strut around to show their slim figure after years of crouching in embarrassment to hide bulges all over a potato-sack body.

"Best I have felt in the last fifteen years . . ."

(REGISTERED NURSE): In one week I have lost 12 pounds on your diet and without any untoward side effects. No hunger. No frustrations, headaches or irritability. I feel great, the best I have felt in the last fifteen years. I started at 158 pounds at 5 feet 4 inches tall. With the first 12 pounds gone I will lose a total of 40 pounds and stay about 115 pounds. I am a registered nurse and have tried all the reducing diets with no success ever until now. I owe you, Dr. Stillman, my life—my husband and family are so happy. We are once again becoming a family loving one another together.

Just as it is thrilling to get comments like this, it is heartbreaking to a doctor particularly to see people ruining their health and their personal and family happiness because they stuff themselves and become monstrosities to themselves and others. Surely food and the palate and the stomach aren't worth that much to you if you are overweight and consider all the plusses of being slim. Please reread this nurse's comments and then start taking that flab off yourself.

Healthful dieting . . .

(WOMAN): Dr. Stillman, your Quick Weight Loss Diet is terrific. For the first time in years I have learned to diet in a healthful fashion. Most important, I now diet without being hungry.

It will help you to realize that the diets I have devised for overweights are not "fad diets" (whatever that means), but have been worked out for over 10,000 patients *to help them slim down and stay thin*. The dieting instructions you will follow did not burst into existence overnight. You can have confidence in my methods taking off your excess pounds quickly and healthfully. You won't feel hungry or deprived if you follow my directions exactly. This has been proved with *people*, with hundreds and thousands of overweights who slimmed down beautifully after they had despaired of ever being slim, attractive and fully vigorous again.

Man gets lovely wife back . . .

(WOMAN): Dr. Stillman, I'm in love with you. But so is my husband—because you gave his wife back to him. With your diet I've lost 50 pounds and I gained back a "young thinking" attitude. In January I was sure I was ready for the glue factory. Everything on me was stiff, and my joints locked. It was painful just to walk around, let alone be a wife and mother. I was 38 years old, but I felt ninety. Anyway, thank you for a wonderful summer. Swimming, housecleaning—even repairwork around the house, such as sanding and varnishing windowsills, came easy—things I used to dread. The swimming had stopped because I couldn't stand to see myself in a bathing suit, the rest because it was easier to just sit.

The transformation of this woman from a fat, sedentary, sick mess of flesh into an attractive, vital, energetic individual is not unusual. If you are in the former category, you should be able to make the same miracle happen for yourself. The simple, usable methods to effect the marvelous change are here—all you have to do is make a beginning—*now*.

Lost 42 pounds in seven weeks . . .

(MAN): My wife purchased your book for me and I went from 267 pounds to 225 pounds in seven weeks—a drop of 42 pounds in that short time. I would like to reach 200, to take off the other 25 pounds and *keep them off*. Incidentally, I am 45 years old, 5 feet 10 inches in height. I am happy to tell people in my area what your methods have done to make me a lighter, happier person.

I am pleased, naturally, that this gentleman is proud and happy about dropping 42 pounds of his excess weight. Before he is finished with quick weight loss dieting, over the long pull, I want to see him get down to his ideal weight of 155-165 pounds. With a total drop of over 100 pounds from his previous enormous oversize, his reducing will be in stages, the first 50 pounds off quickly, then a week or two of Stay-Slim eating, then another 30 pounds off and a week or two of Stay-Slim maintenance dieting, and the final stage of 20 to 30 more pounds off by quick weight loss dieting, and then Stay-Slim eating to keep himself at ideal weight.

After he is down to ideal weight, this man may wish to get rid of extra inches on some problem spots. He will smooth these places away with the Inches-Off Diet. Imagine the burden on his physique of carrying 100 extra pounds of flab—about two-thirds of his ideal weight! Now he can look forward to a more healthful, far more active and probably productive life, and he will look younger than his 45 years instead of appearing ten or more years older, as was probably the case. Chances are, according to insurance statistics—which are based not on theory but on life-and-death facts—that he has added ten or more years to his life.

Lost 25 pounds in three weeks . . .

(WOMAN): I'd like to add my thanks to the list of the many people who have been helped by your recommendations. I lost 25 pounds in three weeks, am on Stay-Slim eating now, then will go back to losing the rest of my overweight.

The significant point here is that this lady took off the first 25 pounds of excess weight in three weeks—*not in the six months or so if she succeeded in losing a pound a week by slow "balanced dieting" methods*. This great drop in weight, the beautifying difference in her figure, the sense of buoyant relief in dropping so much burdensome fat—all have given her the will power and confidence to continue until she is at her most healthful, most attractive ideal weight.

Keep this in mind in relation to your own problems of overweight: By losing 25 pounds, she has put down more than the equivalent of a large iron ball weighing that much which she has been carrying around for years. If you are carrying around "an iron ball" of 25 or more pounds of overweight (or less, as the case may be), you are not only just putting a drag on your aching arms and back. Realize also that the 25 extra pounds of fat clogs and pulls on your overworked heart and other vital internal organs. Like this lady, you can get rid of this awful burden in just three short weeks, even less perhaps, depending on how much excess fat you are carrying. You can accomplish this weight loss in weeks, you don't have to drag on month after month and perhaps fail completely.

Quick weight loss for whole family . . .

(MOTHER): As of today, my husband, daughter and I have been on your dieting method for six days and are continuing. Each of us lost 6 pounds by the third day of dieting your way. As of today I have lost 9½ pounds (over a pound lost per day). I weighed 165½ pounds and now weigh 156 pounds (in less than a week). Thank you for getting me started back to feeling my old self. I am 5 feet 3½ inches tall and always wore a size 8 or 10 dress until three years ago. I had an operation last year and gained more weight and could not snap out of my depressive mood until a woman I met gave me your book to read. I'm heading for further weight loss.

Our daughter, who is only 5 pounds overweight and a size 5 or 7, at first laughed at us. However, when my husband and I each lost 6 pounds by the third day she started to eat our way. She is my height, weighs 115 pounds and will go down to 110 pounds. Thank you for writing the book—I call it "my Bible." For the first time we realized, my husband and I, that overweight is a killer, that we diet not just for appearance's sake. We are 44 and 46 years old, and cannot afford the weight gain we made in the past three years.

This letter spotlights many important points, including the necessity to read every page of this book. It is clear that one of the things motivating this lady and her husband was the realization that overweight can cut life short, as well as spoil one's good looks.

Also, as in this case, too many people put on weight after an operation, become depressed and stay fat, often dangerously so. As soon as the physician says that you are fully recovered (and during recovery, too), you should take off excess pounds to aid a quicker, maximum return to good health and good spirits.

Another lesson in this letter is that people tend to be skeptical about desired results from any dieting. They have been let down too often by slow, dragging and therefore ineffectual methods. I suggest that you take a "show me" attitude like the daughter in this family: When she saw her parents each take off 6 pounds in three days, she went on the diet and accomplished the same herself. Show yourself—prove to yourself by trying my Quick Weight Loss or Inches-Off diets that "nothing succeeds like success." You, too, can have the figure you want—a self-made figure.

"Practical, flexible, realistic" diet . . .

(WRITER): I know you have heard this many hundreds of times before, but I would like to add my word of thanks in saying that your book has offered me the first really practical, flexible, realistic diet in a lifetime of dealing with this problem.

The "flexible" aspect of treatment is something a doctor learns necessarily from dealing with human beings, not strictly with laboratory standards. With my quick weight loss methods I give you practical means for trimming down your overweight, permitting you to shift from one diet to another if that's how you personally can reduce best. You may accomplish the most by alternating my Quick Weight Loss Diet for a few weeks with my Inches-Off Diet for several weeks, then back again. Stay on each diet at least a week for quickest reducing. QWL is an all-protein diet, while Inches-Off is low protein.

By switching, you get a complete change of food variety, yet both take off weight rapidly. It is *not* undesirable to jump from one way of eating to another. The body adjusts speedily and marvelously—it is a marvelous mechanism. My whole purpose,

and certainly yours, is to *get that excess weight off*. You can be
sure of accomplishing that with my instructions and your cooperation.

Lose weight easily and painlessly . . .

(WOMAN): I believe that your book will become "the Bible"
of all those who wish to lose weight easily and painlessly. After
trying one diet after another for the past five years, I can truly
state that yours has met the ideal weight loss method. Following
your method for only five days I know that I will succeed without any effort to attain a loss of 25 pounds.

Success with my patients proved to me over the years that a
practical method that works for most overweights should be
relatively "easy" and "painless," as well as result in quick weight
loss. On both my Quick Weight Loss Diet and Inches-Off Diet
you eat as much as you want (without stuffing yourself, of
course) and you don't count calories. You don't feel hungry—
in fact, your appetite generally decreases—so it is quite "easy"
to ward off temptation and you are not likely to suffer the "pain"
of aching for more food. You will find that appetite gratification
is a much overrated item anyhow compared with a slim, attractive figure and a new surge of health and vigor.

Lost 13 pounds in under a week . . .

(WOMAN): I'm pleased to say that after not quite a week
on your diet, I have lost 13 pounds. I am twenty years old and
started on your diet at 160 pounds—I am 5 feet 6 inches tall.
I intend to lose a good deal more, as I am convinced. My goal
is 130 pounds—realistically. I would like to reach 120-125, but
if I make 130, I'll be happy. Incidentally, for the first time in
eight years of off-and-on dieting (since age twelve), I *know* I'll
win the Battle of the Bulge this time, thanks to you!

This bright young lady, I predict, will attain her ideal weight
of 120 pounds and will be very "happy" about it. She has the
proof in her quick weight loss, and she has the confidence in this
method—two assets which apparently she never had in her eight
previous years of dieting. This off-and-on dieting failure is not

uncommon with youngsters, since they, even more than better-adjusted adults, are prone to require quick results or they give up—in other areas as well as dieting. How would you like to be 13 pounds lighter in less than a week from today? Simply follow this young lady's example.

Rule One: Get that weight off!

(WOMAN): I read through your book completely and put myself on your diet *with phenomenal results*. The diet corroborates many things my own doctor told me about dieting over the last twenty years, chiefly, "Get that weight off, I don't care how." I have lost very successfully, will lose 10 more pounds and then will use your method of maintenance eating.

I agree thoroughly with the lady's physician that the important goal is to "Get that weight off," no matter how (even starvation under a doctor's supervision can be very effective and healthful). As stated before, I recommend medical checkup before and after dieting. I cannot help but regret that this woman, like many others, had to endure twenty years of overweight before reducing successfully.

Lost youth regained . . .

(YOUNG WIFE AND MOTHER): I want you to know that this is the first love letter I've written to a man other than my wonderful husband. I love you. In less than a week on your diet method I lost my first 11 pounds. At that time I was interested in going down to 125 pounds. Now my goal is 105 pounds. I will be 105 in just a few weeks because I'm now 116 pounds.

I remained faithful to the diet for two weeks, and then I treated myself to tastes of everything I thought I missed, only to find that I missed your diet. I haven't been 116 pounds since junior high school. I am a 29-year-old mother of three. Now I look as if I could be in high school. In fact a sixteen-year-old asked me for a date last week.

My husband and I are thrilled with my dieting results. He lost 14 pounds in just five days on your diet. He is now 150 pounds and he looks about 22 years old. You have changed my life and I don't know how to thank you. Once again, allow me to say I love you.

Even my wife said that she didn't object to "love letters" like this one. I would like to call to your attention a very pertinent lesson if you have been carrying around excess weight for years. It's too bad that this young woman, for one, had to put up with her overweight for twelve long years when she might long ago have attained the feeling of zest and happiness she expresses now. If you have been delaying dieting, I urge you to start now and see how much less of you there is just one week from the day you are reading these words.

"Constant Battle of the Bulge" . . .

(WOMAN): My life since I was 26 years old has been a constant "Battle of the Bulge." I have tried every kind of diet that I read about, and dieted so faithfully that I would reach a point of looking a little better and then would gain it all back plus some. With my ears always peeled for a new easy way to lose weight, I started out really dieting by your method, and I haven't cheated once. This morning I was proud to see that I had dropped 10½ pounds in the first week.

I find that I am not hungry at all. My doctor advised taking the weight off, as I have arthritis. He approves of the diet, and I feel so good, healthy, no bloat, and good elimination. I wish to express my thanks to you, and hope that in a few weeks I will have attained my goal. I am only 5 feet 3 inches, so I really have to take off at least 25-30 pounds more. Hope it continues the way it has started.

I can promise this lady that she will see the results she wants. She has proof that she can lose weight, and the quick weight loss method has given her the will power to keep dieting. Her improved health and appearance have provided the incentive to keep losing pounds.

This case, like so many others, proves also that instead of a sick person (in her case arthritis and other ills) feeling weaker from dieting, the increase in health and well-being starts speedily as pounds of fat come off. It makes medical sense and every other kind of sense that excess fat weighs down and impedes proper body functioning rather than helping it. Every kind of dependable fact proves that, by and large (the larger the worse), the fat person is *not* a healthier person.

Far greater weight loss than expected . . .

(DIETICIAN): My own experiences would make good reading. I am 63 years old, 5 feet 1 inch in height and weighed 194½ pounds. Today, the beginning of my fifth week on your diet, I weigh 175 pounds, a loss of 19½ pounds. I just can't believe it. Before the diet I was crippled with arthritis—now not a pain nor an ache. Can you believe it? (I can't.) I'm hoping the aches won't return.

On your diet method I haven't any desire for anything else to eat. I suppose because I'm getting results and feel good too. I saw my doctor, who had been treating me for obesity, high blood pressure and other problems, including exhaustion. Thank goodness she approved of your diet. Checkup after three weeks showed that my diastolic pressure came down a few points and she tells me it will come down more as I reduce more.

Last evening I made a study of the number of calories I consumed daily. I've kept a detailed study of my food consumption but I hadn't counted calories. I was amazed that I had eaten only an average of 818 calories a day with so much food to eat. I couldn't believe it. When I figured it out I had lost far more than the calorie-count would indicate. So you see how delighted I am at the 19½-pound loss.

This lady's comments bring up several points for emphasis. In the first place, it is natural that your all-over physical condition and your bodily functioning should improve as unhealthy burdensome fat is removed. However, there can be no promise or guarantee by me or anyone else that all your ills will automatically be cured. Arthritis, for example, may be due to many reasons, and overweight is just one complicating factor. Getting down to ideal weight is a great health boon, no question about it, but don't count on it to get rid of all your troubles.

Secondly, no matter what diet you are on, if you stuff yourself with the permitted foods you won't lose weight as rapidly, and if you overstuff to great excess you may not lose any weight at all. The less you eat of permitted foods on any diet, the more speedily you will shed excess pounds. Always keep that in mind or you'll just be kidding everybody, yourself most of all, and you must blame yourself for failure, not the dieting method.

Thirdly, if you are overweight, you should start reducing at once. Every day that you keep that excess fat on and in your body puts an extra 24-hour drag on your heart, other organs and your entire system. There may be breakdown and serious complications due to overweight any day. Other tragic problems may also be brought on by unattractive flab, as illustrated by this unhappy comment from a very fat, very sad lady: "There are easier ways to lose weight than the way I lost 165 pounds in one day—the day my husband left me." On the other hand, you can follow the philosophy of a noted industrialist who said, "My eyes and thoughts are always on the future—because that's where I will spend the rest of my life." You can enjoy a better tomorrow and tomorrow and tomorrow by starting to take off pounds and inches today.

3

What Takes Inches Off Quickly

Taking extra inches off your hips, buttocks, stomach, legs, shoulders and arms can be accomplished with the special Inches-Off Diet at most any adult age. In respect to "well padded" regions of the body, the *Journal of the American Medical Association* stated: "After middle age, especially in women, the accumulation of fat appears to have a selective preference for the buttocks, resulting in so-called 'middle-age spread.'"

The effective Inches-Off Diet form of reducing dimensions can be used not only after middle age but at any adult age, since young men and women are not exempt from bulky problem spots in common figure areas. A great percentage of individuals need spot reducing, and not only in the region of the buttocks, hips and protruding stomach.

You can switch to this special method of dieting after you have trimmed down to your ideal weight in pounds through my basic Quick Weight Loss Diet or other diets in this book. You can, if you wish, get down to your ideal weight through the Inches-Off Diet itself, as follows.

If you are overweight . . .

If you weigh more than you should according to my ideal weight listings in Chapter 1, I recommend that you get down to your desired weight in the proved quickest possible way, safely

47

How Inches Come Off With Quick Weight Loss and Inches-Off Dieting

1. Excess fat removed by Quick Weight Loss dieting takes many inches off all over the body, as indicated here on midsection, buttocks and legs.

2. The Inches-Off Diet pulls fat out from between the muscles and reduces the muscle mass.

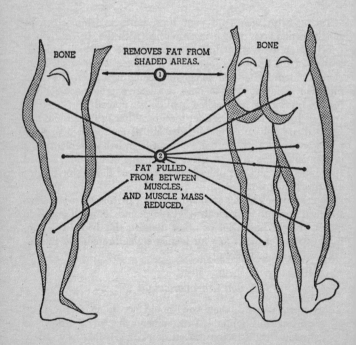

BONE

REMOVES FAT FROM SHADED AREAS. ①

BONE

FAT PULLED FROM BETWEEN MUSCLES, AND MUSCLE MASS REDUCED. ②

Diagram-Sketch of Back Muscles of Thigh and Leg

Inches-Off Dieting pulls fat out of the muscle areas (see arrows) ...slims the legs, thighs, calves, ankles. In the same way, Inches-Off dieting takes extra inches off the midsection, shoulders, arms, and other muscle mass "problem spots."

and healthfully, with my basic Quick Weight Loss Diet. You'll find this famous diet included in this book, along with several variations of the Quick Weight Loss Diet that have never appeared in any book before.

Any of my quick weight loss diets will take pounds and inches off you in a hurry right from the start. As you lose excess pounds, naturally you also lose inches. You will note this clearly as you see the weight go down on the scale. Your figure starts slimming down beautifully, as reflected in the mirror. The inches start vanishing, which is readily apparent from the fact that your clothing becomes loose all over your figure. You will see and feel a marvelous difference.

Once you get down to your desired weight, you may—as so many people do—still want to reduce the width of padded hips, bulging buttocks, protruding stomach, extra-heavy shoulders, arms, legs, thighs, calves, whatever your personal inches-off problem may be. That is when you go on the Inches-Off Diet.

The Inches-Off Diet is also a quick-reducing diet if you are overweight. You may go on it right from the start for your whole reducing program if you prefer the permitted foods to those on the basic Quick Weight Loss Diet. Or you may alternate one week on one diet, the next week on the other, and so on, during the weight-reducing period. You'll note that the foods listed are quite different for each of these two diets. The separate instructions must be followed as detailed for each diet.

If you're at desired weight . . .

Whichever of my diets you use, when you're down to your desired weight and want to take off some more inches in problem spots, then you go on my Inches-Off Diet. At your ideal weight, this diet supplies enough calories so that you stay slim without taking off much or any weight. However, you will see the extra *inches* go—that is your goal.

It's a fact that many individuals, women particularly, whether overweight or at their desired weight, consider it a "curse" to have oversize hips and thighs, and other bulky spots. Ordinary methods of reducing, when you have taken a number of pounds off your figure, slim down those problem areas to a good extent but not to the satisfaction of many figure-conscious women and a surprising number of men. They want, understandably, the over-all "young" narrow look without undesirable bulges here and there.

The problem areas of the body tend to be large and heavy for a number of reasons but mostly because of excessive muscle mass. Ordinary reducing diminishes the measurements in the muscle masses and other areas because there is a considerable amount of fat interspersed between the muscle fibres. Losing this fat is desirable from every viewpoint, but it is not enough to achieve the desired slimmer dimensions for some.

A means must be used that will get rid of some of the muscle mass itself. That's why I created the Inches-Off Diet for my patients with "problem figures." The person must get down to ideal weight, and then eat foods that have two features. First, the foods should contain the minimal amounts of protein. Second, the proteins in these foods should be those which are a little more difficult for the body to utilize.

Science, anyone?

The explanation of the way the Inches-Off Diet works inter-nally involves a little "scientific" understanding that you can skip if you like, but it may be interesting to you: The body requires protein for good health, there's no question about that. There is also no question about the fact that the body needs very little protein for the wear and tear of ordinary living—that is, to make new hair, skin, nails, certain membranes and juices essential to the body's functioning. Some protein is needed to replace the amount that is used up in each cell, in all tissues and organs of the body.

However, the body is a great miser. It *reuses* all proteins that are broken down so that constant heavy intake of proteins for replenishment is not needed. To make this clear, here is a rough parallel: Many ornamental water fountains and some air-condi-tioning systems in commercial buildings recirculate and reuse the original supplies of water over and over again, requiring little extra water to keep functioning properly. By reusing internal proteins, the body can also get along on few additional supplies of proteins daily.

The body normally requires about ½ gram of protein daily for each pound of body weight, in order to be in desirable nitrogen balance. This means that a woman weighing 120 pounds should eat about 60 grams of protein daily (or about 2 ounces). If more than this quantity of protein is eaten, it is either wasted or deposited as fat if the diet contains more calories than your body uses.

While this explanation is so oversimplified that it doesn't qualify as exact "science," it is given to reassure you that a great intake of proteins is not essential to maintain health and vigor for the normal person.

It is important to understand that Inches-Off is a low-protein diet, not a no-protein diet. You do get some proteins, far more than enough proteins to sustain and promote excellent health, from the permitted foods on the Inches-Off Diet. But it is important that you do not eat more protein than is advised in detailed instructions later, or the purpose of the diet will be defeated.

Growing youngsters, particularly of pre-school age, women who are pregnant and those who are nursing babies, need more than ½ gram of protein daily for each pound of weight. The same applies, of course, to people in deprived areas who have long been starved or undernourished due to lack of food or who confine their dieting year after year to foods that lack sufficient protein. These are special cases and do not relate to the "normal" person in civilized areas.

The Inches-Off Diet is recommended for people of normal health. As with any form of dieting, I advise medical checkups before and after restricted eating for the purpose of reducing, just as I urge annual checkups by a physician for every individual no matter how healthy he appears to be.

Many fine low-protein foods . . .

In order to accomplish the greater muscle-mass reduction that results in loss of extra inches, the Inches-Off Diet utilizes foods which have the least amount of grade-A protein. Such protein exists in abundance in all animal foods—meats, chicken, turkey, fish, milk, cheese. You will be following a *low* protein diet made up chiefly of vegetables, fruits, cereals, sugars and a small amount of fats and oils. (The proteins in these types of food are also more difficult for the body to metabolize.) By following instructions exactly, you will keep your daily protein intake within the 20 grams maximum permitted.

The result is a diet that is not only low in calories so that weight does not go up, but also very low in proteins. Thanks to this combination, extra inches come off the heavy pelvic, shoulder, leg and other muscular areas. The explanation may not be quite clear or essential to the average person. What does count to you is that extra inches can come off your problem spots, as has been accomplished for hundreds of my patients on the Inches-Off Diet.

Similar types of minimum protein dieting have been developed and used for the past 25 years and more by physicians. These have usually been devised for patients suffering from high blood pressure and retention of protein waste products. Others have found such dieting effective in many cases of kidney disease (nephritis), as noted in various scientific studies. In cases of protein or nitrogen retention (uremic patients), an article in *Medical World News* states, "For these . . . a new rigid low-protein diet could spell the difference between life and death." Such patients must avoid an accumulation of protein products in the blood.

While fine results were recorded in such studies in respect to high blood pressure, retention of protein waste products and kidney diseases, the effects on muscle mass generally went unnoticed. It was my great personal interest and experience in reducing, figure trimming and figure changing that alerted me to the changes in the muscle mass of individuals on low-protein eating. As I tried and perfected special diets for my patients with oversize problems, they not only lost weight but *the actual measurements about the buttock and hip areas, shoulders, thighs and legs were reduced considerably*.

It is significant that year after year most of the genuine vegetarians, fruitarians and cereal eaters remain slim, healthy and shapely (not those, for example, who call themselves vegetarians but eat eggs, milk and other animal products). Without realizing it, these true vegetarians and the like eat a minimal amount of protein and are almost always in what doctors call "negative nitrogen balance."

Repeated results and findings have proved that for the person without any special medical problem, low-protein dieting can go on year after year, if desired, without harmful effects. To my knowledge, aside from an all-fruit-juice diet or fasting, the only way of eating which will reduce the massive shoulders, buttocks and other muscle-mass areas is low-protein eating such as is found in my Inches-Off Diet.

Proved successful . . .

My Inches-Off method of dieting has been proved successful with thousands of my oversize patients with problems in the muscle-mass spots. This diet should work for you if you follow the simple instructions exactly. You can usually get wonderful results, something you've tried for and have never been able to accomplish before. This is not wishful thinking. It has happened with my patients who had been unsuccessful previously in smoothing out and trimming down buttocks, thighs and other problem spots after getting down to their desired weights. The diet should do the same for you.

How much *extra* dimension reduction can you expect on the Inches-Off Diet? Once you are down to your desired weight, this diet should enable you to take off:

> *. . . about 4 extra inches from your shoulders . . .*
> *. . . about 6 to 10 extra inches around waist, buttocks and hips . . .*
> *. . . about 4 extra inches in the thighs . . .*
> *. . . about 2 extra inches in the calves . . .*
> *. . . extra trimming of ankles, arms, wrists.*

These extra inches of reduction on my Inches-Off Diet are in addition to the inches lost on the reducing diet that brought you down from overweight to your desired weight.

Since people are not built exactly alike, they cannot all expect to achieve a "perfection" of ultra-slim dimensions according to those, let's say, of the "ideal" Miss America. That is hardly a common goal. I take it that you wish to achieve the loveliest possible figure for yourself, based on your natural body conformations. On the Inches-Off Diet, you can take *extra inches off* what you may have considered your minimum "normal" measurements in the past.

You cannot remake a usually heavy leg into a pencil-thin limb, nor can I promise you this. But you *can* reduce your dimensions to slim down problem areas to the degree stated in inches in preceding paragraphs. That should be a most pleasant and desirable prospect for you, a goal certainly worth working toward, and one which the Inches-Off Diet can help you attain.

How the inches come off . . .

When you go from overweight to ideal weight on any diet, you lose a sizable amount of subcutaneous fat—that's the fat directly under the skin. As you lose this fat, you lose inches also. When you've lost that fat, in order to take extra inches off in problem spots it is necessary to lose *muscle-mass* fibres and tissue. That's what happens on the Inches-Off Diet once you are down to your ideal weight.

One aspect of the inches-off transformation is due to the fact that many fat cells when dormant are not distinguishable from muscle-fibre cells. A function of the Inches-Off Diet is to help convert the bulging fat cells back to the original muscle-fibre cells. This conversion acts to reduce the heavy muscle mass considerably.

The Inches-Off Diet pulls extra fat out from *between the muscles*. The goal is to pull 1 or 2 ounces of fat from between the muscles daily. This acts to reduce the dimensions of the buttocks, stomach, hips, shoulders, arms and legs. On the diet, at ideal weight, you can lose ½ to 1 pound per week from the muscle areas, depending on their bulk in your case. You maintain your desired weight but you slim the problem areas gradually. This amounts to a slimming, trimming difference in dimensions eventually totaling a good number of inches, as previously listed. Your eyes will see the difference, and the tape measure will prove it.

Since Inches-Off dieting is very low in protein (while provid-

ing enough protein for good health and vigor), the body is forced
to use proteins in the muscle areas. This process also pulls fat
out of those areas of muscle masses. As a result, extra inches
come off.

Not 100 percent protein-free . . .

I believe that it must be stressed repeatedly that while the
Inches-Off Diet is low in protein, it is not 100 percent free of
protein. A completely protein-free diet is neither advisable nor
possible. Most animal and vegetable foods contain some protein.
Some foods are without protein—the list includes sugar, molasses,
syrups, fats, butter and oils. A diet based on only these foods
would be impossible to devise sensibly, as well as being inad-
visable.

The less protein there is in a diet, the more protein the body
extracts from the organs and muscles. As stated, on my Inches-
Off Diet which is low in protein, the individual who is not overweight but at ideal weight will maintain that desired weight
while losing extra inches from the overlarge buttocks, shoulders,
stomach and other bulky places on the body.

Will exercise take off the extra inches?

"But, Doctor, even though I'm down to my ideal weight, my
buttocks still bulge more than I like, and I have those heavy,
muscular shoulders, arms, thighs and legs." Hearing statements
like that from some patients caused me to do extensive research
and create a method that would trim down inches in those common problem spots, a method that could work for most everybody.

Many claims have been made that the oversize inches can be
taken off by strenuous exercise, massage, vibrating machines and
other assorted means. In my experience such approaches are
unproductive and unsatisfactory as a whole. Exercise in moderation can be helpful in firming areas of the body to a small degree,
and for your vigorous health. Therefore I provide some carefully
selected and devised exercises, with *proper* instructions, in Chapter 9. Such exercising is just a supplement to the Inches-Off Diet.

No amount of exercising in itself will reduce muscle masses as desired. In fact, if you exercise too much and too strenuously, you will probably build up the muscles and add inches instead of trimming them away. What you need is sufficient muscle exercises but not muscle builders. Moderate exercise, as suggested later, can be both healthful for your entire system and helpful in slimming and beautifying your dimensions.

Count on girdle control to remove bulges?

You cannot "spot reduce" effectively or permanently just with a "super-control" girdle. When double elastic panels, special belts, or other construction devices push the fat *in* at one place it must swell or pop *out* to some extent at another. If you use powerful elastic to slim the sides of your thighs, for example, the displaced flesh may bulge out at the fronts of your thighs.

Elastic control garments can be a makeshift and temporary aid, but only proper dieting control can take off the inches in problem spots as well as all over your body. Furthermore, if you are overweight and you keep pushing the fat around with force-ful girdles to accommodate your dresses, the fat still remains to burden your heart, lungs, circulation and various other organs. Any way you pat, pull or push it, excess flesh is unhealthy as well as uncomfortable and unbecoming.

Understanding muscle-mass reducing . . .

Muscle is made up primarily of protein or meat, or what doctors call "the lean mass." A vital point in understanding the problem is to realize that fat is interspersed with muscle. You can see this in the beef you get at the butcher shop when the meat is cut against the grain and fat shows between the fibres and tissues. In beef this is generally called "marbleized meat" be-cause of the similarity in appearance to the grain or markings in some marble.

It becomes clear that if the fat is removed from between the muscle fibres and tissues, the bulk becomes less and the mass shrinks in outside dimensions. When the areas are the buttocks, hips, stomach, shoulders, thighs or legs, actual inches come off as the low-protein diet pulls fat out of the muscle area.

When the low-protein Inches-Off Diet is followed, muscles do not lose their strength. Have no fear of that. Contrary to the belief of some, the need for protein is not even increased by muscular work. The muscles need other elements, which are provided by the Inches-Off Diet, but they don't require extra protein.

Just follow the diet and all instructions that are given in necessary detail. Those extra unwanted inches should come off the problem spots on your figure.

4

Your Quick Inches-Off Diet

You can use the Inches-Off Diet to get weight off in a hurry by keeping the total calories low. The calorie-count total depends on how much you eat. When you aim for *quick reducing* on this diet, you should eat about half as much in quantity of foods as you find in the Inches-Off daily-eating listings that follow in this chapter. These listings are primarily for taking off the *inches* after you have reduced to your desired weight.

Alternate the Inches-Off and QWL Diets if you prefer . . .

You will note that the low-protein foods you are permitted on the Inches-Off Diet are almost exactly the opposite of the high-protein foods you would eat on the basic Quick Weight Loss Diet (Chapter 5). Therefore you may find it very effective in reducing quickly, and to keep reducing until you're down to your wanted weight, to eat one week on the basic Quick Weight Loss Diet, second week on the Inches-Off Diet, third week on the Quick Weight Loss Diet, and so on.

You'll see the pounds dropping on the bathroom scale day after day and week after week by sticking to either of these diets or alternating them weekly. You will also see the inches of unwanted flesh vanishing, and your dimensions rapidly diminishing to a slim, attractive figure—the number of pounds and inches varying, of course, according to how much you are overweight at the start. In any case, you will achieve your first goal—*to get those ugly excess pounds off quickly.*

On to taking extra inches off . . .

Now, at the point where you're down to your ideal weight, you will go on the Inches-Off Diet and stay on it until you achieve the dimensions you want. You'll take off extra inches from oversize shoulders, arms, stomach, buttocks, hips, legs, thighs, calves and ankles. Read the following over carefully, and then read again, for these are important points to follow to arrive at your best possible size, figure, beauty.

INCHES-OFF GUIDELINES

1. **Eat only the low-protein foods listed.** You'll find in the listings a large and delicious variety of vegetables, fruits and a number of other foods that may be a surprise to you—a pleasant surprise. But, if you are tempted by foods not listed and wonder whether they are permitted, stop wondering—just don't eat any foods that are not on the "permitted" lists.

2. **Take special note of the "NO" foods.** Don't eat any of the "no" foods at any time when you're on the Inches-Off Diet. If you eat those forbidden foods, you will prevent the low-protein system from working most efficiently to take those unwanted inches off your problem spots.

3. **Eat to satisfy, not to stuff.** You'll find that you are permitted just about as many vegetables and fresh or artificially sweetened fruits (those on the extensive "permitted" list) as you want. This does not give you license to stuff yourself at any point—it means that you may eat enough to satisfy, or "fill," you and then you stop right there. If you keep stuffing, you'll be adding undesirable calories and eventually piling on ounces and pounds.

4. **Get quicker results by spreading out meals.** With low-protein eating, as with most all types of foods, you're better off spreading out your daily food over six smaller meals a day than three larger meals. You'll lose pounds and inches *quicker* by spreading out the same daily quantity total. However, if it's necessary or

convenient or desirable for you to eat the permitted foods in three meals a day, you'll achieve the reducing results you want, although not quite as rapidly.

5. For quicker results, choose lower-calorie foods. As you'll see in the listings of vegetables and fruits, for example, you can have any of those noted. For the quickest loss of pounds and inches, choose those (check the calorie listings) which are lowest in calories. For instance, a cup of cooked cauliflower is 30 calories, while a cup of cooked brussels sprouts is 60 calories. Thus, while brussels sprouts are low in calories, they have twice as many as cauliflower, but fewer than cooked onions or beets. It's up to you whether you wish to play this little "extra-savings" game or not. If you don't want to take the time, it's not really necessary. You can be guided simply by the "permitted" list, which makes it quick and easy to choose the foods you eat.

6. Go on the Inches-Off Diet for six weeks. You won't get the results you want if—once you are down to your ideal weight—you go on the Inches-Off Diet for a week, then slip off, then go back later, and so on. You must stay on the diet for six weeks. With this type of dieting you won't see the extra inches begin to vanish until you have been on the diet for a week or more. Remember, you are at your desired weight, and the Inches-Off system is now "pulling" extra fat out of the muscle masses, also reducing the size of the muscle cell by pulling out some of the protein. After the first week, those problem spots will begin to lose dimensions and inches. You can stop at anytime after one or more weeks—once you have trimmed your problem spots enough to suit you.

7. After six weeks a checkup is desirable. I've had hundreds of patients on the Inches-Off Diet without their incurring any medical problems. They have lost inches and looked and felt better than ever before, since I devised the diet for just such results. Many people on this kind of low-protein eating, such as true vegetarians and fruitarians, have lived long, vigorous lives and stayed slim and exceptionally healthy. However, I recommend that, after six weeks on the Inches-Off Diet, you have your doctor make a very simple blood test to see that sufficient protein is maintained in the blood, and the amount of albumin and globulin in the blood are normal. You will undoubtedly be normal, but have the blood test made as a reassurance.

8. Go back on the diet for six more weeks if needed. You can go off the Inches-Off Diet for a week or two, if you like, then back on it for another six weeks. After six more weeks on the Inches-Off Diet, now a total of twelve weeks, see your doctor for another blood test. Your blood count and protein content will undoubtedly be normal. Meanwhile, as each week proceeds, you will be losing more of the heaviness in your problem areas. You'll be seeing a wonderful change if you're following the Inches-Off Diet correctly.

9. Go back on the diet for two more weeks. You will now have completed a total of almost 100 days on the Inches-Off Diet. If you have eaten correctly, as directed, and not exceeded the daily calorie count to maintain your ideal weight, your problem spots should have slimmed down considerably. Measurements, as well as your own eye, will show you that you have taken inches off the muscle-mass areas—shoulders, arms, buttocks-stomach-hip region, legs, thighs and calves. If you wish to slim those problem areas even more, go back on the Inches-Off Diet any time you like, it's a very healthful way of eating.

10. Go on normal, balanced, Stay-Slim eating. After the 100 days of Inches-Off eating, you can go on regular variety eating, which includes meat, poultry, fish, eggs and other foods. Be sure that you keep your daily eating within your Stay-Slim calorie count, otherwise you'll start putting on excess pounds again. Eat this way for two weeks, then if you want to take off still more inches and reduce your dimensions in the muscle-mass areas, start your Inches-Off Diet all over again, as instructed. Realize that this is fine, delicious, healthful eating, including fruits, vegetables and other fine foods that sustain many people for a slim, vigorous, lengthy lifetime.

11. Drink plenty of liquids. On the Inches-Off Diet, as on all reducing diets (and even on regular balanced eating), it is important to drink plenty of liquids. The fluid not only washes out waste matter from the system but is also filling, helping you to keep dieting and not to want foods that you shouldn't have in order to take off inches and pounds. On the Inches-Off Diet, enjoy at least 8 to 10 cups or glasses of tea, coffee, and low-calorie carbonated beverages every day. This is no hardship, since most people normally consume 4 to 5 cups or glasses of coffee, tea, and carbonated beverages daily. To keep calories down, use artificially sweetened sodas and juices and sweeten your tea and coffee artificially, if at all, and drink it without cream or milk (a dash of cream or a spoonful of non-dairy creamer is permitted if you feel you "must" have it).

12. **Take a vitamin-mineral pill daily.** While it is not likely that you will incur any shortage of vitamins and minerals from the wholesome foods on the Inches-Off Diet, I recommend that you take a daily vitamin-mineral pill, tablet or capsule. If you are over forty years old, you may take a high-potency vitamin-mineral pill daily.

13. **Exercise moderately.** You will find exercises in Chapter 9 that will help to firm your figure and promote good health and vigor. It is vital that you pursue an active, alert but moderate way of living. *Don't exercise strenuously* or overexercise at any time, since this will build up your muscle masses and tend to augment rather than diminish your dimensions. You've seen pictures of the Muscle Beach specimens with their bulging masses of muscles due to weight-lifting and other strenuous exercises. Walking several miles a day (not necessarily all in one stretch) is good moderate exercise as well as an aid to your well-being.

14. **If you have any medical problem,** do not go on the low-protein Inches-Off Diet without your doctor's checkup and permission. This low-protein form of dieting is not, as stated before, for pre-school and growing youngsters, for pregnant women or for nursing mothers. It is not for people afflicted with kidney diseases, liver diseases, fevers, hemorrhages, colitis, diarrhea, ulcers of the stomach and intestines, running skin diseases, other illnesses that your physician has diagnosed. It hardly needs saying that with any illness or history of medical complications, you will check with your physician and follow his recommendations for treatment, care, diet and other functions and activities.

THE INCHES-OFF DIET

Make up your menus and your daily eating on the Inches-Off Diet from the following permitted, wholesome, healthful foods.

Eat moderate portions, not stuffing yourself or overeating at any time.

The less you eat, the more quickly you will lose pounds until you are down to your ideal weight.

Eat enough to stay at your desired weight once you have reached it. Cut down on the portions and amount you eat if you find yourself gaining weight as you weigh yourself daily.

Eat the permitted foods only and you will trim inches off your muscle-mass areas—shoulders, arms, buttocks region, legs, thighs, calves—wherever you are too bulky.

I have found many patients enthusiastic about the Inches-Off Diet not only because of a gratifying loss of pounds and inches, but also because it is a simple, satisfying way of eating. With a wide variety of fine, enjoyable foods, meals are easy to prepare. Particularly by staying with only the vegetables and fruits, results are extra quick and constant.

FOODS PERMITTED

Vegetables

Artichokes
Asparagus
Beans, Green
Beans, String
Bean, Wax
Beet greens
Beets, diced
Brussels Sprouts
Cabbage
Carrots
Cauliflower
Celery
Chard
Chicory

Chinese Cabbage
Chives
Cucumbers
Dandelion Greens
Eggplant
Endive
Kale
Lettuce
Mushrooms
Okra
Onions
Parsley
Parsnips
Peppers

Potatoes
  (sparingly)
Pumpkin
Radishes
Sauerkraut
Spinach
Squash
Strained Vegetables
Tomatoes
Turnip greens
Turnips
Watercress
Zucchini

Fruits

If fruits are canned, use brands packed in water and artificially sweetened.

Apples
Apple Sauce

Apricots
Bananas

Blackberries
Blueberries

Canteloupe	Honeydew Melon	Pears
Cherries	Huckleberries	Persimmons
Crabapples	Lemons	Pineapple
Cranberries	Limes	Plums
Cranberry Sauce	Loganberries	Prunes
Currants	Mangoes	Raisins (sparingly)
Fruit Salad	Mulberries	Raspberries
Gooseberries	Muskmelon	Rhubarb
Grapefruit	Nectarines	Strawberries
Grapes	Oranges	Tangerines
Guavas	Papayas	Watermelon
	Peaches	

Soups

All vegetable soups.	Fruit	Bouillon, Broth,
Asparagus	Mushroom	Consommé; clear,
Beet (Bortsch)	Onion	no bits of meat,
Celery	Tomato	chicken, seafood,
		and so on.

Vegetable Juices

All juices made from vegetables on the permitted list, including tomato juice, sauerkraut juice, combination-vegetable juices, and so on.

Fruit Spreads

All jams, jellies, marmalades, preserves, "fruit butter," made from the permitted fruits (see listing). Use sparingly if made with sugar; use more generously if artificially sweetened (the difference is in calories, not in protein).

Miscellaneous Permitted Items

Catsup	Mustard	Salad Dressings,
Chili Sauce	Olives	Low-Calorie
Chow Chow	Pickles, Dill, Sour,	Tomato Sauce
Horseradish	Sweet	(no proteins such
	Relishes	as meat, cheese)

Cereals (Small Portions)

Most hot and cold cereals are permitted in small portions, but NOT cereals marked "contains protein." Permitted cereals include:

Cream of Rice	Flakes—Bran, Rice, Wheat
Cream of Wheat	Oatmeal
Farina	Puffed—Rice, Wheat, Corn, Bran

Breads

Don't eat more than one slice of bread or toast, or one small biscuit or muffin per meal, because of high calorie content. No cheese breads or any marked "contains protein."

Biscuits	Melba Toast	Soda Bread
Bran	Muffins	White
Corn	Rye	Whole Wheat

Crackers (Small Portions)

Graham	Pretzel Sticks	Soda Crackers
Matzos	Rye Wafers	

Cookies (Small Portions)

Bland cookies but not any marked "contains protein." Eat no more than one cookie at a meal (two if very small size) because of high-calorie content.

Animal Crackers	Ginger Wafers	Tea Biscuits
Arrowroot	Lady Fingers	Vanilla Wafers
Chocolate Wafers	Lemon Wafers	Zweibach

Very-Small-Portion Foods

These foods are permitted, since they are low in protein, but must be used *very sparingly*, if at all, because of their high-calorie content. You will fail to lose inches and pounds if you use these foods liberally. If you use cream, for instance, use only a dash in your coffee; if you use butter, just a little on a piece of toast; use your common sense similarly with sugar, syrups, oils, and so on.

Brown Sugar	Molasses	Spaghetti
Butter	Olive Oil	Sugar
Cream	Popcorn	Sugar Syrups
Creamers,	Puddings,	Sweet Potato
non-dairy	artificially	Tapioca
Flour	sweetened	Vegetable Oil
Honey	Rice	
Mince Meat		

"NO" Foods (Not Permitted)

Don't eat any of these foods while on the Inches-Off Diet:

Avocado	Eggs	Milk
Beans (except	Fish	Nuts
green, string,	Gelatin	Peas
wax)	Lentils	Poultry
Cheeses	Margarine	Turkey
Chicken	Meats	Seafood
Coconut		

MAKE UP YOUR INCHES-OFF MENUS

From the listings of permitted foods—and by-passing the "no" (not permitted) foods—choose what you will eat each day on the diet.

You can plan ahead a full day at a time, or make up your meals as you go along, whatever your usual custom is when you're eating "normally."

You'll see how easy it is to stick with your Inches-Off Diet as you serve regular family meals. You simply skip the meats and poultry and fish you serve your family, and take an extra portion of vegetables, fruits and other permitted foods.

Keep your meal-planning simple; there are plenty of healthful, delicious foods from which to choose for every meal.

To take off pounds quickly when you're overweight, keep your own meals and portions small until you're at desired weight. The less food you eat and the smaller the portions, the more quickly you'll lose—and those pounds will come off rapidly on the Inches-Off Diet.

When you're at your desired weight, to take extra inches off just eat enough total calories per day to stay at that weight without gaining or losing. Weigh yourself every day. If you start to gain, cut down on the amount of food and size of portions. If you begin to lose below your ideal weight, increase the amounts and portions of the permitted foods. As you maintain your desired weight, you'll take off the unwanted inches in problem spots, thanks to the Inches-Off Diet.

Sample Menus

To save calories, use artificial sweetening, if any, in coffee and cereals. If you must have cream in your coffee, use just a dash or a little non-dairy powdered substitute (don't use milk). On cereal, use as little cream as possible, perhaps thinned out with water, but don't use any milk.

BREAKFASTS

(1)	(2)	(3)
4 oz. Fruit Juice Toast, 1 slice 　with jam, jelly Coffee, Tea, as 　much as desired.	1 Sliced Orange Cold Cereal (small) Coffee, Tea, as 　much as desired.	½ Melon Cooked Cereal 　(small) Coffee, Tea, as 　much as desired.

LUNCHES

(1)	(2)	(3)
½ melon, grapefruit 　or watermelon Tossed salad, mixed 　vegetables with 　vinegar and 　lemon, or low- 　calorie dressing Coffee, Tea	Fruit Salad 2 soda crackers 　with jam Coffee, Tea	Tomato stuffed 　with vegetables Toast, 1 slice 　with jam Stewed fruit Coffee, Tea

DINNERS

(1)	(2)	(3)
Tomato Soup	Half grapefruit	Fruit cup
Hot vegetable plate	Baked rice with	Vegetable plate incl.
Sliced orange	vegetables	baked potato
Coffee, Tea	Coffee, Tea	Coffee, Tea

Snacks

If you feel that you must have something to eat between meals and in mid-evening, you have a wide choice:

> A small piece of fruit, raw or baked or stewed, artificially-sweetened canned fruit, melon.
> Vegetable snacks such as carrot sticks, raw cauliflower, celery sticks, olives.
> Small cookies, no more than one or two a day.
> Bouillon, consommé, broth—clear soups only, with meat, poultry, fish, or seafood bases.
> All the artificially sweetened carbonated beverages you want, up to 5 to 10 glasses a day. Artificially sweetened fruit juices in moderation (to keep down calories). All the coffee and tea, artificially sweetened, without cream or milk, all you can drink, the more the better.

Cocktail Bonus

If you enjoy a cocktail or a glass of wine or beer or a drink of whiskey—Scotch, bourbon, rye, and so on—you may have it, preferably limited to one drink a day because of calories. Alcoholic drinks straight, or mixed as cocktails, do not contain protein. If you overdo the number of alcoholic drinks you have daily, you'll be adding calories and you'll go above your ideal weight.

If you prefer to use 100 calories or so for a cocktail, then you must give up some food of about the same number of calories—that's up to you. Of course, all such calorie substitution must be done in moderation, as you don't get the same food values in an alcoholic drink as you do from fruits, vegetables and other foods permitted on the diet. However, Inches-Off is one diet on which you can have your cocktail and lose or maintain your weight (depending on total number of calories you consume daily), while still losing those unwanted inches.

A *wide choice* . . .

The preceding menus are just a few samples to give you a general idea of the wide variety of delicious servings you can enjoy on the Inches-Off Diet.

To repeat, at your ideal weight, how much you consume in calories will affect whether you stay at ideal weight or start to gain. Check your weight on the scale every morning before breakfast. If you're going over your ideal weight, cut down on quantities (and calories) you consume of the permitted foods. If you're losing pounds beyond your ideal weight, increase your daily intake of the permitted foods.

Keep checking with the Ideal Weight/Daily Calories table in Chapter 1 as your guide. Stay at that weight, follow the Inches-Off Diet as instructed and you will soon see those bulky problem spots begin to diminish.

Inches-Off Diet Recipes

Note the recipes that follow and the ingredients used as a guide to creating your own recipes and also to adapting recipes in cookbooks and newspaper food features.

As you probably know, and if not you will certainly discover, you can cut down on the butter, oils and other high-calorie ingredients in many cookbook recipes and still produce delicious dishes that are lower in calories, more readily digested and more healthful than with the suggested quantities of high-calorie rich ingredients. More and more, good cooks are becoming convinced that a dish doesn't have to be very rich and highly flavored to provide gourmet eating. The true gourmet appreciates fresh, natural flavors increasingly. The good cook realizes that no matter how good a dish that contains rich high-calorie ingredients may taste, if it is very fattening, not readily digestible or healthful, it is not something she should serve to herself, her family, or her guests.

Using the foods on the permitted list of the Inches-Off Diet, you can make hundreds, in fact limitless numbers, of tasty, satisfying recipes and servings. Just a few recipes are given here as an indication and starting point for your guidance.

A SAMPLING OF INCHES-OFF RECIPES

KINGLY CABBAGE

8 cups cabbage, finely chopped
½ tsp. dry prepared mustard
½ tsp. gran. sugar
¼ tsp. salt
2 tbsp. butter
1 tsp. lemon juice

Shred cabbage and cook. In another saucepan, mix mustard, sugar, and salt with butter, heat slowly, stirring constantly. When smooth, stir in lemon juice. Pour sauce over cooked cabbage, mix with fork. Serves 4-6.

VEGETABLES À LA KING

2 tbsp. safflower oil margarine
½ cup dry breadcrumbs
6 green onions and tops, sliced
1 medium cucumber, peeled and sliced
3 lg. ripe tomatoes, peeled and sliced
3 tbsp. chopped celery
½ tsp. salt
½ tsp. sugar
¼ tsp. pepper

Melt 1 tablespoon margarine in 8-inch skillet. Add breadcrumbs, stir over low heat until lightly browned, remove from skillet and save. Melt remaining 1 tbsp. margarine in same skillet and cook onions over low heat until tender. Layer remaining vegetables and seasoning in casserole with onions. Bake in 375° moderate oven about 30 min. or until vegetables are tender. Sprinkle breadcrumbs on for last 10 min. of cooking. Serves 4.

VEGETABLE STEW

1 tsp. butter
4 cups finely shredded cabbage
1 cup thinly sliced celery
1 thinly sliced peeled medium onion
½ green pepper cut in thin strips
2 cups diced ripe peeled tomatoes
1 tsp. salt
⅛ tsp. pepper

Heat butter in large skillet, add cabbage, celery, onion, green-pepper strips, tomatoes, salt, pepper. Cover skillet and cook about 5 min. until vegetables are all tender, stirring once or twice while cooking. Serve at once. Serves 4.

CAULIFLOWER IN TOMATO SAUCE

4 tbsp. minced onion	⅛ tsp. pepper
1 tsp. butter	1 can tomatoes
2 tsp. flour	1 large head cauliflower
1½ tsp. salt	

Sauté onion in the butter until tender, stir in flour, add 1 tsp. salt, the pepper and tomatoes. Cook uncovered, stir often until thick and smooth. Cook cauliflower in water separately with remaining ½ tsp salt. Place cauliflower on serving dish and spoon half of sauce over it, remainder around base. Serves 6.

BROILED MUSHROOMS

½ lb. fresh mushrooms	pepper, nutmeg to taste
1 tsp. butter	1 lemon, juice
salt to taste	

Wash mushrooms, remove stems. Place mushrooms rounded side down on shallow baking dish. Combine other ingredients in melted butter, brush into mushrooms. Broil until tender. Serves 3-4.

BEETS À LA CASSEROLE

4 cups pared, diced raw beets	¼ cup boiling water
1 cup chopped onions	1 tsp. butter
1½ tsp. salt	

Arrange beets and onions in covered 1½ qt. casserole. Add salt, boiling water (more water later if needed), butter. Cover, bake in 375° preheated oven for 80 min. Serves 6.

DICED BEETS

1 lb. diced raw beets.
½ cup water
¼ tsp. salt

Cook for 40 min. adding more water if necessary. Drain and serve hot. Serves 4.

GRATED BEETS

2 cups beets, grated	1 tsp. honey
4 tbsp. water	salt to taste

Cook beets in saucepan in water for 15 min. Add salt. Pour honey over hot beets, stir with fork. Serves 4.

ZUCCHINI SLICES

2 lbs. zucchini	½ tsp. salt
1 tsp. butter or oil	¼ tsp. basil

Scrub zucchini and, with skin left on, cut into ½-inch slices. Add with salt to ½ inch boiling water in saucepan. Cover, cook 10 min., drain. Add butter or oil, sprinkle with basil. Serves 4-6.

VEGETABLE COMBINATION

1 cup cooked or canned tomatoes	¼ cup chopped green pepper
1½ cups cooked or canned snap beans	1 tbsp. chopped onion
	1 tsp. butter
	salt and pepper to taste

Heat butter and brown onion and green pepper, add tomatoes and snap beans. Cook 20 min. Serves 4.

BROILED TOMATOES

4 medium-sized tomatoes	¼ tsp. salt
1 tsp. monosodium glutamate	½ tsp sugar

Cut tomatoes in half. Sprinkle with ms, salt and sugar, broil 20 min. under preheated broiler. Serves 4-8.

BROILED EGGGPLANT

1 lb. eggplant
1 tsp. oil
¼ tsp. salt

Peel eggplant, slice thin, brush oil over slices, add salt. Broil in oven. Serves 6.

VEGETABLES IN CASSEROLE

6 sliced green onions and tops
1 cup breadcrumbs
1 med. cucumber peeled and
  sliced
4 large tomatoes peeled and
  sliced
3 tbsp. celery chopped
1 tbsp. butter or margarine
½ tsp. salt
½ tsp. sugar
¼ tsp. pepper

Melt butter or margarine in 8-inch saucepan. Add ½ cup breadcrumbs, cook until lightly brown. Combine all ingredients in casserole, bake in 375° oven for 30 min. Spread other ½ cup breadcrumbs on top for last 10 min. cooking. Serves 4.

COOKED CARROTS

1 lb. carrots washed and scraped
½ tsp. salt
¼ tsp. pepper

Cut carrots in slices or strips if desired. Heat ½ cup water, add
salt and carrots, simmer 30 min. Drain, add pepper. Serves 4.

COOKED CELERY

6 stalks celery cut lengthwise
½ cup boiling water
1 chicken-flavor bouillon cube
¼ tsp. basil

Place all in saucepan, cover and cook 20 min., adding more water
if needed. Serves 2.

STEWED CUCUMBERS

2 medium cucumbers
1 tbsp. vinegar
¼ cube bouillon
½ cup water
salt to taste

Peel cucumbers and slice. Soak in vinegar a few hours before
cooking. Drain cucumbers, add salt, put in consommé, simmer
10 min. Serves 4.

CURRIED CABBAGE

6 cups finely shredded cabbge
1 tsp. butter
4 tsp. flour
pepper to taste
¾ tsp. curry powder
4 tbsp. minced onion
1 tsp. salt
¾ cup water

Cook cabbage until tender. Melt butter in double boiler, stir in next five ingredients until smooth. Add water while stirring over boiling water. Heap cabbage in serving dish, pour curry sauce over it. Toss. Serves 4.

SCALLOPED POTATOES

6 potatoes	2 cups water
1 large onion	2 tbsp. flour
pepper to taste	1 tsp. butter
½ tsp. salt	

Wash and pare potatoes and cut in very thin slices. Place potatoes in a butter-greased pan, sprinkle with salt and pepper. Sauté onions in butter until slightly brown, add to potatoes. Cover and bake in 375° oven 30 min. Remove cover, add flour first dissolved in ¼ glass water. Continue baking 15 min. longer until potatoes are tender and brown crust has formed at top. Serves 6.

BAKED SQUASH

1 acorn squash
¼ tsp. butter
salt and pepper to taste

Wash squash and place in small baking dish. Add water to ½-inch depth and bake in 375° oven 30 min. until skin is tender. Remove from oven, cut in half, remove seeds. Dot with butter, sprinkle with salt and pepper. Serves 2.

STEWED TOMATOES

2 medium tomatoes or 1 cup canned tomatoes
1 small onion
salt, pepper, sugar to taste

Wash and peel tomatoes, cut in quarters, place in small saucepan. Add sliced onion and salt, pepper, sugar. Cook over low heat 10 min. Serves 2.

A SAMPLING OF INCHES-OFF SOUPS

All these soups have 50 or fewer calories per serving. All soups may be diluted further by adding more water along with more salt or spices to compensate.

MINESTRONE SOUP

2 pints vegetable stock
½ tsp. oil
4 peeled tomatoes cut in small pieces
3 celery stalks
3 carrots
2 sm. onions, diced

1 tbsp. tomato puree
1 potato, diced
½ small cabbage, diced
6 small flowerets cauliflower
1-2 tbsp. parsley
salt to taste
pinch of brown sugar

Sauté carrots, onions, celery until slightly brown. Add salt, tomato, tomato purée. Simmer 30 min., then add potato, cauliflower, cabbage, and pinch of brown sugar, simmer for another 20 min. Add parsley to garnish. Serves 4-6.

TOMATO POTPOURRI

2 cups tomatoes, cut up
1 cup carrots, diced
2 tbsp. chopped onion
1 cup spinach, chopped

1 cup celery, chopped
2½ cups water
1 tsp. Worcestershire sauce

Cook all vegetables in water until tender, add spinach and Worcestershire sauce, cook 10 min. Serves 4.

CLAM-VEGETABLE SOUP

Don't use any clams, whole or pieces.

2 cups clam juice
½ cup tomato juice
½ tsp. onion grated
1 tbsp. celery grated

2 tbsp. lemon juice
¼ tsp. salt, or to taste
1 tsp. grated horseradish
dash Worcestershire sauce

Combine ingredients with warm clam juice, stir and strain after a few minutes. Serve hot or as a chilled cocktail. Serves 4.

MUSHROOM BOUILLON

2 cups boiling water
1½ cups minced mushrooms
4 bouillon cubes

Dissolve bouillon cubes in boiling water, add minced mushrooms, cook until tender. Serves 3.

MEAT OR CHICKEN SOUP

3½ lbs. soup meat or chicken
½ cup onions, chopped
1 cup carrots, diced
½ cup celery chopped with
  leaves

½ cup cabbage, chopped
6 mushrooms, sliced
1 tomato cut up
4 qts. water

Put meat or chicken with bones in a large soup pot with water, cover and bring water to boil. Skim off fat. Add vegetables and cook until meat or chicken is tender. Remove ingredients and strain. Chill and remove all fat. Use as broth or soup stock. Don't eat the meat or chicken, just use in making soup (someone not on the Inches-Off Diet will eat it). Serves 8.

PLAIN BORSCHT

4½ cups water
2½ cups beets, shredded
4 bouillon cubes

5 tbsp. lemon juice
1 tsp. salt
pepper, pinch

Combine bouillon, water, beets, and simmer 15 min. Add lemon juice. Serve hot or cold. Serves 6. (Some stores have low-calorie borscht in jars; don't add sour cream or milk.)

VEGETABLE SOUP

1 cup potato, diced
½ cup cabbage, chopped
½ cup onions, chopped
½ cup green beans, sliced
1 cup celery, chopped
½ cup fresh peas

½ cup carrots, diced
2 cups tomato juice
4 cups water
½ tsp. salt
dash of paprika

Cook all vegetables for 1 hour in tomato juice, add water, salt, simmer for ½ hour. Serves 6-8.

FRUIT SOUP

6 cups water
1 cup applesauce
½ cup orange juice
½ cup peaches, puréed

½ cup pineapple juice
2 tbsp. lemon juice
1 tsp. or to taste artificial-
  sweetener solution

Combine all ingredients in saucepan, simmer for 15 min. Garnish with sprigs of mint. Serves 4-6.

When meat or vegetable soups are desired, you may use vegetable, chicken or meat bouillon cubes in 1 cup of boiling water.

Use these few sample recipes as a guideline for the wide range of tasteful, healthful dishes you can prepare for pleasant, effective Inches-Off dieting.

INCHES-OFF ALL-VEGETABLE DIET

This Inches-Off All-Vegetable Diet is excellent for reducing quickly if you're overweight, or for taking extra inches off after you're down to your ideal weight through the basic Quick Weight Loss Diet or any other effective method.

Here's all there is to it: Eat vegetables only, and only those on the Inches-Off permitted list (no avocados, no beans other than green, string or wax beans, no lentils, no sweet potatoes).

Eat as much as you want of any of the permitted vegetables of your choice, up to six meals daily. This means exactly what it states—as much as you want of the permitted vegetables, up to six meals daily.

Drink a good deal of water and unlimited quantities of non-caloric liquids—coffee, tea, carbonated beverages that have fewer than 3 calories per 8-ounce container.

You can make these vegetables, and combinations of vegetables, more interesting to the taste with herbs and spices, and a sprinkling of low-calorie dressings.

You may vary the vegetables with fruits, but only those fruits of lower rather than higher calorie-count in the range of fruits (see calorie tables).

If you stick with this diet exactly as stated, you will lose pounds quickly down to your ideal weight. If you continue this all-vegetable way of eating, you can be certain that you will never again be heavy.

On this diet you get only a small quantity of protein, but enough to keep the average person in good, continuing health and vigor. With this low-protein eating, the body pulls protein and fat out of the interstices (very small, narrow spaces) of the muscles, while the muscles remain healthy and strong. *The inches come off* and your body will be as lean as possible. The problem spots of shoulders, buttocks, stomach, hips, legs, thighs and calves, and any other places will become flattened out as much as your natural formations permit.

Warning: This Inches-Off All-Vegetable Diet will become less effective, and possibly won't do the job you want on problem spots, if you start to relax and add forbidden foods. Some people on this diet, who still call themselves vegetarians, start to add some vegetable-oil dressings, bread, butter, cheese, eggs, nuts, milk and other foods not on the permitted list. With those additions, the weight can go up and the inches start piling on again. Remember, to get the attractive slimness you want all over, there can be no extras, no deviations.

If you go on this diet and fail to lose pounds and inches, and to take off extra inches at the problem places, you are definitely a "poor loser"—and the fault is undoubtedly your own for not sticking to the diet exactly as instructed. Once you establish the enjoyable routine of this kind of healthful eating, you're likely to say that the great improvement in your figure and vitality makes it very worthwhile.

Inches-Off Made Easy . . .

It is clear to you by now, I'm sure, that you can forget past theories that do not include special eating, about diminishing the dimensions of your figure including the too-common muscle-mass "problem spots." All the figure massage, steam baths, pounding at your flesh, electrical devices and *overstrenuous* exercising tend to build up muscle instead of slimming down arms, legs, buttocks. All these are inefficient and very short term.

There are two types of dieting, other than my Inches-Off Diet, that will take extra inches off. One is a diet consisting of nothing but sweetened juices in quantity totaling under 500 calories a day; frequent medical checkup is desirable. The other is a fasting routine which, if undertaken for more than one or two days, should be under medical supervision. Both these methods are difficult and highly impractical for most people.

The Inches-Off Diet is a pleasant way of eating—and of eating sufficient quantities daily—for most anyone who wants to be slim and as trim as possible all over the body. By pulling fat out of

5

The Famous Original Basic
Quick Weight Loss Diet

The diet you're about to begin
Made a once-heavy lady so thin
That when she essayed
To drink lemonade—
She slipped through the straw and fell in.

I cannot promise you that you'll be slim enough to "slip through a straw"—nor would you want to. But no reducing method ever worked out, in my opinion, can equal my basic Quick Weight Loss Diet in taking off pounds rapidly, surely, healthfully. I would not consider a diet book of mine as helpful and effective as reducing instructions can possibly be without including this diet.

The basic Quick Weight Loss Diet from my previous book, *The Doctor's Quick Weight Loss Diet,* is given here with some variations and additions. Many of the new points were spurred by questions from readers and audiences whom I have addressed all over the U.S. and Canada, including Hawaii, Alaska, Puerto Rico. I have also incorporated the results of my continuous further investigations and findings. From such research, experiences and results, I know that these additions will be helpful.

The expanded diet and instructions will, I am certain, be of considerable extra value to you in assisting you to solve your overweight problems. In the next chapter "New Quick Weight

Loss Variety Diets," you will find information that has never before appeared in a book.

You will see that as the basic Quick Weight Loss Diet takes off your excess pounds, it also reduces your dimensions wonderfully as a matter of course. It has accomplished this double natural benefit for over 10,000 of my overweight patients over the past 45 years, as well as for hundreds of thousands of others through my writings. Very soon after you start on the Quick Weight Loss Diet, you will weigh surprisingly less, as the numbers and pounds marked on your bathroom scale will prove to you. Also, you will look better in the mirror and in clothing, and you will start to feel better all over.

The ideal combination that I recommend to you strongly is this:

(1) Take excess pounds off speedily with the Quick Weight Loss Diet.

(2) Then, take extra inches off, smoothing out problem spots in the muscle masses—shoulders, arms, buttocks, hips, abdomen, legs, thighs and calves—with my Inches-Off Diet.

SWIFT BENEFITS ON THE QWL DIET . . .

You lose 5 to 10 percent of your weight the first week on the Quick Weight Loss Diet. The amount depends on how many excess pounds you're carrying at the start.

You take off 5, 10, 15 or more pounds a week on the QWL Diet. Using the 5- to 10-percent loss rule, if you are considerably overweight at 160 pounds on the scale, you will lose 8 to 16 pounds the first week if you follow the simple instructions.

You should lose 5 pounds each week on the average, week after week, on this diet. Most overweights lose 5 pounds in just a few days, and 10 pounds or more in a week at the start. Figuring conservatively, you can count on averaging out a minimum of 5 pounds lost per week. Therefore, if your goal is a 5-pound loss, that number of pounds should vanish in a week or less. Ten pounds should come off in two weeks or less. You should drop 15 pounds in three weeks or less, and so on.

A loss of 25 pounds a week is about the maximum experienced by any of my usual patients on the Quick Weight Loss Diet (there have been even greater weekly weight losses in unusual instances). My records are filled with cases—mostly of people like you, not abnormal overweights, although I have also treated many of the very obese—of women and men taking off 20 pounds and much more in a month, 30 pounds in six weeks, 40 pounds in two short months, and so on.

Your loss may vary 3 to 10 pounds or more a week while you are on the diet. Just stay with the diet, making sure that you are following instructions exactly. You will average 5 pounds or more weight lost a week. After a few weeks on the diet you might reach a week where you lose 2 pounds, but the next week it could be 7 pounds and the following week 6 pounds, so you maintain the 5-pound average.

Don't deviate from QWL directions, or eat foods not permitted. In that case you cannot expect the weight loss you want. Get back on the diet correctly, eat moderately of the permitted foods, drink plenty of water and other beverages and you cannot help but lose weight rapidly.

Weigh yourself nude each morning to note the daily—yes, daily—loss of weight. If you are not losing, chances are you are eating wrong. You may be stuffing yourself with the permitted foods; realize that while you are allowed as much as you want of the foods on the list, if you stuff yourself, then you are only defeating your own purposes.

If you come to a standstill one week after losing many pounds during previous weeks, don't get upset about it. Keep on your QWL Diet and usually you will lose *a lot more weight* in the next week or two. The standstill was probably a temporary water retention, which sometimes happens. Check your intake of food to make sure you are not eating (1) some forbidden foods, (2) snacking excessively during the day and evening and (3) eating overabundant portions. Be patient and you will attain that 5-pound-or-more average weight loss week after week.

Your appetite decreases usually after you are on the Quick Weight Loss Diet a few days. It becomes easier to diet instead of more difficult, because you are permitted plentiful quantities of satisfying foods. Repeatedly, overweights report that they are "surprised" that they soon lose their old compulsions to overeat.

They generally don't have the "irresistible" cravings for rich sweets and other high-calorie foods.

Take off weight gains immediately. Watch out for the "3-pound danger signal!" Once you are down to your ideal weight, get on the scale first thing every morning, unclothed. If the scale shows on any day that you have gained 3 or more pounds over your ideal weight go back on the Quick Weight Loss Diet at once. Within a couple of days you will remove the excess pounds and be back to your ideal weight. This quick removal of any new weight gain is just one of the reasons why many actresses and actors in motion pictures, television and the theater use and recommend the Quick Weight Loss Diet. If they start putting on the least bit of extra flesh, they can remove it in no time at all before it starts to show in the public eye and threaten to ruin a career.

Take off weekend weight gains at once. It is not uncommon for people to have a big weekend of increasing eating and drinking. It becomes especially important to check your weight upon arising Monday morning. If you have gained above your ideal weight, go back on the QWL Diet right away until you remove those excess pounds. If you let more weight creep up on you day after day, taking off the extra pounds can become a problem for you. Don't put it off! Go back on the QWL Diet as soon as the numbers on the scale rise above what they should be.

Remove vacation excess rapidly. On a vacation, cruise, a business convention, and so on, exceptionally heavy eating and drinking can increase your weight alarmingly. When you step on the scales a week later and are shocked that you have gained 10 pounds, take action. Don't put it off. That weight is usually easy to take off in a week on the Quick Weight Loss Diet. Typical case: An executive left home for a business convention on a Sunday after checking his weight at 160 on the scale that morning. When he returned the following Saturday night, he weighed in upon arising Sunday at 170 pounds and was shocked at the 10-pound gain. He went back on the QWL Diet that very day, starting with breakfast. The following Friday morning, after five days of dieting exactly according to instructions, he weighed his ideal 160 pounds again. His belly was flattened out and he said that he felt like "a new man."

WHY *the* QWL *Diet takes off more pounds* . . .

You lose more weight than on other diets with the same reduced calorie intake. The basic reason is that this method of eating on the Quick Weight Loss Diet builds up in your system what is referred to medically as "high specific dynamic action." This comes about because the QWL Diet is made up entirely of protein, foods which I have selected specifically for eating separately and in combination to reduce you most rapidly.

This all-protein way of eating burns up fat more efficiently, from a metabolic and chemical viewpoint, than other types of foods. If you add any carbohydrates at all, even as a snack—such as in sugar, sweets, crackers, breads, grains—that not only "dampens the fire," but, in effect, puts it out. As a result, the fat is not burned up so rapidly.

Dieting by the QWL system burns up about *275 more calories daily* than a diet that contains the same number of calories but includes other elements, such as the carbohydrates in sugar, vegetables, fruits, cereals and other common foods. In other words, if you consume 1200 calories daily on the X-Diet (pick any name), which includes carbohydrates, compared with 1200 calories a day on the QWL Diet, you would still be burning up 275 more calories per day by quick weight loss eating than on the X-Diet—even though you took in the same number of calories that day on either one.

The QWL method is healthful, as your system is not deprived of any essential elements for the time you're on the diet (you don't stay on the diet forever). Your internal mechanism uses up and converts your own body fat into small amounts of carbohydrate or sugar. It also converts your body fat into energy or fuel, and breaks down body fat into fatty acids that provide your system with its energy and heat when you don't take in carbohydrates or sugars. The fat is "melted" out of the storage, or fat, centers by this dieting method. The less you eat, the more you use up excess fat stored in your body—a very good reason to go for smaller rather than excess portions of the permitted foods.

As the body loses extra fat by this way of eating, it also withdraws extra intercellular water, which explains why there is usually more frequent urination. As a result, the body is lighter from the fat and water loss, and you feel lighter and peppier in a remarkably short time. The heart beats more easily, and the lungs breathe and blood flows more easily, too.

This system, with its high efficiency and rapid usage of internal fat from your storage centers, lags if you break the diet by eating foods containing carbohydrates: sugar, alcohol, other forbidden foods.

THE BASIC QUICK WEIGHT LOSS DIET

This is the dieting method I have perfected that takes off more weight more quickly than any other way of dieting I know or have heard about through my years of medical practice and intensive study. You reduce speedily, safely, pleasantly.

You *don't* count calories (although calories do count). Instead, you eat as much as you want, without stuffing yourself, of the all-protein foods listed—and no other foods while you're on the diet.

Make up your meals to suit your own taste and convenience from the foods listed here:

1. LEAN MEATS—baked, boiled or broiled—all visible fat removed. In preparing, don't use any butter, mayonnaise, oils or any other fats. (Check details later on specific questionable meats that many dieters have asked me about.)

2. CHICKEN, TURKEY—boiled, broiled or roasted. Remove all skin, preferably before cooking, but certainly before eating. Remove fat repeatedly, as when boiling chicken. In cooking, don't use any butter, margarine, oils or any fats at all.

3. LEAN FISH—baked, boiled or broiled. In cooking, don't use any butter, margarine, oils, fats of any kind. (Read details on following pages about smoked fish, cooking with wine and other questions that I'm often asked.)

4. SEAFOOD—including clams, crabs, lobsters, mussels, oysters, shrimps and seafood variations such as crab legs, lobster tails, prawns. Prepare baked, boiled or

broiled, definitely not pan-fried or deep-fat-fried, breaded, or any such fatty methods—no fried soft-shell crabs, for example, nor recipes like deviled crab cakes or others containing any ingredients not in the listing of permitted foods.

5. EGGS—prepare in any way that does not use butter, margarine, oils, bacon fat, any fats whatsoever. You may have hard-boiled eggs, preferably, or soft- or medium-boiled. Eggs may be poached, coddled, or baked or fried in non-stick, no-fat utensils—scrambled, sunny-side up, omelet, whatever your preference may be as long as no fats at all are used.

6. COTTAGE CHEESE, POT CHEESE, FARMER CHEESE, also SKIM-MILK CHEESES in moderation. "CREAMED COTTAGE CHEESE," which is the most popular cheese in this category and permitted on the QWL Diet, is made with a very small percentage of skim milk or whole milk added in preparation for increased moistness (there is not enough milk used to interfere with the quick-reducing process in the human system).

POT CHEESE is cottage cheese without any milk added.

FARMER CHEESE is cottage cheese pressed into a firm bar for cutting. There is no milk added.

SKIM-MILK CHEESES are marked "made with skim milk" on the label. Check the labels of brands at cheese counters—if marked "part skim milk," it is better not to include the cheese on this diet.

7. BROTH, CHICKEN CONSOMME, BEEF BOUILLON—in cubes, powders, liquids. Check the labels before buying any brand, to make sure that the product is low-calorie and that no fats are used in preparation. Homemade consommé, broth, bouillon, made from chicken, meat, fish, without vegetables or other forbidden-food additions and with all the fat removed, are excellent for this diet. Clear soups, or any others, with any vegetable or fruit content or base are not permitted.

8. LOW-CALORIE, ARTIFICIALLY SWEETENED GELATIN DESSERT—you may use if limited to one or two average servings per day. Don't use any toppings, such as

whipped cream or other whipped products, sauces, and so on.

9. AVERAGE A HALF-GLASS OF WATER HOURLY. It is absolutely necessary that you drink at least 8 glasses of water daily—which averages out to drinking only a half-glass of water per waking hour, something anyone can certainly do easily. The more water you drink, the better for losing weight most quickly.

The reason for drinking water illustrates how much more effective than others this diet is. QWL sets up an internal process that burns up much more body fat than most other diets. This naturally produces waste products, or "ashes" of burnt fat. The intake of water washes out these waste products, and also helps prevent and relieve any dryness or undesirable taste in the mouth due to the burning up of fat in your system.

10. COFFEE, TEA—drink as much as you want, without cream, milk or sugar. You may sweeten with artificial non-caloric substitutes to your taste, as much as you wish. Check the labels and don't use any sugar substitute containing "carbohydrates." You may drink cup after cup of coffee (caffeine-free, if you prefer) and tea all day and all evening long. It's a good idea to have a cup or two *before* meals as well as during, after and between meals. Added to the water, this fluid aids in removing waste matter.

11. NON-CALORIC CARBONATED BEVERAGES—drink flavored sodas, club soda, seltzer, vichy—as much as you want all day and all evening, up to 5 to 10 glasses a day of artificially sweetened sodas. Added to your water intake, artificially sweetened sodas and plain soda aid the desirable flow of liquids through your system. Also, the cold sodas are refreshing and help satisfy a "sweet tooth." Check the labels. Artificially sweetened sodas that are marked "1 calorie per 8 ounces" or figures about as low as that are considered "no-calorie" and are permitted. But beware of so-called "low-calorie" or "lower-in-calories" or "reduced-calorie" beverages that actually contain dozens of calories per bottle when you read the

fine print on the label (as is often the case with chocolate-flavored beverages).

12. HERBS AND SPICES—salt (and salt variations such as onion, celery and garlic salt), pepper, garlic, basil, bayberry, cloves, dill, marjoram, rosemary, thyme, other common dried herbs and spices, monosodium glutamate, also meat tenderizer, may be used lightly, always in moderation.

13. CATSUP, COCKTAIL SAUCES—use these in moderation (but no sauces containing fats), along with light usage, never in large quantities, of horseradish, prepared mustard, relish, chili sauce. If you heap on sauces and relishes you will spoil the most effective, speediest weight loss results that you want. Don't use any mayonnaise, no creamy or oily salad dressing or other dressings, no oils or fats—not even any "low-calorie" salad dressings or mayonnaise. If the item is not on this 14-point listing, don't use it.

14. VITAMIN-MINERAL TABLET DAILY. It is desirable to take vitamins and minerals daily even though I have never known of any cases of vitamin deficiency among persons on the QWL Diet. Take any form you prefer— tablets, pills, capsules, liquids—any brand that fulfills "average daily vitamin requirements." If you are over age forty, you may take higher-potency "therapeutic" vitamins. You might take this stronger dosage also if you decide to eat very small amounts of the permitted foods in order to drop pounds and inches even more rapidly than usual.

DON'T EAT OR DRINK ANYTHING THAT ISN'T ON THE PRECEDING LISTING OF PERMITTED FOODS. If you think you are following directions and still don't lose weight as promised, then you are probably "cheating," knowingly or otherwise. You had better check carefully whether you are including some foods or drinks that are not permitted and are therefore spoiling the most efficient working of the QWL fat-burning system. If you are stuffing yourself, then you may be taking in more calories than even QWL eating can burn up in your body; cut down quantities and portions to moderate size. It must make good sense to you that if you over-

eat, you cannot expect to see the pounds and inches drop off as
swiftly as you would like.

In making up your meals, you might choose to eat just one
food, such as steak. Or you might combine smaller portions, such
as some shrimp with cocktail sauce, a well-broiled hamburger
and perhaps a little cottage cheese as a side dish. Just don't stuff
yourself at any time.

Use the permitted seasonings to enjoy the fine food thoroughly.
Learn to use the seasonings, spices and herbs in moderation to
suit your personal taste and that of any other dieters in your
family. A few drops of fresh lemon juice (just a few drops, even
a teaspoonful is not permitted) squeezed on broiled fish spar-
kles up the good natural flavor. A bright and successful QWL
dieter suggests a delicious dish of cottage cheese just by adding
a little artificial sweetener and sprinkling on a few dashes of cinnamon (*not* cinnamon sugar).

Variety meats—calves liver, beef liver, kidneys, sweetbreads
and such—are permitted when broiled. If there is any visible fat
at all, remove from the meat before broiling and before eating.
No butter or other fats may be used in preparation or serving.
For moistening, as in cooking in a non-stick, no-fat pan, a little
dry wine may be used. Make sure that cooking is thorough so
that the wine flavor (which indicates alcohol and calories present) just about vanishes.

Frankfurters are permitted, but only all-beef (no pork content
or high-calorie fillers), skinless or with all skin removed before
eating. Prepare boiled or broiled, preferably sliced in half lengthwise if broiling, and with all fat drippings removed. It's fine to
use a little mustard.

Smoked meats, such as baloney (bologna), tongue, corned
beef, pastrami, may be eaten in moderation but only if you
choose all-beef (no pork content), very lean cuts. Trim off any
visible fat, as on corned beef, pastrami and tongue, then broil
and serve after all fat drippings have drained off. If you have a
tendency toward high blood pressure, or if you are a water retainer, it is best that you avoid smoked or other salty foods—
salty meats, smoked fish, highly spiced foods of any kind.

Duck, goose, birds other than chicken and turkey tend to be fatty. If you eat them at all, be sure to remove all skin and eat only the leanest meat. It is just as well to skip these fatty species entirely while dieting.

Canned salmon, tuna, sardines—may be eaten but only if packed in water (label marked "water-packed") or if oil is drained off thoroughly. One method of draining it to let all the oil run off and then pat the food with a paper towel to dry off remaining oil thoroughly. Another method is to place the food in a sieve and hold under slowly running water so that water washes through gradually and drains off the oil. Then pat fish dry with a paper towel. If the brand of salmon, tuna, sardines or other tinned fish or seafood still looks or tastes oily, don't eat it. You are better off with lean, broiled fresh or fresh-frozen fish.

Smoked fish, such as smoked haddock, smoked kippered herring, assorted herrings, smoked salmon, smoked sturgeon, smoked white fish, are not recommended on the QWL Diet. They tend to be fatty and much higher in calories. For example, a moderate portion of smoked eel is about 360 calories, compared with about 160 calories for the same portion of unsmoked eel. With some very lean fish, such as haddock, the difference is not as great; a moderate portion of fresh haddock is about 80 calories, compared with about 105 calories for the same portion of smoked haddock, so the latter is permitted but in smaller portions than the fresh haddock. However, herrings, smoked white fish and other such smoked fishes are fatty and should not be eaten on the QWL Diet.

Hard candies, chewing gum—only the artificially sweetened "sugarless" or "dietetic" types may be eaten at all and then *very sparingly,* a few a day at most. Check the fine print on labels, which must list ingredients and contents. Don't eat *any* gum or candies (no soft candies at all) that are high in "carbohydrates" (as noted on labels) or in "sorbitols" or "mannitols" or "hexitols." These ingredients are eventually metabolized in the system as carbohydrates, although more slowly than usual candies. You'll find that many of these candies and gums with reduced calories still have over 60 percent hexitols, 40 to 60 percent or more of carbohydrates and should not be eaten on the Quick Weight Loss Diet.

Two or more sticks of sugarless chewing gum a day are not harmful to the dieting program. However, unfortunately, some dieters, when told that such gum is permitted, have chewed 30 to 100 sticks a day. Excesses like that can definitely prevent the most efficient working of the reducing process. The same is true if you eat large quantities per day of sugarless or reduced-calorie candy. You're better off staying away from them entirely while on this diet.

Broth, consommé, bouillon are permitted not only at meals but also between meals as long as all fat has been removed in preparation and in heating. These are filling and provide extra liquid, which is desirable. Good for snacks most anytime during the day and evening.

"NO" FOODS (NOT PERMITTED)

What you are *not* permitted to eat is of particular importance in Quick Weight Loss Dieting because elements such as carbohydrates interfere drastically with your speediest weight loss. The "wrong" elements don't just dampen down the protein-fueled "fires" that consume fat, but actually put out those fires. Then your returning to QWL recommended all-protein intake has to make those fires start up all over again. Check and keep checking the "no" foods, and stay away from them (even though many are fine foods in themselves) until you have lost your excess weight and are on Stay-Slim Eating.

No alcohol allowed for the duration of the diet. No whiskey, Scotch, gin, vodka, not even the driest wines or beer (except for a touch used in cooking, as covered elsewhere). After you are down to ideal weight, you can have alcoholic drinks in moderation (a matter of counting calories). Alcoholic drinks in strict moderation are permitted on some other diets in this book.

No rich desserts, no ice cream, ice milk, sherbets, or such.

No soft drinks containing sugar. You can and should enjoy noncaloric artificially sweetened sodas, which help keep the waste matter moving out of your system. According to many tests of people trying to tell whether unmarked glasses contain sugar-soda or artificially sweetened soda, there is no real taste difference in fact, just in the mind. A fair personal test should convince you. Go for the repeated refreshment of many non-caloric sodas, up to 10 glasses a day, in a variety of flavors.

No dairy products permitted other than eggs and the few cheeses allowed in the basic QWL listing—cottage cheese, pot cheese, farmer cheese, and skim-milk cheeses in moderation. No whole milk, skim milk or cream, not even a dash for your coffee or tea. No butter, not even a tiny pat on your steak.

No sugar is to be used, not in coffee, tea or anything else. Use as much non-caloric sweetener as you want, in liquid, but be sure the sweetener is made with *calcium* saccharin and cyclamate rather than *sodium* saccharin and cyclamate (see listings of ingredients and calories printed on the package). No candies, cakes, cookies, mints or any other items containing sugar. I have nothing against sugar as such but its intake can spoil the internal QWL fat-burning system.

No cereals, macaroni products, spaghetti, rice, bread, flour, no grain products. These are all wholesome foods in their place and in small quantities, but they don't belong in QWL eating, which burns up your excess fat most swiftly.

No vegetables or fruits of any kind, neither fresh nor canned, nor in jams, jellies or preserves, nor in any other form. No reduced-calorie jams or jellies or toppings. (You get plenty of these foods on the Inches-Off Diet, which works quite differently in your body in pulling out weight and inches of fat.)

No non-protein "fillers" which probably don't tempt you anyhow. If you see non-protein fillers on the label, don't include the item in this diet. If you're not sure whether the filler is protein or not, don't get the product.

No anything that is not in the basic QWL listing of permitted foods. There is nothing that your body will miss or cannot do without on the Quick Weight Loss Diet if you are a person in normal health. The proteins you eat provide all the fat energy and vitamins ordinarily required by the system. For instance, you get vitamin C in the fresh fish, seafood and meat. I have never found even one person who developed a clinical vitamin or mineral deficiency on QWL eating. This includes individuals who have dropped over 100 pounds of excess weight in three months on this diet. (As I state repeatedly, it is good practice to have a doctor examine you occasionally while you're on any diet.)

IMPORTANT HELPFUL TIPS

When eating in restaurants, you can stay with the QWL Diet easily. You might start dinner with a shrimp, crabmeat or seafood cocktail or clams or oysters on the half shell, without mayonnaise or any such dressing but with cocktail sauce and a little horseradish. Have a lean broiled steak, hamburger, lean roast beef, chicken or fish without the side dishes (a little cottage cheese may be added). Drink coffee or tea, perhaps a cup before dinner as well as during and after the meal. Stop eating at the point where your hunger is satisfied. Don't stuff yourself just because there is more food on the plate—leave it.

If you feel hungry, fill yourself with coffee, tea, no-calorie carbonated beverages, a snack of cottage cheese, half a hard-boiled egg, a cup of bouillon. In a few days after you start the diet, you'll find your appetite decreasing naturally.

If you miss rich tastes, you'll be pleased to note that the desire soon vanishes. You'll rediscover the fine natural flavors of fresh meats, fish and other permitted foods when prepared without butter, oils, other fats. Many dieters, after they get down to ideal weight, find that they prefer the non-buttery, non-greasy natural flavors after they break old, unhealthy habits that brought on the unbecoming, dangerous fat they've finally taken off.

Cooking with wine is permitted but only if the wine is used scantily, in the absolute minimum quantity, and that the wine is used in cooking with heat. As the food cooks, most of the alcohol burns away. If much of the wine flavor remains, then you have used too much, since the flavor indicates that alcohol and calories have remained. The purpose of using the wine in cooking is to help lend moistness to the food, not for any primary purpose of flavoring. If you use wine at all, choose light, dry wines, never sweet or heavy wines. If you use wine too liberally in cooking, you are adding undesirable calories, slowing down your weight-reduction process and fooling yourself most of all.

Cooking with beer or liquor is also permitted only in very small quantities to fluff up some recipes or to moisten foods, and may be used only with heat so that the alcohol and calories cook away. If the taste remains, the food will then have extra, undesirable calories hidden in it, and that is not recommended on the QWL Diet.

Family reducing on the Quick Weight Loss Diet has produced remarkable results for many overweight families, a common problem because all are involved in calorie-rich meals from infancy up, along with family TV snacking, refrigerator raids, constant overeating habits. This diet often works for the whole family even though other diets have failed. The reason is that pounds drop in the QWL way each day, day by day, so it becomes a kind of game, keeping an encouraging weight-loss score—which isn't possible when there is a disheartening loss of only a pound or two a week as on most diets, especially "balanced dieting."

In a typical overweight family report, in the first week the father lost 12 pounds, mother lost 11 pounds, teenage daughter and son lost 8 and 7 pounds, respectively. That's a family loss for four people of 38 pounds a week. I've even heard of one family challenging friends in another overweight family to a QWL race to learn which could lose the most total pounds in a week, thus putting each individual on his mettle in order not to let down the family team. Fine results are also reported by roommates who go on the QWL Diet together.

Spread your daily food intake over six meals instead of the usual three meals a day if you want to lose weight even more speedily on the Quick Weight Loss or most any diet. There is no clear scientific explanation for this result but it is a fact of dieting. If you consume 1,000 calories a day in six meals, you will lose weight more rapidly than if you eat the same 1,000 calories in three meals that day. You will lose more swiftly also if you spread the 1,000 calories (or whatever the quantity may be) over your entire waking time daily, instead of consuming the same amount in three meals a day. But if you stuff yourself with excess quantities all day long, you won't lose weight.

You don't count calories, because you are eating from a list of low-calorie, high-protein foods, and that is self-limiting in its effect without need for counting calories. The method reduces automatically your total calorie intake, and burns up more calories than other combinations of food, as previously explained.

few weeks, then switch to Stay-Slim Eating, back to the QWL Diet for several weeks, then to Stay-Slim Eating, and taking it that way step-by-step until down to ideal weight. I permit this, since people vary and my concern is each one's personal success in achieving healthful, attractive ideal weight.

The chart here illustrates a case of a woman 5 feet 4 inches tall who weighed 160 pounds, that's 45 pounds more than her ideal weight goal of 115 pounds. As you can follow on the chart, she went on the Quick Weight Loss Diet for three weeks and lost 25 pounds. She then preferred to switch to Stay-Slim Eating for two weeks, so I advised a calorie intake daily of about 1300 calories, which is her allotment for ideal weight of 115 pounds (115 x 11 calories per pound). I recommended this rather than calories for her actual weight at that point, which was still too much at 135 pounds (135 x 11 would be about 1500 calories per day).

After the Stay-Slim Eating change for two weeks, she went back to the QWL Diet for three weeks, lost 20 more pounds for a total of 45 pounds less than her original weight of 160 pounds. She resumed Stay-Slim Eating, about 1300 calories per day, and stayed slim, attractive, and as she put it, "felt marvelous."

You might also vary your quick-reducing routine by going on the QWL Diet for three weeks, on the Inches-Off Diet with a different kind of quick-reducing eating for two weeks, then back to the QWL Diet until down to ideal weight.

QWL Dieting after illness . . .

Many people have asked me how soon they can go on the Quick Weight Loss Diet when recovering from an illness. I usually advise that this is something for your personal physician to decide. As you can note, there are fine, natural, healthful foods on the QWL Diet listing, healthful for most individuals, well or ill. Excess pounds are even more harmful for the person who is sick or who is recovering, since overweight is often a barrier to swiftest full recovery.

Particularly if you are ill or have been sick, you should have your doctor check you before going on any diet. The same is true, of course, in respect to resuming work, sports or other activities after illness. Have a checkup and then proceed with confidence.

For example, I have often been asked how soon one may go on the QWL Diet after being down with "mono," or mononucleosis, or the other names for that confusing illness. This is a scare disease, and if an enlarged spleen or liver was not developed, if there was no sign of jaundice, there is nothing objectionable in the Quick Weight Loss foods. However, protein is not recommended to individuals who have nephritis or associated kidney disease—for them the Inches-Off Diet is indicated.

The basic rule still applies, that your physician should check you and advise you accordingly about your individual case, especially after illness.

ADDITIONAL NOTABLE CHECKPOINTS

Regarding waste elimination, realize that on this diet when burning up fat rapidly and flushing it out with plenty of liquids each day there is little residue. If you don't have a bowel movement for a few days (although this won't necessarily happen), don't be disturbed. Nature makes adjustments so that most individuals usually soon have a daily bowel movement again, if that's their habit originally, in spite of reduced residue. If you are bothered by a lack of bowel movement, take some mineral oil or milk of magnesia.

You lose lots of water, and will be urinating more often than usual. This is excellent, as it removes lots of incompletely burned fats and waste from your body. Don't let anyone tell you that your lost weight is only lost water. You are dumping lots of fat along with the water. This goes on week after week on the diet as you lose 10, 20 or more pounds. This "water loss" reasoning is mostly given by overweights who are reluctant to diet. They use the excuse and then keep their unhealthy, unsightly excess fat while they give fake reasons for not going on a proved diet. Those who are determined not to diet will always find something else to blame—except their own overeating.

My advice is to stop thinking about whether your loss of weight is "fat loss" or "water loss" or any other kind of loss. Just keep following my instructions and you will keep losing pounds.

You will be delighted as the scale shows you dropping to your ideal weight, and your mirror reflects your slimmed-down, more attractive figure. That's what really matters for the sake of your good looks and good health.

A *swift surge of well-being* is generally experienced soon after you go on the Quick Weight Loss Diet, in a day or two by many. The protein-fueled "fires" start burning fat out of your fat storage centers in a hurry, move out waste matter, relieve the bloated abdominal and generally sluggish feeling so many overweights suffer from. Many fat individuals say that they didn't realize how poorly they were feeling until QWL dieting swiftly made them feel so much better. A frequent comment is: "I'm fully alive again, I didn't realize that I was living half-dead!" In a surprisingly short time of QWL dieting, you're likely to start *looking* better too, in face and body. People will start saying to you, "You're looking just great—what's happening to you?"

If you are allergic to any of the foods in the Quick Weight Loss basic listing, skip them and eat the others. You have plenty of choice. If you are allergic to some types of shellfish, eat those that don't affect you, along with lots of lean fish. Skip eggs if you are allergic to them (that applies only to a very small percentage of people). Also, if your cholesterol count is high (as your doctor would have informed you), don't eat more than four eggs a week.

If you feel any adverse effects from QWL dieting (very few people do), realize that most of them are imaginary, usually reflecting a mental or emotional resistance to dieting and depriving yourself of the rich foods that made you fat and have been undermining your health. If you get a dry, unpleasant taste in your mouth, you aren't drinking enough water. Drink those 8 glasses or more of water a day, plus other beverages, and any such undesirable taste will go away.

If you feel a bit tired or sleepy (which shouldn't happen), take a brief rest and then get active again. Most likely you will feel the opposite of fatigue—a wave of new energy. If you feel a slight light-headedness from rising suddenly from a lying-down position, just rise slowly instead. Any such sensation, even if real instead of imaginary, will soon disappear as you keep dieting. If you keep feeling fatigued, it might possibly be that your system needs a bit of sugar, such as 1 or 2 ounces of orange juice. If such tiredness persists, switch to the Inches-Off Diet or other quick weight loss diets. If you are concerned about any unusual symptoms at all, have your doctor check you. I repeat, undesirable symptoms are *unusual* among people I've checked on this diet—and that means thousands of men and women in person.

Be active when dieting, as you should be at all times. Walk, work, move about. Don't lie around. Don't sleep more than eight hours a day. Start acting like the more alive, alert, more attractive person that your slimmed-down self will be.

Don't confuse the QWL Diet, or any of the diets in this book, with "miracle" overweight cures, so-called "fad diets" (whatever that may mean), or any other form of unproved "sensational, phenomenal, fantastic" dieting. I developed the Quick Weight Loss methods of all-protein and other dieting through my 45 years of medical practice (primarily as an internist, not as a "diet doctor"). The Quick Weight Loss Diet, along with every other dieting method I recommend, is based on *results* with over 10,000 of my own patients, including women, men and youngsters.

My proved successes provide one reason why you can expect exceptional weight loss on the QWL, Inches-Off and other diets detailed here. *You will get results,* usually better than you ever dreamed possible. All my methods require are your personal cooperation, made easy for you by simple, practical, easy-to-use instructions. Thousands upon thousands of overweights who often failed before have succeeded in attaining ideal weight and improved attractiveness and health with my quick weight loss methods. So can you.

Carry a copy of the basic Quick Weight Loss Diet, copied from these pages. But don't stop there. Keep checking the instructions in this entire chapter and all the other pages of the book as reminder and encouragement. This rereading will help keep you on the right road to your ideal weight and toward staying slim once you attain your goal.

Your cooperation assures success . . .

"The Quick Weight Loss Diet took off my 47 pounds of excess weight which I failed to lose on many other diets over the past

10 years"—that kind of happy statement by a woman patient has been repeated to me in person and in letters countless times. The same gratifying success can be yours if you follow instructions exactly with my methods.

Your quick loss in weight is your swift gain in health, better looks, an all-around uplifting feeling of vigor and zest in living. The sooner you start on this basic Quick Weight Loss Diet, or any of my quick-reducing diets, including the Inches-Off Diet, the sooner you will attain the goal of improved beauty and well-being that you want so much. Never will others say of you again, as the joke goes, "If travel is broadening, she must have been around the world a dozen times. . . ."

Happier days (and nights) to you!

6

New Quick Weight Loss Variety Diets

Variety's the very spice of life,
That gives it all its flavour.
— Cowper

About 2,400 years ago the Greek poet Euripides wrote: *"Variety is sweet in all things."* There is no point in disagreeing with these venerable gentlemen, since I have at times heard from dieters, "Your Quick Weight Loss Diet is wonderful, is taking off my weight and inches swiftly and beautifully—but can't I have just a little more variety in foods?"

Some QWL dieters have told me that they miss mostly the taste of milk. Others yearn for a vegetable or two, or for a piece of fruit. In some cases, I know that this may make the difference between the overweight staying on the QWL Diet and falling off, even if only temporarily (as the pounds start piling on and the inches start massing up on the figure as reflected in the mirror, most of these men and women go back to QWL dieting quite eagerly to see the pounds and inches begin vanishing again in a hurry).

As I point out repeatedly, my concern is not to theorize about reducing people, but to get results—*to get that weight off.* Accordingly, I have created for some patients a number of Quick Weight Loss Variety Diets. As you will see, these start with the most effective reducing method, my basic Quick Weight Loss

Diet, with detailed directions about adding a few foods for the variety you may crave now and then. You won't lose weight quite as rapidly with the QWL Variety Diets as with the basic QWL Diet, but you'll still be taking off pounds and inches quite rapidly if you stay within the bounds of the instructions.

WHY all-protein dieting works quickest . . .

It's worthwhile for you to take a few minutes to review the sound reasons why QWL all-protein dieting reduces you most rapidly. As a thinking individual, this knowledge can help you to sustain your dieting:

1. Protein is more filling than other elements, so that your desire to eat more is reduced. Instead of "the more I eat the more I want"—which overweights often say about pastries, sweets and other rich foods—the opposite usually happens with all-protein eating. Many have told me, "To my own amazement, I find that on the QWL Diet, the less I eat the less I want." You benefit, too, by breaking past high-calorie eating habits and turning to a new, more healthful way of eating in the future.

2. Protein burns up fat more quickly and more efficiently in your system, as previously explained.

3. Protein pulls more fat out of the fat depots in your body.

4. Protein stops the accumulation of fat deposits in your system more efficiently.

5. A complete break with the past is provided by my QWL all-protein eating. Experience proves that it is easier for most overweights to break away completely from their past overeating habits which made them fat than to cut down on portions, to keep eating the same as before, more or less, but in smaller quantities. For most overweights, that simply doesn't work.

6. Helps produce a more effective system of eliminating liquids and waste matter from your body, avoiding swelling and bloating.

7. You lose remarkably quickly—QWL all-protein dieting usually causes you to lose as much weight in the

first ten to fourteen days as if you were on a fasting or
"starvation" diet—yet you are eating plentifully.

8. You need little will power, because the swift drop of
pounds on the scale each morning, which you see with
your own eyes, gives you the "won't" power to keep you
from going back to the overeating ways that made you
fat and keeps you on this quick-reducing method.

9. Protein cannot be deposited, is readily excreted by
the system. Quite the opposite, sugar and carbohydrates
in food intake turn to fat. The fat is deposited as fat. On
the all-protein diet you not only lose weight rapidly but
you also start looking better and feeling better, lighter
and livelier rapidly, as fat deposits are stopped and fats
are pulled out of the depots.

Keep in mind that when you go on one or the other of the
Quick Weight Loss Variety Diets, you will be on high-protein
eating rather than all-protein dieting. Your loss in weight and
inches will not be as rapid, but will still result in quick weight
loss. Taking the pounds off rapidly is always my concern, since
this spells reducing success, which I find doesn't happen if loss
is only a pound or two a week.

The key to success with the QWL Variety Diets is that you
make sure not to let yourself go in eating the extra foods permitted. Remember that if you start to stuff yourself a little, and
then a little more and more, you will defeat your purpose (and
mine), and the pounds and inches will come off more slowly. So
please follow the precautions against overeating precisely, for
the sake of your own most beautiful figure and feeling of buoyant
health and well-being.

QUICK WEIGHT LOSS VARIETY DIETS

This is the basic food listing from which you start all the QWL
Variety Diets. Read the details about these foods and their
preparation and usage in the preceding chapter; for the sake
of brevity I will not repeat all the details here.

1. Lean meats.
2. Chicken, turkey.

3. Lean fish.
4. Seafood.
5. Eggs.
6. Cottage cheese, pot cheese, farmer cheese.
7. Broth, consommé, bouillon.
8. Artificially sweetened gelatin.
9. Average half-glass water hourly.
10. Coffee, tea.
11. Non-caloric sodas.
12. Herbs and spices.
13. Catsup, cocktail sauces.
14. Vitamin-mineral tablet daily.

On the QWL Variety Diets you may eat all the preceding foods, following all the instructions in the preceding chapter—*and add other foods* as follows.

However, this caution is extremely important: Don't increase the total *quantity* of food you would eat on the basic Quick Weight Loss Diet. When you add something, such as a portion of vegetable or a piece of fruit, reduce the amount of meat or fish or eggs or other permitted food that you would have eaten to fill, not stuff, your stomach.

Your intake in total calories, even though you don't count calories on the QWL system, is still low enough to reduce you rapidly, although not as quickly as on the basic QWL Diet. If the number of pounds a week you lose is too diminished on a QWL Variety Diet, cut down on the portions and amounts you're eating or go right back on the basic QWL Diet.

Like some of my other successful dieters, you may wish to stay on the basic Quick Weight Loss Diet for a couple of weeks, then shift to one of the QWL Variety Diets for a week or two, back to the basic diet for a couple of weeks, and so on. This is a pleasant, easy system for quick weight reduction for many women, men and youngsters.

QWL VEGETABLE-FRUIT VARIETY DIET

Choose the general range of your eating from the Quick Weight Loss basic 14-point listing.

You may add one cup a day of vegetables of your choice from the listing that follows shortly. Choose a full cup of one vegetable, or a half-cup each of two vegetables. Eat that amount of vegetables either cooked or raw, as you prefer.

You may season the vegetables lightly with herbs and spices. You may use catsup sparingly, or a small quantity of vinegar if you like. You may add a very small quantity of low-calorie salad dressing, but be sure it's the low-calorie kind, not a rich mayonnaise or oily dressing.

Don't use butter, margarine, ·oils, fats of any kind on the vegetables.

Eat the vegetables at one meal per day, not all through the day. You might enjoy the vegetables at lunch one day, at dinner the next—it's up to you.

Fruits permitted in the listing may be substituted for the vegetables one day, as you wish. Again, you must observe the caution of moderate portions. "Apple" means a medium-size apple, not one of the giants that may contain two or more times as many calories as the small to medium apple. You must use good sense and restraint to get the slimming results you want so much.

You get infinite variety with this addition of vegetables and fruits. You may have a hot vegetable or two (depending on quantities) one day, the next day a small salad of lettuce, or lettuce and tomato, or raw spinach salad with a few raw carrot sticks, or endive with small chunks of apple, many other combinations; the following day a half grapefruit, or small piece of melon, or a sliced medium apple or a baked apple (without sugar but artificially sweetened), or a cup of strawberries or other berries.

You can create many different dishes, such as combining cottage cheese or hard-boiled egg with vegetable or fruit in a gelatin mold, using· no-sugar unflavored or flavored gelatin, adding artificial sweetener or no-calorie flavorings, having a cold salad of a small quantity of chilled vegetables and chunks of fruit on lettuce, combining watercress and radishes, making a vegetable soup of clear broth or bouillon or consommé with a small quantity of fresh vegetables heated in the broth . . . and so on if you must satisfy a yearning for variety.

Choose in moderation from the following listings:

Lowest-Calorie Vegetables
(no more than a cup-a-day total)

Asparagus
Bamboo Shoots
Beans—Green,
  String, Wax
Broccoli
Cabbage
Carrots
Cauliflower
Celery

Chard
Chicory
Chinese Cabbage
Cucumber
Endive
Fennel
Lettuce
Mushrooms

Okra, canned
Radishes
Sauerkraut
Spinach
Summer Squash
Tomatoes
Watercress
Zucchini

Medium-Calorie Vegetables
(less than a cup-a-day total)

Artichoke
Beans, Snap
Beets
Brussels Sprouts
Chives
Eggplant

Kale
Kohlrabi
Leeks
Okra, fresh
Onions
Peas, young

Peppers
Pumpkin
Rutabaga
Squash, winter
Turnips

NO Avocado, Baked Beans, Lima Beans, Corn, Late Peas, Potatoes, Sweet Potatoes, Yams.

Fruits
(moderate portions, instead of vegetables, not in addition to vegetables)

Apple, medium
Applesauce, ½ cup
Apricots, 3
Banana, half
Blackberries, ½ cup
Blueberries, ½ cup
Canteloupe, half medium
Cherries, ½ cup
Grapefruit, half, no sugar
Grapefruit juice, ½ cup
Grapes, ½ cup
Honeydew, medium slice

Lemon juice, no sugar
Orange, half
Orange juice, ½ cup, no sugar
Peach
Pear, half medium
Pineapple, ½ cup, no sugar
Pineapple juice, ½ cup
Plums, 2
Raspberries, red, ½ cup
Strawberries, ½ cup
Tangerine
Watermelon, small slice

No dates, figs, prunes, raisins; NO canned fruits in heavy

syrup; NO sugar-added juices or sauces (use artificial sweetening in any form); NO sugar added to any fruits, juices, sauces.

You may cook the fruits permitted in most any form such as stewed or baked, but don't add any sugar nor sugar syrups, no butter or oil or fats of any kind; any kind of no-calorie artificial sweetening is allowed.

Plenty of beverages must be taken each day with the QWL Vegetable-Fruit Diet as with all quick weight loss diets, and preferably with any diet. Drink about an average of half a glass of water every waking hour—that's about 8 glasses of water a day. Drink plenty of non-caloric sodas in many refreshing flavors. Drink lots of coffee and tea, as much as you want, without sugar, milk or cream.

QWL SKIM-MILK VARIETY DIET

A small but nevertheless a definite percentage of overweights on the Quick Weight Loss Diet have expressed, after a few weeks on the diet, a desire for some milk to give them greater variety. For them and for you, if you are in this category, I have worked out the QWL Skim-Milk Variety Diet, which has proved very satisfactory to them as a reducing aid. I recommend that the milk and milk products be taken in moderation. After a week on the QWL Skim-Milk Variety Diet, I advise returning to the basic QWL Diet for a couple of weeks, then back to the Skim-Milk system for a week, and so on, as an effective and swift reducing plan.

Don't drink any whole milk or eat any whole-milk cheeses; no cream, of course. You may have one or two 6-ounce glasses a day of skim milk or buttermilk or one or two portions of unflavored yogurt. You don't lose any food values in skim milk, all you give up (and you certainly want to) is the fat in whole milk. Skim milks are greatly improved in flavor, so that it is difficult to distinguish the taste from whole milk.

Skim milk adds variety for many dishes. You can make a very satisfying dish in a no-fat, no-stick frying pan with scrambled eggs, a bit of skim milk and cottage cheese slowly cooked and mixed to provide a fluffy concoction. You may add a little skim milk on this diet to your coffee or tea, along with artificial sweetening.

Use skim-milk cheeses with this diet moderately, but more liberally than permitted on the basic QWL Diet. Adding some ricotta or mozzarella cheese to egg, chicken and meat dishes may improve the variety greatly for you. Skim milk cheeses contain a carbohydrate (lactose) that interferes with speediest reducing; you're better off with cottage cheese, pot cheese and farmer cheese. Don't use too much of the skim-milk cheeses at any one meal or on any one day or you'll be adding too many calories and cutting down on your weight loss speed.

Yogurt may be used as a side dish, as a portion in itself, or as an ingredient in recipes involving other QWL foods only—but use only unflavored kind, *not the flavored or fruit* types. The flavored and fruit types can contain a great many additional calories that you must avoid. Start with plain yogurt and, if you prefer, flavor it yourself with non-caloric sweeteners and flavorings, or with a small addition of artificially sweetened low-calorie jellies or jams.

This is a sizable change and a very welcome one for some overweights, adding skim milk or skim-milk cheeses, or yogurt (not all of them at the same meals) during the day on the QWL Skim Milk Variety Diet. Keep in mind always that you are adding calories and diminishing the swift reducing power of the all-protein fat-burning system within your body. However, a change to this from the basic QWL Diet one week out of three, or as you work it out to suit yourself best, can result in the most effective long-range quick-reducing program for you.

QWL SLICE-OF-BREAD VARIETY DIET

For some strange or not-so-strange reason, considering eating habits since childhood, some QWL dieters miss bread the most. One obese lady who came to my office with her husband was "one of the world's biggest bread-eaters" (as she put it). I could believe it—for as she came through the door it was a rather tight fit. Her husband suggested flippantly, "You'd better go out sideways" —and she remarked sadly, "I have no 'sideways.'"

Her problem, as with so many other overweights, was not that the bread and cakes and cookies and rich desserts alone piled the calories and pounds on her, but that she added quantities of bread products to all the other foods she ate. I promised her that she could have a slice of bread after a few weeks on the basic Quick Weight Loss Diet. Happily, she immediately started losing so much weight, about 20 pounds the first week, 12 pounds the next week, and averaging between 5 and 10 pounds lost a week after the first few weeks that she forgot all about the bread she thought she couldn't live without.

However, if you have a yearning for a slice of bread after a few weeks on the basic QWL Diet, you may switch for a week at a time to the QWL Slice-of-Bread Variety Diet. You may have one slice of Protein Bread every day. This may not sound like much of an allowance now, but after you have diminished your eating on quick weight loss dieting of any kind, you will find that one slice of bread a day as an additional substitute satisfies any such craving you may have.

I recommend that you have half a slice of the Protein Bread at breakfast, plain or toasted. You may spread on a little artificially sweetened low-calorie jelly or jam or preserves, adding enough for flavoring and moistening without piling it on. You may enjoy the other half-slice of Protein Bread at lunch or dinner or as a mid-afternoon or evening snack with several cups of coffee or tea, again adding a little artificially sweetened jelly or jam if you wish.

As with all the QWL Variety Diets, when you add the slice of bread, consider it a substitute for something else rather than 'an addition to what you would otherwise eat. Cut down some on your cottage cheese or egg or meat or whatever you have planned, or simply take smaller portions of the other foods.

QWL COCKTAIL-WINE-WHISKEY VARIETY DIET

When one of my overweight patients kept begging me to let him have "one drink," he used the lame old excuse that "whiskey makes me see double but feel single." I pointed out that heavy consumption of alcohol on top of overeating helps to double the weight, too, for disastrous results. However, I do permit some overweights when dieting to vary the basic QWL Diet by taking one alcoholic drink a day after a while.

This QWL Cocktail-Wine-Whiskey Variety Diet has proved to be a welcome change for some of my dieters, who enjoy a daily drink out of proportion to the calorie content. If you feel that way, you may switch to this diet one week out of every three, staying on the basic QWL Diet for the other two weeks. In that way, your weight loss will continue to be encouragingly swift, even if not as sharp a drop on the scales as it could be.

One drink a day means just that—one alcoholic drink of 1 ounce of hard liquor, at whatever time you wish each day, but not two or three or more. If you can't stop at one moderate-size drink a day, then don't start at all or you'll fail to lose weight rapidly. You may make that drink any type—Scotch, bourbon, rye, gin, vodka, brandy, or a glass of wine or beer, or a mixed cocktail. Consult the calorie tables and choose the dry, not sweet, lower-calorie wines and cocktails.

Consider the alcoholic drink a substitute rather than an addition on your diet, taking a smaller portion than normal of one of the permitted foods on the basic QWL Diet.

Mixing the Variety Diets . . .

Keep in mind that with all the QWL Variety, you are breaking the all-protein fat-burning system and affecting the metabolism, which pulls more fats out of the fat-deposit centers in your body. You may therefore switch from one to the other of the Variety diets each day if you like.

Thus, you may stay on any of the diets, such as the QWL Vegetable-Fruit Variety Diet, for a week and then go back to the basic QWL Diet for two weeks. Or you might go on the QWL Vegetable-Fruit Variety Diet for a day or two, the QWL Skim-Milk Variety Diet for a day or two, on to the QWL Cocktail Variety Diet for a day or two, and so on. Mix as you see fit.

In any case, watch that bathroom scale each morning. If you reach the 3-pound-over danger signal, go right back on the basic QWL Diet, or cut down on the amounts of foods (and therefore calories) you are consuming.

7

More Speedy Slimming Diets for Your Personal Choice

A child of nine, apparently agreeing with the old adage that "you are what you eat," wrote down her observations concerning the world about her: "All people are made alike. They are made of bones, flesh and dinners. Only the dinners are different."

Not only are the dinners different, but people are different in following instructions effectively, as any other physician will agree. Since my purpose throughout my years of practice and in my writings has been to get those pounds off my overweight patients, I know that people react differently in their attitudes about specific diets. Therefore I give you a choice of the ways to get that weight off fast, including additional diets in this chapter.

Many of the diets that follow are based on low-calorie intake, for if you eat only between 400 and 700 calories a day, then you will achieve quick weight loss. As one such dieter noted in a memo he left for his secretary: "I've gone out to lunch. I'll be back in 227 calories." Because it works so well for many overweights, I'm here providing some detailed day-by-day menus for taking weight off rapidly, along with other ways of dieting that have worked well for my patients. You can never say that you didn't lose weight because you didn't have enough choice of ways that take off pounds and inches quickly.

7-DAY QUICK WEIGHT LOSS DIETS

Here are schedules for a full week of meals. I have set these directions down in detail in meal-by-meal, day-by-day order, as I find that some overweights reduce well by this means. They stay with the diet faithfully for the entire period of a week, since it takes weight off day by day, one or more pounds a day.

This is right in line with my quick-reducing methods. It is true of all my quick weight loss and inches-off diets. When the numbers go down, down, down, day after day, that's your built-in will power which so many overweights claim they don't have. You won't need it by my methods.

See for yourself, on these 7-Day QWL Diets as with the others. As your weight diminishes, you keep dieting one more day, and another, then another, until you reach your desired figure. This is entirely different from old-fashioned "balanced dieting" whereby you lose only a pound or two a week. In that situation, most people wail, "What's the use?" Then they fall off their diets. By contrast, quick weight loss changes that you see on the scale daily, and even in your mirror, give you the staying power to keep dieting.

How to Diet . . .

When you start on my 7-day QWL Diets, promise yourself that you'll stay on the schedule for the full week, but concentrate only on each day's dieting. On Monday morning, check what you're permitted that day. Eat those foods, and only those foods. Don't be concerned about how you'll get through the next day. Think the same way when you arise on Tuesday—take care of just that day's eating, not the next.

By the third day, a surprising thing happens to most people on this diet. Instead of having increased desire for food, the appetite decreases. You get along pleasantly on less. Before you know it, the week is over and you're pounds lighter and lovelier. Friends will remark about how much slimmer and prettier you look. Note how much healthier you feel, more vigorous and alive, as the burdensome fat melts away. Instead of being weaker from the weight loss, you'll feel stronger, like a "new person."

7-DAY QWL DIETS CHECKLIST

Eat the foods on the menu listing; in addition, check these extras:

1. Take one vitamin-mineral pill a day while on the diet. If you're over 45, take the "high-potency" type.

2. Drink at least a half-glass of liquid every waking hour on the average. In other words, drink 8 to 10 glasses of liquid daily in any form permitted on the diet. That includes water, tea, coffee (no sugar, cream or milk unless listed), no-calorie (or less than 10 calories per 12 ounces) artificially sweetened sodas. The more liquid you drink daily the better, because you're burning up fat more rapidly on this low-calorie eating. The liquid helps wash out the waste matter that is leaving your fat depots each day that you're dieting. Thus, as you're losing that unhealthy fat, the liquids remove it quickly from your system.

3. You may enjoy a portion of artificially sweetened gelatin at lunch and dinner each day. Add that to the daily listing that follows. Mix up flavors if you like, to add a variety of tastes.

4. Between meals, you may also have clear bouillon or broth or consommé twice a day—once in the morning and again in the afternoon. Make it from bouillon cubes, instant broth or granulated bouillon. It's also suggested that you dissolve each portion in 1½ or 2 cups of water in order to consume more liquid and fill you up. Consommé, too, is liquid, of course, and the more no-calorie (or few-calorie) liquids you drink a day, the better for your quick weight loss.

5. Enjoy *plenty* of coffee and tea with your meals. It's a good idea to have a cup or two before eating to help curb your appetite, and another cup or two after the meal. Enjoy regular or caffeine-reduced coffee with as much artificial sweetening as you like within reason. The coffee may be ground or instant. In either case, and this

goes for tea also, skip the sugar, cream or milk unless it's in the listing.

6. No butter, fats, oils or regular dressings are permitted on any vegetables, salads or other foods.

7. Keep in mind that the longer you broil, bake or boil meats, fish and poultry, the more readily they are digested thoroughly. Also, cooked well and thoroughly, the same portion has fewer calories than if cooked "rare."

8. Cut all your food into small pieces and eat slowly, chewing and stretching out the portion for a long time.

9. Aside from the foods and beverages listed in the diet, and the extras advised here, don't eat or drink anything else during the week or more that you're on this diet.

10. It's worth repeating that I've never had a patient show any ill effects from such dieting, only improved health and beauty. However, it's advisable to be checked by a physician for all-around good health before going on any diet.

You can promise yourself this: At the end of a week on this diet, sticking to it exactly, you will lose 5 to 10 percent of your weight, the variation depending on how much excess fat you're carrying. In other words, you'll lose 5 to 10 or more pounds in just one short week. That's a very worthwhile goal, isn't it?

7-DAY QWL DIET NO. 1

Monday (480-calorie total)

Breakfast:

> 1 boiled or poached egg, or may be scrambled or fried without any added fat, in a non-stick pan.
> 1 slice protein bread.
> Coffee with 1 oz. skim milk.

Lunch:

> Hamburger, lean, 3 oz.
> 1 carrot cut in slim sticks.

3 celery stalks.
Tea or coffee (at least 2 cups).

Dinner:

Consommé, 1 cup.
Broiled swordfish steak, 3 oz.
Tossed salad with lemon juice or low-calorie dressing.
Coffee with 1 oz. skim milk.

Tuesday (500-calorie total)

Breakfast:

½ small orange.
1 slice toast thinly spread with low-calorie jam or jelly.
Coffee or tea, 2 cups.

Lunch:

Medium tomato stuffed with crabmeat.
Coffee with 1 oz. skim milk.

Dinner:

¼ broiled chicken (6 oz.)
½ cup green beans.
Coffee or tea, 2 cups, no skim milk.

Wednesday (455-calorie total)

Breakfast:

1 slice of toast thinly spread with low-calorie jam or jelly.
Coffee or tea, 2 cups.

Lunch:

Broiled halibut, 4 oz.
½ cup steamed carrots.
Coffee or tea, at least 2 cups.

Dinner:

> 1 thin slice calves liver, 2 oz., broiled.
> ½ cup Brussels sprouts.
> Coffee or tea, at least 2 cups.

> *Thursday* (440-calorie total)

Breakfast:

> 1 hard-boiled egg.
> Coffee or tea, at least 2 cups, with 1 oz. skim milk in
> each (unless you prefer it black).

Lunch:

> 3-inch wedge of melon, or half-orange, or half-cup straw-
> berries; no sugar.
> 2 tablespoons cottage cheese.
> 1 slice of toast.
> Coffee or tea.

Dinner:

> ¾ cup all-vegetable soup.
> Hamburger, lean, 4 oz., well broiled.
> 6 spears of asparagus.
> Coffee or tea, at least 2 cups.

> *Friday* (490-calorie total)

Breakfast:

> Half grapefruit.
> Coffee or tea, at least 2 cups.

Lunch:

> Boiled shrimp, 4 oz., with 1 tablespoon of cocktail sauce.
> Lettuce leaves, moderate portion.
> 1 slice of toast.
> Coffee or tea.

Dinner:

> 1 cup of clear broth.
> Veal, broiled, 4 oz.
> ½ cup cauliflower.
> 1 medium-size pickle, sour or dill.
> Coffee or tea, at least 2 cups.

> *Saturday* (500-calorie total)

Breakfast:

> Orange juice, half-cup.
> ⅔ cup of oatmeal.
> 1 8-oz. glass of skim milk.
> Coffee or tea.

Lunch:

> 1 hard-boiled egg, sliced thin.
> 1 slice of bread.
> Coffee or tea, at least 2 cups.

Dinner:

> Flounder, broiled, 2 oz.
> Broiled tomato, medium-size.
> Coffee or tea, at least 2 cups.

> *Sunday* (500-calorie total)

Breakfast:

> 1 egg, boiled or poached, or fried without fat.
> 1 slice of toast.
> Coffee or tea, at least 2 cups.

Lunch:

> Half canteloupe, or slice of other melon, or sliced half-
> orange, or half-cup berries.
> 4 tablespoons cottage cheese.
> Coffee or tea.

Dinner:

> Lobster meat, 4 oz.
> 1 medium tomato, sliced, with moderate portion of
> lettuce, with lemon juice or low-calorie dressing.
> 2 slices melba toast, rye or white.
> Coffee or tea, at least 2 cups.

Wherever it is noted that you may have coffee or tea with skim milk, you may take it without the milk if you prefer.

Where you are permitted a slice of bread, it may be toasted or not, as you wish.

A good means of weighing out the number of ounces of food, such as meat and fish, that you are permitted to eat is to get a small, inexpensive postal scale. Soon you will be able to know about what size portion each common food should be for the maximum ounces allowed (once you shape a 3-ounce hamburger, you pretty much know the 3-ounce size, for example).

If you haven't a scale handy, check the pound weight of what you buy, as marked on printed packages, then separate into parts for 4 ounces, 3 ounces, and so on. Unwrap a pound of lean ground meat and make five 3-ounce hamburger patties, wrapping and freezing for future meals. A reminder for size of portions permitted:

> Half-cup or glass is 4 ounces.
> Two tablespoons equal 1 ounce.
> The usual cup or glass measure means 8 ounces liquid.

Go to it now on this 7-Day QWL Diet and you'll see a slimmer you in the mirror and on the scale just one short week from to-day. After the week is up, go on for another week of repeating the diet if you are still over ideal weight; or try one of the following 7-Day variations, keeping in mind the same rules laid down for the preceding; or go on the basic Quick Weight Loss Diet for a week or two.

It's your privilege to choose whatever you prefer, since all these QWL diets will help you get down to your ideal weight.

7-DAY QWL DIET NO. 2

Monday (530-calorie total)

Breakfast:

1 egg, prepared without any fat.
1 slice toast, thinly spread with low-calorie jelly.
Coffee.

Lunch:

½ canteloupe or grapefruit.
¾ cup all-vegetable soup.
½ slice toast.
Tea or coffee, at least 2 cups.

Dinner:

Cup bouillon.
4-oz. boiled or broiled fish.
1 sliced cucumber.
1 low-calorie gelatin dessert.
½ slice toast.
Coffee or tea.

Tuesday (520-calorie total)

Breakfast:

¾ glass skim milk.
1 cup dry cereal (any no-sugar kind).
Coffee.

Lunch:

Vegetable plate—beets, spinach, zucchini.
½ slice toast.
Coffee or tea, 2 or more cups.

Dinner:

> Bouillon, consommé or broth.
> 4 oz. lean meat (broiled, boiled or roasted).
> ½ slice toast.
> Coffee or tea.

Wednesday (430-calorie total)

Breakfast:

> ½ grapefruit.
> Coffee.

Lunch:

> ½ can water-packed tuna.
> 6 stalks of celery.
> Coffee or tea, at least 2 cups.

Dinner:

> ½ cup all-vegetable soup.
> 3 oz. baked broiled or boiled fish.
> 4 oz. of any vegetable except beans, peas, potatoes.
> Coffee.

Thursday (470-calorie total)

Breakfast:

> 1 egg.
> ½ slice toast.
> Coffee.

Lunch:

> 8 tbsp. cottage cheese (sprinkle with cinnamon and
>   artificial sweetening if desired).
> ¼ head lettuce.
> Coffee or tea.

Dinner:

> ½ canteloupe.
> Bouillon.
> 3 oz. broiled chicken (or boiled).
> 1 sliced tomato.
> Coffee or tea.

Friday (535-calorie total)

Breakfast:

> 1 slice toast.
> Artificially sweetened jam.
> Coffee.

Lunch:

> Tossed salad, all greens, low-calorie dressing.
> 1 slice American cheese.
> ½ slice toast.
> Coffee or tea, at least 2 cups.

Dinner:

> Bouillon, consommé or broth.
> 3 oz. lean-meat patty.
> 1 cup carrots.
> 1 cup green beans.
> Coffee or tea.

Saturday (495-calorie total)

Breakfast:

> 1 egg.
> 1 slice toast.
> Coffee.

Lunch:

1 oz. processed cheese.
1 sliced tomato on lettuce.
½ slice toast.
Coffee or tea, at least 2 cups.

Dinner:

Bouillon.
½ head lettuce with low-calorie dressing.
4 oz. boiled or broiled chicken.
½ slice toast.
Coffee or tea.

Sunday (500-calorie total)

Breakfast:

1 egg.
½ sliced orange.
Coffee.

Lunch:

½ grapefruit.
4 tbsp. cottage cheese on
¼ head lettuce.
1 slice protein bread.
Coffee or tea, at least 2 cups.

Dinner:

10 boiled shrimp on lettuce with 1 tbsp. cocktail sauce.
1 sliced tomato.
2 Melba toast.
Coffee or tea.

Before Retiring:

1 of any fresh fruit in season.

7-DAY QWL DIET NO. 3

Monday (600-calorie total)

Breakfast:

    1 slice toast.
    Artificially sweetened jam.
    Coffee with skim milk.

Lunch:

    Tossed salad with low-calorie dressing.
    1 oz. any cheese.
    ½ slice toast.
    Coffee or tea, at least 2 cups.

Dinner:

    Clear soup.
    2 cups cooked vegetables.
    3 oz. lean meat.
    Coffee or tea.

Snack Before Retiring:

    Apple or ½ canteloupe.

Tuesday (485-calorie total)

Breakfast:

    ½ grapefruit.
    Coffee.

Lunch:

    ½ can water-packed tuna.
    6 stalks celery.
    Coffee or tea, at least 2 cups.

Dinner:

> Clear broth.
> ½ melon.
> 3 oz. boiled or broiled fish.
> ½ cup cooked vegetable.
> Coffee or tea.

Snack Before Retiring:

> 1 apple or pear.

> *Wednesday* (470-calorie total)

Breakfast:

> 1 egg.
> ½ slice toast.
> Coffee.

Lunch:

> 4 oz. cottage cheese, with cinnamon and artificial
>   sweetening.
> ¼ head lettuce.
> Coffee or tea, at least 2 cups.

Lunch:

> ½ melon.
> Clear soup.
> 3 oz. chicken.
> 1 sliced tomato.
> Coffee.

> *Thursday* (540-calorie total)

Breakfast:

> 1 glass skim milk.
> 1 cup dry cereal.
> Coffee.

Lunch:

> Plate of three hot vegetables, such as beets, carrots, green beans.
> ½ slice toast.
> Coffee or tea, at least 2 cups.

Dinner:

> Clear broth.
> Lean-meat patty.
> ½ slice toast.
> Coffee or tea.

> *Friday* (585-calorie total)

Breakfast:

> 1 egg.
> 1 slice toast.
> Coffee.

Lunch:

> ½ canteloupe.
> Vegetable soup.
> ½ slice toast.
> Coffee or tea, at least 2 cups.

Dinner:

> Clear broth.
> 4 oz. fish, boiled or broiled.
> 1 sliced cucumber.
> 1 slice toast.
> Serving of artificially sweetened gelatin dessert.
> Coffee or tea.

> *Saturday* (600-calorie total)

Breakfast:

> 1 egg.

1 slice toast.
Coffee.

Lunch:

1 oz. of any cheese.
1 sliced tomato and lettuce.
½ slice toast.
Coffee or tea, at least 2 cups.

Dinner:

Vegetable soup.
3 oz. chicken.
¼ head lettuce with low-calorie dressing.
½ slice toast.
Coffee or tea.

Sunday (500-calorie total)

Breakfast:

½ sliced orange.
½ slice toast with artificially sweetened jelly.
Coffee.

Lunch:

½ canteloupe.
Vegetable plate, three hot vegetables.
½ slice toast.
Coffee or tea, at least 2 cups.

Dinner:

½ grapefruit or 1 sliced apple.
3 oz. chicken.
Tossed salad with low-calorie dressing.
Artificially sweetened gelatin dessert.
Coffee or tea.

7-DAY QWL DIET NO. 4

Monday (500-calorie total)

Breakfast:

>   1 slice toast with 1 tbsp. artificially sweetened jam.
>   Coffee with 1 oz. skim milk.

Lunch:

>   Salad of ½ head lettuce, ½ green pepper, 1 tomato, 1
>   cucumber, with low-calorie dressing.
>   Coffee or tea, at least 2 cups.

Dinner:

>   1 cup hot sauerkraut.
>   Boiled potato.
>   1 can asparagus tips, 4 oz.
>   ½ grapefruit.
>   Coffee or tea.

>   *Tuesday* (490-calorie total)

Breakfast:

>   ½ grapefruit.
>   Coffee.

Lunch:

>   Hot vegetable plate, carrots, green beans, spinach.
>   ½ slice bread.
>   ½ melon.
>   Coffee or tea, at least 2 cups.

Dinner:

>   Baked or boiled potato, or 1 cup spaghetti with 1 tbsp.
>   catsup.

1 cup eggplant with little vinegar, ½ cup beets
1 fresh fruit such as medium apple, pear or orange.
Coffee or tea.

Wednesday (460-calorie total)

Breakfast:

1 sliced orange.
Coffee.

Lunch:

1 cup all-vegetable soup.
1 slice rye bread.
Coffee or tea, at least 2 cups.

Dinner:

Hot vegetable plate, three vegetables.
½ melon.
Coffee or tea.

Thursday (300-calorie total)

This day is very low in calories for those who want to lose pounds very quickly. If this is too difficult for you, repeat one of the other days of the week's dieting.

Breakfast, Lunch, Dinner, Before retiring:

Have a glass of buttermilk those four times of the day, that's all. This is an effective one-day quick-reducing break for many of my dieters.

Friday (315-calorie total)

Breakfast:

½ grapefruit.
Coffee.

Lunch:

Tossed salad, greens only, with low-calorie dressing or
lemon juice.
1 slice bread.
Coffee or tea, at least 2 cups.

Dinner:

1 cup all-vegetable soup.
4-oz. can of asparagus tips.
Coffee or tea.

Saturday (320-calorie total)

Breakfast:

1 egg.
Coffee.

Lunch:

3 oz. cottage cheese on lettuce.
2 Melba toast.
Coffee or tea, at least 2 cups.

Dinner:

Baked or boiled potato with 2 oz. beets, 2 oz. spinach,
and ½ cup okra.
Coffee or tea.

Sunday (365-calorie total)

Breakfast:

2 tbsp. cottage cheese.
½ slice toast.
Coffee.

Lunch:

> 1 cup all-vegetable soup.
> ½ slice bread.
> Coffee or tea, at least 2 cups.

Dinner:

> ½ grapefruit.
> 1 egg.
> 1 slice bread.
> Coffee or tea.

Reminders for 7-day dieting . . .

You can make up your own 7-day diet at the beginning of each week if that routine is the way you prefer to reduce, using my listings as guidance in making your own selections. You can reshuffle any of the days from the preceding diets to form a week's eating. Or you may prefer to refer to your calorie tables and make up your own QWL diets averaging about 500 calories a day or less—the fewer calories, the quicker you slim down, of course. Just *don't* make up a 7-day NO-reducing diet like the self-deluding lady who decided to lose a pound a day by staying the same weight but turning back the numbers on the scale a pound each morning.

> • • • Keep drinking plenty of water and other beverages when dieting, at least 5 glasses a day, preferably twice that.
>
> • • • You may use low-calorie dressings in small amounts with all your salads, or fresh lemon juice.
>
> • • • Drink loads of coffee and tea, preferably at least 2 cups at each meal, perhaps one before the meal and one with or after.
>
> • • • Don't forget your vitamin pill with breakfast daily.
>
> • • • When you are permitted bread, it's better to make it protein bread, plain or toasted, as you prefer.
>
> • • • You may have artificially sweetened sodas at meals instead of coffee or tea, if you prefer.
>
> • • • A few servings a day of consommé or bouillon, and

single portions of artificially sweetened gelatin dessert, are permitted.

Have no fears . . .

Some of the quick weight loss diets in this chapter, such as the Repetition QWL Diets that follow and others, may seem somewhat strange and insufficient to you. Please remember that I have had many patients on every one of the diets recommended to you. All have benefited greatly in becoming slimmer and more attractive in a very short time. All have achieved better health after such dieting than before.

To attain those worthy goals for yourself, just follow instructions on these pages. Drink plenty of the permitted liquids each day of dieting; take your daily vitamins; and watch your depressing overweight disappear.

I must remind you again that these "bizarre diets," as some might call them, are—like all my quick weight loss diets—for people who have no wasting disease, just the too-common waistline disease of overweight. That is, the diets are for all overweights except those who are or should be under medical care for a specific, possibly serious, ailment.

Furthermore, while these diets will improve your health by taking off burdensome pounds of fat and flab from your body and organs, I don't want you to attribute to my methods some magical *curative* value. Also, don't connect these diets to any philosophical, religious or faith elements, or hostility to doctors. These diets are all based on sound medical practice and good sense, with one primary goal: *to get that overweight off.* There is nothing antagonistic or mystical about them, no mumbo-jumbo, no "miracles"—even though the astonishing and gratifying quick weight loss may strike you as a miracle for you personally.

If you develop any unusual complaint while on *any* diet (mine or another), if you encounter troublesome symptoms that you've never had before, consult your doctor immediately—without fail. Don't continue on the diet. Don't take laxatives or colonics. Don't go to any type of faith healer or pseudo-medico. See a qualified medical doctor.

Keep in mind always that humans may get sick whether they

are dieting or not. No diet is a cure-all. If a problem appears, get the best medical help and care promptly. That applies to non-dieters as well.

REPETITION QUICK WEIGHT LOSS DIETS

You may be one of these overweights who can stick with a diet best, and lose weight astonishingly fast, when you're limited to one or two foods a day and eat those foods at every meal. Numbers of my patients have found this the way to dieting success. Since my goal is to help you take off excess pounds quickly and healthfully, I've created a wide choice of Repetition Quick Weight Loss Diets for you.

These are very simple diets, very low-calorie—ranging from as little as 180 to a top of 420 calories per day, averaging only 270 calories per day. If you can stay on Repetition dieting for a week and you're burdened with excess pounds, you should lose from 7 to 14 pounds per week, 1 to 2 pounds a day, depending on how overweight you are. That big, quick loss is certainly a worthy target to shoot for. Many factors are working for you on these days.

In the first place, planning of varied menus is practically eliminated. You can tell yourself each day, "This is what I'm going to eat—and that's all, brother!" The choices per day are so limited that there's no worry about consuming too many calories.

Secondly, with these limited diets you automatically thrust temptation aside. It's as though you have put on blinders for the day and have blocked out everything but the one or two foods that you're permitted to have. Also, the quantity of each food you can eat is strictly regulated—simple, clear, no confusion whatever.

Thirdly, you lose your appetite in a hurry on a Repetition Diet. Rather than becoming hungrier, you find after just a couple of days that your desire for more food diminishes, you don't look forward to filling your stomach. This may be difficult for you to believe but you'll find it's so, as proved to me in hundreds of cases.

On all these Repetition Diets, the will-power factor again is built in. The fact that you see the numbers on the scale dropping delightfully by the second or third day, and going down-down-

down day after day, is the prime encouragement to stay with your restricted diet and away from high-calorie foods that would pile on that fat again.

I purposely provide over a dozen Repetition QWL Diets for your choice so that you can swing from the Egg Diet on Monday to the Tuna-Lettuce Diet on Tuesday, and so on—the selection and rotation is up to you. If you want to stay on just one of the diets, such as the Melon-Cottage Cheese Diet every day for a week, you'll succeed in losing weight rapidly.

You don't have to be concerned about the need to stay on a Repetition Diet for months. One week or a few weeks will get you started on your weight loss campaign, then you can switch to the basic Quick Weight Loss Diet, or one or more of the Quick Weight Loss Variety Diets, then to the Inches-Off Diet, as you decide. One thing is sure, you'll get that weight off in a remarkably short time and improve your appearance and health wonderfully.

INSTRUCTIONS FOR ALL REPETITION DIETS

Daily Vitamin Pill: You'll note that each diet includes a daily vitamin pill. This should be a high-potency pill combining vitamins and minerals. I have never found a vitamin deficiency among any of my dieting patients, including those who have reduced on my Repetition Diets. However, I recommend the daily high-potency pill as a simple extra protective measure.

Beverages—minimum of 8 to 10 glasses a day: On these very low-calorie, limited Repetition Diets, your system is burning off at at a high rate. The waste materials thus created in the system must be washed away—accomplished by drinking often throughout your waking hours. You must take a total of at least 8 to 10 glasses of liquids per day, including these choices:

   – Water, as much as you can drink comfortably.
   – Artificially sweetened carbonated beverages that contain no more than one half calorie per fluid ounce (most non-sugar sodas contain only a small fraction of a calorie per ounce)—check the label. Enjoy plain soda or seltzer, or a wide variety of delicious flavors. *You can drink many glasses of artificially sweetened, low-calorie*

sodas per day as you wish—all day long, all evening,
every waking hour—up to 10 glasses a day.

– Coffee, as many cups a day as you wish without
cream or milk or sugar but with as much artificial sweetening as you like, within reason. If the caffeine in coffee
bothers you, drink the type of coffee from which caffeine
has been removed.

– Tea, as many cups of tea a day as you like, without
cream or milk or sugar. Use as much artificial sweetening as desired, within reason. Enjoy any type of tea you
like best, a variety of kinds during the day if you prefer
to savor their subtle flavors—Ceylon, Orange Pekoe,
Earl Grey, Darjeeling, Formosa Oolong—there are many
for your choice. You'll find that drinking quantities of
tea, many times a day, at meals and between meals, is
both filling and satisfying.

Don't leap to the conclusion that you have to be drinking
water and beverages continuously—8 glasses at a time, for example, to carry it to extremes. Drinking 10 glasses or cups of beverage a day amounts to only about half a glassful per waking hour.
Thinking of it another way, if you drink only 3 glasses of water
the entire day, 4 cups of coffee or tea at meals and at coffee-
breaks, and 3 glasses of carbonated beverages, you're already
up to 10 glasses a day —and you can go on from there to limitless
quantities daily. Flushing out your system with such liquids is
necessary and healthful for quick-loss diets, and good for anyone at any time.

In addition to the repetition foods and liquids permitted on
these diets, you may have two or three moderate-size servings
daily of *low-calorie, artificially sweetened gelatin dessert,* with
meals or between meals, in a variety of flavors. You may have
each day *two servings of instant consommé,* broth or bouillon
made with cubes, powders or liquids. To dilute each serving,
add to consommé more liquid—I suggest that you dissolve each
cube in 1½ to 2 cups of hot water instead of 1 cup of water. This
fills you up more. Enjoy the consommé with meals or between
meals, as you please.

No other extras: A prime rule on my Repetition Diets is that
each day you eat only what is specified for that day, no larger

portions than listed, no additional foods except the gelatin and consommé. If you deviate from that you'll be ruining the desired quick weight loss on that diet, and you should then choose one of my other quick weight loss diets in the book that permits you larger portions and greater variety.

Here are over a dozen Repetition Diets that have proved successful in reducing men and women quickly:

EGG DIET
(225 calories a day)

1 egg—three times a day.
Water, coffee, tea, non-caloric sodas.
1 vitamin pill.

SKIM-MILK DIET
(225 calories a day)

1 glass of skim milk—three times a day.
Water, coffee, tea, non-caloric sodas.
1 vitamin pill.

BUTTERMILK DIET
(300 calories a day)

1 glass of buttermilk—four times a day.
Water, coffee, tea, non-caloric sodas.
1 vitamin pill.

COTTAGE CHEESE DIET
(180 calories a day)

4 tablespoons cottage cheese per portion—three times a day.
Water, coffee, tea, non-caloric sodas.
1 vitamin pill.

MEAT-VEGETABLE DIET
(410 calories a day)

1 hamburger, 3 oz., lean, well-broiled, twice a day.
½ cup green vegetable with each hamburger.

Water, coffee, tea, non-caloric sodas.
1 vitamin pill.

CHICKEN-VEGETABLE DIET
(200 calories a day)

1 chicken leg (without skin)—twice daily.
½ cup green vegetables with each chicken leg.
Water, coffee, tea, non-caloric sodas.
1 vitamin pill.

FISH-TOMATO DIET
(300 calories a day)

Fish (moderate, 4 oz.), baked or broiled—twice daily.
2 medium-sized tomatoes—1 with each fish meal.
Water, coffee, tea, non-caloric sodas.
1 vitamin pill.

MELON-COTTAGE CHEESE DIET
(240 calories a day)

½ melon with 2 tablespoons of cottage cheese—3 times a day.
Water, coffee, tea, non-caloric sodas.
1 vitamin pill.

BANANA DIET
(270 calories a day)

1 banana—3 times a day.
Water, coffee, tea, non-caloric sodas.
1 vitamin pill.

CRABMEAT-LETTUCE DIET
(420 calories a day)

1 moderate portion of crabmeat—twice a day.
¼ head of lettuce—twice a day, with crabmeat.
Water, coffee, tea, non-caloric sodas.
1 vitamin pill.

SHRIMP-LETTUCE DIET
(300 calories a day)

12 medium-size shrimps—twice daily.
¼ head of lettuce—twice daily with shrimps.
Water, coffee, tea, non-caloric sodas.
1 vitamin pill.

TUNA-LETTUCE DIET
(290 calories a day)

Solid white tuna, water-packed, 4 oz.—twice daily.
¼ head of lettuce—twice daily with tuna.
Water, coffee, tea, non-caloric sodas.
1 vitamin pill.

SALMON-LETTUCE DIET
(375 calories a day)

Salmon, water-packed, 4 oz.—twice daily.
¼ head of lettuce—twice daily with salmon.
Water, coffee, tea, non-caloric sodas.
1 vitamin pill.

STEAK-VEGETABLE DIET
(400 calories a day)

Steak, lean, broiled, 3 oz.—twice daily.
½ cup green vegetables—twice daily with steak.
Water, coffee, tea, non-caloric sodas.
1 vitamin pill.

On all Repetition QWL Diets, you may scatter your meals at any time you wish during the day. For example, on the Fish-Tomato Diet, if you prefer to have your fish at breakfast and dinner, skipping fish at lunchtime—suit yourself.

Keep filling yourself up at meals and between meals with plenty of the permitted beverages.

Enjoy plenty of moderate exercise each day—do a lot of brisk walking.

Keep busy outdoors as well as indoors.

Don't think of the food you're missing but of the more attractive looks and more vigorous health that will soon be yours.

Keep in mind that by the third day of Repetition dieting, any appetite will be diminishing remarkably. You'll start to see the numbers dropping on the scale as you weigh yourself each morning.

You don't have to follow the same Repetition Diet every day. Make up a weekly schedule if you wish, mixing or repeating the diets according to your personal desires. Here, as examples, are listings covering two weeks of Repetition dieting—but you can make up your own schedule:

REPETITION DIETS WEEK NO. 1

MONDAY—EGG DIET.

TUESDAY—TUNA-LETTUCE DIET.

WEDNESDAY—COTTAGE CHEESE DIET.

THURSDAY—MEAT-VEGETABLE DIET.

FRIDAY—SHRIMP-LETTUCE DIET.

SATURDAY—MELON-COTTAGE CHEESE DIET.

SUNDAY—CHICKEN-VEGETABLE DIET.

REPETITION DIETS WEEK NO. 2

MONDAY—SKIMMED MILK DIET.

TUESDAY—SALMON-LETTUCE DIET.

WEDNESDAY—BANANA DIET.

THURSDAY—STEAK-VEGETABLE DIET.

FRIDAY—CRABMEAT-LETTUCE DIET.

SATURDAY—BUTTERMILK DIET.

SUNDAY—FISH-TOMATO DIET.

Ignore the old saying "Use not vain repetitions." I can assure you that your adherence to any or all of my Repetition QWL Diets will not be in vain. Just one week or less will take off an average of 10 pounds of overweight. You'll read the proof in the diminishing numbers on your bathroom scale, and the fact that you can get into that smaller-size dress (or too-tight suit) that you were about to throw away.

Yes, one week of Repetition dieting can make a remarkable reduction in your waistline, so much so that the majority of my Repetition dieters go on eagerly to the next week of this kind of quick weight loss eating. This is usually the case even though they thought at the start that they could never endure one week on the diet, let alone more.

FASTING QWL DIET

To those patients who have a very strong motivation to reduce quickly, and to prove they can by getting 4 or 5 pounds off in a couple of days, I frequently suggest one or two days on my Fasting QWL Diet before switching to any other dieting method. You can lose an average of about 4 pounds (2 to 7 pounds generally) in 48 hours (my basic Quick Weight Loss Diet takes off almost as many pounds as rapidly as fasting).

When you have no solid food at all for a day or two, you lose a lot of the feeling of bloat and discomfort that often accompanies considerable excess weight. You start feeling lighter and better, with a wonderful sense of relief due to starting to get rid of the constant burden of fat.

A day or two of fasting seems to accelerate the metabolism and prepares the system to burn up food more easily after the fasting. Also, going entirely without solid food diminishes your appetite in a hurry so that you're not hungry in spite of not eating; this may strike you as a strange phenomenon but it invariably turns out that way. With a lessened appetite, you're a step nearer to success when you shift to the quick weight loss diet of your choice.

I don't recommend fasting more than one or two days except under medical supervision. Fasting is primarily for the obese, those who are dozens of pounds overweight. It is usually too exhausting for the obese to exercise or undertake a sizable increase in activity that would help take off weight. By fasting, they drop pounds quickly and retain a driving desire to keep taking off pounds instead of stuffing themselves.

In one of the tests of eleven obese persons on a fasting routine under medical supervision, they lost 14 to 33 pounds in ten days. Nine out of eleven stayed on the fasting diet for twelve to 117 days. Rather than becoming ill, most all improved in health as weight dropped off, the body feeding on its own fat. (Some patients, who were predisposed to gout before fasting, developed gout and received medication.)

Typical results are given in an article in the *Journal of the American Medical Association:* "All reports have emphasized that prolonged fasts are easily tolerated, little discomfort is experienced, and no serious adverse effects are observed." So you certainly need not be concerned about becoming weak or ill from one or two days of fasting. Like others, you'll probably feel much better after 24 to 48 hours of no food at all.

On my Fasting QWL Diet, follow these simple rules for one or two days, preferably for two days:

- . . . Don't eat any solid food at all, but keep drinking large quantities of liquid hour after hour. The liquids help wash waste products out of your system and give you a feeling of being full so that you don't crave food.
- . . . Drink at least 8 to 10 glasses daily, and as much more water as you can during your waking hours.
- . . . You may have three servings each day of clear consommé, broth or bouillon, made with cubes, powder or liquid. Make each portion with 1½ cups of water instead of 1 cup of water for milder flavor and more liquid per portion.
- . . . Drink as much coffee and tea during the day as you wish, the more the better (no-caffeine coffee if you prefer); no cream, milk or sugar, but as much artificial sweetening as you wish, within reason.
- . . . Drink lots of non-caloric artificially sweetened carbonated beverages, a variety of flavors if you like, up to 10 glasses a day. They give refreshment as well as aiding the liquid flow through your system and helping to keep you feeling full enough so that you don't miss solid food.
- . . . Take one or two high-potency vitamin-mineral tablets each day on the fasting diet.
- . . . Go about your affairs normally, walking and work-

ing and being active but no more so than usual.
You should be feeling fine, with the gratifying
sense that you are shedding pounds each day.

After 24 to 48 hours on the Fasting QWL Diet, switch to
the basic Quick Weight Loss Diet, or the Inches-Off Diet, or
any quick weight loss diet of your choice from these pages. The
fasting is a worthwhile preliminary to these other quick-reducing
diets which give you plenty of good, solid food and yet will take
off pounds and trim off inches rapidly.

TWO-MEALS-A-DAY QWL DIET

This type of quick weight loss diet has had some popularity
in Italy, particularly, where it was publicized. I have worked out
a version which a number of my patients have used with good
results, taking off 1 to 1½ pounds a day, 7 to 10 pounds a week,
depending on the amount of overweight at the start. This kind
of dieting is especially appealing to those who want nothing for
breakfast except coffee or tea.

The Two-Meals-A-Day QWL Diet is simplicity itself. You eat
the same meal for lunch and dinner but provide a variety from
day to day by changing the meats, chicken, fish or seafood and
choosing different vegetables at meals. Eat two meals a day (just
black coffee at breakfast, which is hardly a "meal"), both selected
from this listing:

1. Cup of clear soup—consommé, broth or bouillon.
2. 4 oz. lean meat, chicken, turkey, fish or seafood.
3. 1 cup of a low-calorie vegetable; no butter, oil, fats.
4. 2 slices Melba toast.
5. 1 medium-size apple or orange.
6. Coffee or tea, with 1 tbsp. skim milk if desired.

Drink plenty of water and no-calorie, artificially sweetened
carbonated beverages all through waking hours.

As a mid-afternoon and an evening snack, you may have a
portion of low-calorie, artificially sweetened gelatin dessert.

You may use low-calorie salad dressing in moderation, or a
little fresh lemon juice.

Take a vitamin-mineral tablet daily.

You will lose weight rapidly and feel good all through your reducing period on the Two-Meals-A-Day QWL Diet.

RICE QUICK WEIGHT LOSS DIET

Considerable success has been attained with rice dieting not only in reducing overweights but also as an important aid in treating high blood pressure. Although rice is certainly not a low-calorie food, you are permitted a great deal of this bland grain on the Rice QWL Diet, but your weight goes down rapidly for several reasons. Since no salt is allowed in cooking, the rice is so bland to the taste that you don't overeat, especially as there is monotony in having the same basic food meal after meal, even with some flavoring. You don't eat any of the butter, other fats or heavy sauces that are usually used to drench the plain rice and give it appealing flavor (along with loads of extra, burdensome calories). The rice fills you up quickly, so that you have no desire for more than limited quantities, adding up to few calories.

You will find that it requires far more will power than to stay on the basic Quick Weight Loss Diet or the Inches-Off Diet, since the rice is so bland and flavorless. However, if you like rice, this is a quick-reducing as well as healthful way of taking off 1, 1½ or more pounds a day, day after day, the amount depending on how much extra fat you are carrying at the start.

I suggest to my patients that they cook the regular or extra long grain natural rice, including partly-cooked processed rice, rather than the so-called "instant" brands. The natural white rice which you should use (not brown rice) has more flavor than "instant" rice, and costs a good deal less per ounce (check according to the number of ounces printed on the package, rather than size of package, as the "instant" rices bulk up more yet provide fewer portions of cooked rice at serving time).

The rice is more flavorful and satisfying if fresh-cooked at each meal. However, many of the rice brands, especially the long grain rice, may be cooked in unsalted water in the morning and stay fresh and fairly firm in the refrigerator for reheating at lunch and dinner. Here are your basic directions to follow to lose weight rapidly:

Breakfast, lunch and dinner—in general, you eat the same amount of food at each meal, using the same menu consisting of
- up to ⅓ pound of cooked rice per meal (you will probably find that you don't eat that quantity).
- 8 oz. of fruit juice from the permitted list.
- 3 oz. of fruit.

For example, a typical meal would consist of
- up to ⅓ pound of rice.
- 8 oz. of orange juice.
- 3 oz. of stewed prunes.

If you find that this diet is too monotonous to stay on, you can add a moderate portion (½ cup to 1 cup) of one of the permitted vegetables listed later at each meal. You will still lose weight, since the vegetable will probably replace some of the rice you would eat.

Only the foods listed may be eaten on the Rice QWL Diet. If not listed, don't eat it. Drink as much as you wish of water, coffee and tea without cream, milk or sugar; and non-caloric carbonated beverages. Be sure to avoid the following as well as foods not listed:

No nuts, dates, avocadoes.
No vegetable juices.
No butter, fats, oils of any kind.
No candies other than a little homemade hard candy (no candies at all containing butter or other fats).
No ice cream or other rich desserts.
No salt at any time (salt substitute may be used).
No fried foods at all.
No catsup; just a little pepper or mustard or horseradish may be used but only very sparingly.
No frozen vegetables, only fresh vegetables.
No brown sugar, no maple syrup or other sugar syrups; you may use white sugar, cinnamon, nutmeg, sparingly.

Drink a great deal each day, as much as you want, of water and low-calorie carbonated beverages, at least 8 to 10 glasses a day.

Take a high-potency vitamin-mineral tablet each day while on this diet.

You may spread the food permitted for the three meals, same total quantity, over six meals a day if you prefer, and you will lose weight even faster on the six-meals-daily schedule.

The following are listings of permitted juices, fruits and vegetables:

Juices

Apple	Grape	Peach
Apricot	Grapefruit	Pear
Cranberry	Orange	Pineapple

Fruits

Apples	Currants	Pear
Apricots, not dried	Figs, not dried	Pineapple
Banana	Gooseberries	Plums
Blackberries	Grapefruit	Prunes, stewed
Blueberries	Grapes	Raspberries
Canteloupe	Honeydew Melon	Strawberries
Cherries	Melons, all kinds	Watermelon
Cranberries	Peach	

Fruits may be raw, baked, canned, stewed.

Vegetables

Asparagus	Cauliflower	Peppers, Green
Beets	Collards	Spinach
Broccoli	Cucumbers	Squash, all types
Brussels Sprouts	Eggplant	Tomatoes
Cabbage	Lettuce	Turnips
Carrots	Onions	Zucchini

TYPICAL DAY'S MENU

Breakfast:

3 oz. mixed stewed fruits.
1 cup cooked rice,
    with sugar and cinnamon.
4 oz. orange juice.

Lunch:

> 3 oz. fresh fruit.
> 1 cup rice.
> 8 oz. canned pear juice.

Dinner:

> 1 cup rice (with sugar, if desired).
> 3 oz. canned pineapple.
> 6 oz. mixed vegetables (or one vegetable).
> 4 oz. apple juice.

You may add variety to the diet by fixing rice with sugar and cinnamon, fruit and rice mixed together, vegetables and rice mixed together—any such combination you wish to create.

Vegetables may be cooked and served separately, eating a half-cup of spinach and a half-cup of squash, for example, rather than a full cup of either; or you may serve mixed vegetables. But remember that no salt is to be used in cooking vegetables or anything else. Salt substitute may be used for flavoring.

Although it is desirable to have 3 oz. of three different fruits through the day to make up the total 9 oz. of fruit for the day, you may have just one fruit serving if you wish, such as a half-grapefruit at breakfast or a sliced orange, or a larger wedge of melon, and so on.

You will find that you lose weight rapidly on the Rice QWL Diet, and pleasantly—no "skinny" or scrawny look. You rarely, probably never, feel hunger pangs, because you feel full, and the salt-free food isn't that appealing to the appetite. You will feel well-fed but never bloated or overfull unless you stuff yourself as few people ever do on this kind of eating.

This is an excellent inches-off diet, as well as taking off pounds rapidly. This type of eating, when you are down to ideal weight, works well to pull more fat out of the muscle areas, slimming your dimensions and taking extra inches off beautifully.

8

QWL Diets for
Specific Health Problems

Hundreds of years ago it was written by wise men: "Health and good estate of body are above gold, and a strong body above infinite wealth." Emerson echoed, "The first wealth is health." You certainly know by now from the facts I have presented that to help promote good health and vigor as well as beauty, one of the primary rules is to *keep your weight down*. In sickness, getting down to ideal weight and staying that way may well be a matter of life or death.

My own story bears repeating as an example. Decades ago, when I was considerably overweight, I was the victim of a severe heart attack. It was my good fortune to survive and have another chance at living and regaining my health. As a physician I realized that I had better take off the excess pounds quickly or I might never again have a chance. I succeeded in getting down to ideal weight, and I've remained there ever since.

It became my crusade, although my basic practice was as an internist (specializing in internal medicine), to get overweight patients who came in with other sicknesses to take excess pounds off quickly while I was treating their other ills. I mention this to emphasize that while everyone should take off overweight, I consider it crucially important for those with specific illnesses.

The following diets cover some of the more common afflictions. I present them as a general guide that can be helpful to you if you have any of these problems. I must emphasize again, as I do time after time in this book, that your primary instructions should come from the doctor who has examined you personally and knows your individual case. This applies to all diets.

Check my suggestions with your physician; they can be helpful to you in expanding your knowledge by knowing what kind of dieting has helped others with heart troubles and other problems.

ANTI-HEART ATTACK DIET

The American Heart Association has advised: "Reduction or control of fat consumption under medical supervision with reasonable substitution of polyunsaturated for saturated fats is recommended as a possible means of preventing atherosclerosis and decreasing the risk of heart attacks and strokes."

While there are many forms and causes in respect to heart attacks, I am concerned here primarily with coronary-artery disease due to arteriosclerosis (related to atherosclerosis), that is, hardening of the arteries. Any or all heart diseases may be aggravated by overweight. My diet suggestions are specifically directed to combat the great killer, arteriosclerosis, affecting "angina" patients. This can be helped by the type of diet as concerns both quantity and quality of foods.

Two prominent factors tend to reduce the flow of blood through the coronary vessels, thus leading to heart disease. First, there is damage to the walls of the coronary arteries due to deposits of a fatty-like substance. Second, these deposits cause the arteries to be narrowed, and increase the chances of the blood becoming a coagulated mass and forming a clot that may completely obstruct the flow of blood to the heart muscles—causing a "heart attack." It is best, of course, to watch the diet from an early age to help to prevent such fat deposits.

Fat in the system is increased after the eating of any meal, with or without fat. The more fat in the food you have eaten, naturally the more fat in your system after the meal. This leads to three recommendations as a guide:

    (1) Don't eat foods that contain an excess amount of fat.
    (2) Don't overload your body at any time with a large,

heavy meal—that includes special occasions and holidays. Avoid the large, heavy meal, which is more likely to bring on a heart attack.

(3) It is better to eat smaller meals more often than one large and three small meals a day, or three larger meals a day. The more food you put into your stomach at any one time, the more likely it is that you may overload your system, including your blood vessels and other organs, and promote heart troubles. I cannot overemphasize this. If you learn nothing else from this book, it's worth it to have absorbed this point as a signal in your eating for the rest of your life.

By not overloading your stomach and blood vessels, you will help counteract arteriosclerosis, and you will certainly lose weight. A moderate amount of exercise, such as walking after a meal—never anything strenuous—will also tend to burn up some of the free fatty acids floating around in the bloodstream after eating.

Other factors may also aggravate heart troubles, such as smoking, which is particularly dangerous for the heart patient. Excessive emotional reactions such as anger, tension, constant severe pressure in daily living, may be injurious. Diseases such as diabetes and hypertension (high blood pressure) are likely to be complicating in heart problems and should be checked closely by a physician.

ANTI-HEART ATTACK QWL DIET

This type of dieting is very simple, effective and healthful with most any condition, even other than heart problems, or for the person of average health. It might be called an example of a polyunsaturated low-calorie diet that helps promote good health as it takes off excess pounds rapidly. Your daily diet amounts to about 600 calories total.

Make up your daily menus from the foods on this list only:

* 8 oz. tomato juice or other vegetable juice.
* 3 cups low-calorie vegetables, cooked or raw.

or

* Fresh fruits totaling about 100 calories a day (or 100-calorie daily total of vegetables and fruits).
* 1 slice of bread, any type.

* 6 oz. lean meat, poultry, fish or seafood (total in this category of 240 calories daily).
* 6 tbsp. cottage cheese.
* 1 pat of diet margarine.
* 1 egg, no more than four days a week, may be substituted those days for the meat, poultry or fish.
* Coffee or tea, no sugar, milk or cream.

Typical Day

Breakfast:

½ canteloupe.
1 slice toast.
½ pat diet margarine.
Coffee or tea.

Lunch:

6 tbsp. cottage cheese.
Lettuce and tomato salad with a little corn oil dressing or other low-calorie salad dressing.
Coffee or tea.

Dinner:

3 oz. lean ground beef.
3 cups vegetables.
Coffee or tea.

Another Day

Breakfast:

4 oz. tomato juice.
1 slice toast with 1 tsp. low-calorie jam.
Coffee or tea.

Lunch:

½ grapefruit.
3 oz. lean fish.

1 cup vegetable.
Coffee or tea.

Dinner:

3 oz. poultry, remove skin and fat.
4 cups vegetables, or a salad.
Low-calorie gelatin dessert.
Coffee or tea.

Another Day

Breakfast:

Medium orange, sliced.
1 slice toast with 1 tsp. low-calorie jelly.
Coffee or tea.

Lunch:

Fresh-fruit cup.
3 oz. water-packed or drained tuna fish.
Lettuce with low-calorie dressing.
Coffee or tea.

Dinner:

Slice honeydew melon.
3 oz. chicken, turkey or seafood.
2 cups vegetables.
Low-calorie gelatin dessert.
Coffee or tea.

HELPFUL TIPS

2 cups per day bouillon, consommé or broth, made with cubes, powder or fat-free liquid, permitted between meals.

2 portions low-calorie gelatin dessert daily may be enjoyed with or between meals as snacks.

Drink lots of liquid all through your waking hours—water, coffee and tea without sugar or milk or cream (as much artificial sweetening as you want, within reason), and low-calorie, artificially sweetened carbonated beverages of assorted flavors.

Flavor your salads if you wish with a little low-calorie salad dressing, fresh-squeezed lemon juice, a little vinegar, salt, pepper and herbs to your taste.

An ounce of liquor a few times a week is permitted, but the equivalent in calories must then be eliminated from foods taken in the day's eating in order to assure quick weight loss.

Avoid smoking, emotional upsets and prolonged pressure.

Never have a large meal even if you stay within your daily calorie limit by saving up all your calories for one meal; this overburdens the system and may bring on a heart attack if you are susceptible.

Don't use salt or any spices in large quantities. Use just a little salt or a salt substitute.

Avoid animal fats and saturated fats—this means you must do without whole milk, cream, butter, whole-milk cheeses, fatty meats, fatty poultry, duck and goose, mayonnaise, gravies, heavy sauces and dressings; no more than 4 eggs a week; no fried foods, no heavy oils, no buttery foods, no rich desserts.

Dry cereal with ½ cup skim milk may be taken three days a week, substituting for other foods and therefore eliminating that number of calories from the day's diet; for instance, you may have ½ cup dry cereal with skim milk instead of a slice of bread.

Exercise moderately each day—walking is about the best exercise. Make it your business to be active, not lie around; sleep no more than eight hours of the 24, but never subject yourself to strenuous activity or exercise that exhausts you.

When you are down to ideal weight, you may increase your daily calorie intake to stay at that weight (see Ideal Weight and Calorie Table in first chapter), choosing from the foods permitted in the basic daily listing here for the Anti-Heart Attack QWL Diet. You will be far more likely to live healthily ever after, proving the proverb "He who hath good health is young."

ANTI-HIGH BLOOD PRESSURE QWL DIET

To help combat and control hypertension or high blood pressure (checked regularly by your physician, who will tell you if you have this condition), use the Rice QWL Diet given in Chapter 7. This diet is recommended particularly if you have a tendency toward any problems generally associated with high blood pressure. This type of eating will probably bring down your high blood pressure readings as it takes off burdensome extra pounds of fat. Of course, other factors may be involved with hypertension, so be sure to follow the advice of your doctor. This condition must never be neglected, as it may also be symptomatic of related serious ills.

Whatever treatment may be prescribed for high blood pressure, it's a "must" to take off excess pounds immediately and as rapidly as possible. The basis for any reducing diet for those with hypertension is low calorie, low salt, low fat. There are basic rules to be followed.

Use artificial sweeteners and artificially sweetened, low-calorie carbonated beverages as much as you want, within reason, but make sure to check the labels and *avoid any artificial sweetening that contains sodium of any kind*. For example, some sweeteners (all show ingredients on the package) contain "sodium cyclamate" and should not be used if you have hypertension; a listing of "calcium cyclamate" instead makes the product permissible on your anti-high-blood-pressure dieting.

Drink plenty of water and other beverages without sodium. Select lean meats and poultry, trimming off all fat and skin. No oils. No fried foods. No gravies. No pies or pastries. No smoked fish. No pork products. No canned products unless salt free, water-packed instead of with oils.

Avoid overexciting yourself as much as possible. Try to live a relaxed, composed life, within the limits of being an alert, active individual, participating in what goes on about you. Get some mild exercise daily, such as walking, but no strenuous or exhausting activity. Cereals and low-sodium bread are permitted, but no cakes or rich desserts.

For the sake of reducing daily calorie intake, and for most healthful eating, limit drastically any use of butter, whole-milk cheeses, margarine, dressings and bread, but be sure that any of these you eat have *no sodium*. No-sodium foods are usually identified on the package as "salt-free."

Avoid monosodium glutamate.

No catsup or other such items that contain salt.

Vegetables, fruit and rice are excellent foods on any diet for those who have high blood pressure.

SALT-FREE QWL DIET

Choose from the foods permitted in the preceding listing, limiting your intake to about 600 calories a day to lose pounds quickly. Make up your own daily menus from these guides— here's a sample day:

Breakfast:

>   2 oz. orange juice or 4 oz. tomato juice.
>   1 oz. of dry cereal or cooked cereal and half-glass of skim milk.
>   Coffee or tea.

Lunch:

>   Fruit salad.
>   1 cup low-calorie vegetable, cooked or raw.
>   2 oz. broiled lean meat.
>   Coffee or tea.

Dinner:

>   4 oz. of fish broiled (low salt), or
>   4 oz. of lean chicken or turkey (low salt).
>   1 cup low-calorie vegetable, cooked or raw.
>   Tossed salad with a little fresh lemon juice.
>   Coffee or tea.

This is just a sample day. The list of permitted foods leaves you plenty of choice. For example, your breakfast the next day might be a complete departure from the preceding fruit and cereal meal, choosing instead a slice of low-sodium bread, plain or toasted, with 8 tablespoons of creamed cottage cheese and coffee or tea. Average out your calories so that you don't exceed about 600 calories a day, such as 150 calories at breakfast, 200 at lunch and 250 at dinner, juggling as you see fit.

Once you are down to your ideal weight, boost your calorie

intake to stay at that weight. Make up your enlarged meals from the same list of permitted foods in order to keep your hypertension down. As in most dieting, spreading your calories over six meals and/or snacks (six total feedings) a day is the more healthful way.

RICE-VEGETABLE FRUIT QWL DIET

An excellent inches-off diet, as well as a quick weight loss diet that combats hypertension, is the combination of rice, low-calorie vegetables and low-calorie fruits, with an occasional small serving of white bread (non-protein). Follow the rules give in the preceding diet for avoiding salt (sodium). This diet will get you down to ideal weight quickly, and then take extra inches off by pulling more fat and protein out of your muscle-mass areas.

Here, too, the basis for success is low-calorie, low-fat, low-salt eating. You eat small meals, keep the calories down to under 500 per day. You are permitted snacks of raw carrot strips, a small piece of fresh fruit occasionally, a cup of low-salt bouillon, broth or consommé (but beware of high salt content!). Keep active each day with plenty of walking at a moderate pace.

Make up your own daily menus, keeping to fewer than 500 calories total, relying primarily on vegetables, fruit and fruit juices and rice, as follows:

Typical Day

Breakfast:

> ½ cup of cooked rice.
> 2 oz. fruit juice.
> Coffee or tea.

Lunch:

> Tossed salad with a little vinegar or lemon juice, or one serving of canteloupe (half), slice of melon, half grapefruit, apple, or other piece of fresh fruit.
> Coffee or tea.

Dinner:

> ½-cup rice.
> 2 cups of any low-calorie vegetables.
> Fruit cup or piece of fruit or stewed fruit, no sugar or salt.
> Coffee or tea.

Another Day

Breakfast:

> 4 oz. tomato juice, or half grapefruit.
> Coffee or tea.

Lunch:

> Fruit salad.
> Coffee or tea.

Dinner:

> 2 oz. fruit juice.
> ½ cup rice.
> Sliced tomato and sliced cucumber.
> Slice of melon.
> Coffee or tea.

Another Day

Breakfast:

> 4 oz. fruit juice.
> 1 slice white bread (non-protein) with 1 tsp. low-calorie jelly.
> Coffee or tea.

Lunch:

> Cup bouillon, very bland.
> 2 cups vegetables.
> 2 crackers, no-sodium.

Apple, or another piece of fresh fruit.
Coffee or tea.

Dinner:

½ canteloupe or ½ grapefruit.
Mixed salad, a little vinegar or lemon juice.
1 slice non-protein bread with 1 tsp. dietetic jam.
Coffee or tea.

Remember that each day you are better off spreading the food through the day with snacks between meals instead of eating more at mealtime. Take a high-potency vitamin-mineral tablet each day on any of these diets.

ANTI-ULCER QWL DIETING

When you have stomach pains, which may be indications of an ulcer, see your doctor immediately instead of worrying about your condition. He will tell you whether or not you have an ulcer, and will instruct you on eating and care. Whatever treatment you follow, your physician should check you often to make sure that the ulcer is under control and healing, that the treatment is effective. Otherwise very serious trouble may develop.

In modern living a good many overweights develop gastric or duodenal ulcers. These people usually eat too much, indulge in hot, spicy foods, drink excess amounts of strong coffee and tea, cola drinks, beer and alcoholic beverages. They may dose themselves frequently with aspirin and other drugs that are acid in nature. In addition, they are usually under tension, burdened by business or other worries, live the opposite of a peaceful existence.

While the full story of the causes of ulcers is not known, there are certain approaches which will help to heal the ulcers and help prevent their recurrence. First, the individual must have physical and emotional rest, even if it is necessary to remove the patient to a different, tranquil environment.

Second, a bland diet involving frequent feedings is desirable.

Third, some antacids should be taken frequently, and perhaps some tranquilizing medication, all of which your physician will prescribe (no medication should be taken without a prescription and specific instructions).

Fourth, if the patient .is overweight, those excess pounds should come off rapidly. In contradiction, some people complain that they have been put on diets involving such foods as whole milk and cream, which *add weight* while they are trying to get rid of the ulcer. This is not only highly undesirable but clearly unnecessary. I have had great success over the years with patients on two different types of diets that not only help eliminate the ulcer but also take off weight at the same time, as follows (please check these diets with your doctor beforehand):

ALL-PROTEIN ANTI-ULCER QWL DIET

As with all anti-ulcer dieting, frequent feeding is a vital element of the success of this diet. You eat lean (fat removed) meat, fish, chicken, turkey, sweetbreads, liver—*ground up before eating.* Cottage cheese and mashed hard-boiled eggs are also important in the diet. This all-protein eating removes excess weight rapidly, neutralizes acids and helps heal the ulcer quickly. The permitted foods may be substituted and rotated for those on the following listing, in quantities stated: .

> 8 A.M.—one mashed hard-boiled egg, 2 to 3 cups of weak tea, with a little skim milk added to the tea, or to the same quantity of very weak coffee.
>
> 10 A.M.—2 oz. of broiled, lean, finely chopped meat, several glasses of water, very weak tea.
>
> 12 *noon*—2 oz. of mashed liver, water, very weak tea.
>
> 2 P.M.—2 oz. mashed fish, lots of water and weak tea.
>
> 4 P.M.—1 mashed hard-boiled egg, water and weak tea.
>
> 6 P.M.—2 oz. finely cut chicken or turkey, all skin removed, water and weak tea.
>
> 8 P.M.—2 oz. cottage cheese, water and weak tea.
>
> 10 P.M.—2 oz. cottage cheese, water and weak tea.
>
> *During night*—if awake, 1 mashed hard-boiled egg, water.

As stated, an important part of quickly diminishing the contractions of stomach and intestines and helping the ulcer to heal most rapidly is the routine of small, frequent feedings. Overweight is eliminated in a hurry, and patients usually start feeling better remarkably soon. The physician's checkup, which is essential, will confirm this.

LOW-PROTEIN ANTI-ULCER DIET

For those who prefer foods other than the animal foods on the all-protein anti-ulcer diet, an effective reducing and healing routine can be based on foods such as skim milk, soft cereals, softened crackers and toast and puréed fruit and vegetables without any seeds or skin. With such a diet it is essential for the desired quick weight loss that helps healing to keep the daily calorie total under 750 calories.

Limited intake of these foods is essential, spread over the day and evening in about nine feedings, as in this sample daily menu:

> 8 A.M.—1 glass of skim milk, weak tea.
>
> 10 A.M.—1 mashed banana.
>
> 12 *noon*—½ glass skim milk, 2 tablespoons rice or a finely ground, bland hot cereal such as farina.
>
> 2 P.M.—1 glass buttermilk.
>
> 4 P.M.—½ glass buttermilk in which is soaked and softened two bland crackers.
>
> 6 P.M.—1 mashed hard-boiled egg, 2 or 3 cups of weak tea.
>
> 8 P.M.—1 portion of low-calorie gelatin dessert.
>
> 10 P.M.—1 glass buttermilk.
>
> 2 A.M. (or when awake)—1 glass skim milk.

You may substitute for the foods and feedings above small portions of tomato juice, bland cereals, ½ potato mashed, 4-oz. portions of creamed cottage cheese, puréed vegetables, puréed fruits without skin or pits, weak fruit juices.

Tea and coffee should always be served very weak.

A vitamin-mineral tablet should be taken daily.

No cola drinks are permitted, not even the low-calorie, artificially sweetened colas.

You may drink, other than colas, any of the low-calorie artificially sweetened carbonated beverages, up to 10 glasses a day.

No smoking at all is allowed.

No aspirin or other drugs that promote acidity.

Antacids and tranquilizers are permitted, but only as prescribed or advised by your physician.

Always get into a relaxed state when eating or drinking on any anti-ulcer dieting.

I advise drinking some water and weak tea before any feeding.

Try to get a quarter-hour to half-hour rest during the day.

Don't combine any two feedings into one, or eat any large quantities at one time; small, frequent feedings as scheduled are important.

Don't eat any fried foods, no spices or sharp seasonings.

No alcoholic beverages at all.

The diets with their small, frequent feedings under conditions of relaxation should be continued for at least three months. After that the same quantities of food may be eaten in five or six meals a day instead of the nine meals specified.

Checked often by your physician, you can look forward to a remarkably quick and pleasant recovery—along with loss of excess pounds and a slimmer, more attractive figure in a hurry—on either of these anti-ulcer diets, especially the high-protein diet.

ANTI-"STOMACH TROUBLES" QWL DIET

(Gastrointestinal Diseases)

You must see your personal physician for any painful or persistent stomach troubles; this discussion may be helpful to those who are often beset by stomach ills and who like to be informed about common health problems. Here are some of the most familiar stomach afflictions that often affect those who are considerably overweight and should reduce, without fail, for health and comfort.

Gastroenteritis may occur when the stomach and intestines are red and inflamed. This acute and chronic inflammation is a common complaint of overweights. It is generally due to intake of an excessive amount of food, alcohol, beer, spices and fried foods. An outpouring of gastric and pancreatic juices produces heartburn, sour taste, belching and a bloated feeling. This is aggravated further if the food is old, reheated, or infected by bacteria, as is often the case with custards, eclairs, mayonnaise, chicken salads and exposed meat. Such tainted foods are too frequently encountered when *traveling* abroad or in areas where restaurants have inadequate refrigeration or leave food out buffet-style in warm or hot air for hours. (Warning: stay away from such custard-type foods even when you see a tempting but unrefrigerated display!)

The bacterial count in such foods can be excessively high, and the resultant toxins and irritants in the foods can readily make one nauseated, uncomfortable, stomach distended, followed by vomiting and general misery. Simple, effective treatment and relief requires refraining from eating *anything* for 6 to 12 hours. After that, don't eat any solid foods, but you may sip spoonfuls of cracked-ice water, or sip a little hot weak tea. When the stomach settles down, possibly after a day of no solid food, only bland foods in small portions and quantities should be taken. Otherwise the discomfort and illness may continue for weeks and even months, as too many people, *especially travelers*, know.

Ulceration involves a break in the lining of the stomach or intestines. This may be single, as in the stomach or duodenum, or a combination of the two, or it may be many breaks known as *ulcerative colitis*, because most of the lesions are in the large colon.

Diarrhea may result from constant agitation and irritability of the linings due to nervousness or bacterial invasion.

Atonic colitis (ballooning) or *spastic colitis* (spasm) involve a ballooning out and possibly spasms or feeling of tightness in the cecum, which is the beginning of the large intestines.

Diverticulosis involves outpocketing or the development of small pouches along the colon where the food may lodge, often occurring in the elderly and creating inflammation in the areas. The right diets can definitely soothe or calm the savage membranes, and should be followed at the first sign of trouble, along with an examination by a doctor. It is significant that many of the victims of these stomach complaints are excessively overweight and will aggravate the condition dangerously by continuing to eat heavily. Those burdensome, complicating extra pounds of fat should come off in a hurry.

These are the essential points in treatment and relief:

    1. Bland foods.

. 2. No roughage.

3. Frequent small feedings, no big meals.

4. If severe, take sedatives or tranquilizers or anti-peristaltic drugs to lessen the mucous secretions, as prescribed by a doctor (to repeat, this discussion and suggestions are merely supplements to seeing your doctor and getting his specific instructions).

QWL Dieting for Acute and Chronic Indigestion

The following is based on the assumption that you have seen your physician and that no serious cause for your condition has been found. Foods allowed should be easily digestible, bland, never spicy or acid, to be eaten only in very small quantities at each feeding. No harsh medicines or harsh, irritating foods should be taken. All servings should be finely chopped, mashed or puréed. Avoid skin, pits, any fibrous foods.

These foods are permitted only after the stomach has settled, after at least a day of no solid foods, and only sips of ice water and weak tea as liquids:

* Soups, vegetable stock only, bland, not highly flavored.
* Soft-boiled, hard-boiled (mashed), or soft-scrambled eggs made in a no-fat pan.
* Toast, cut into very small, soft pieces.
* Small chopped-meat patties (two 3 oz.), well-broiled, cut into small pieces when eating.
* Sliced chicken or turkey, no skin or fat, 1 to 2 ounces cut into small pieces.
* Fish, after first week, baked, boiled or broiled (never fried), mashed or in small pieces.
* Vegetables with all skin, pits and roughage removed, soft-cooked. Mashed potatoes, yams, are helpful in small portions, kept bland, no spices or fats.
* Bananas, mashed or in small pieces, or softened by cooking.
* Skim milk, cottage cheese, no heavy or spiced cheeses.
* Desserts—low-calorie artificially sweetened gelatin; artificially sweetened, skim-milk rice pudding, very soft.
* Juices—only bland vegetable juices—no fruit juices of

any kind for the first week, bland fruit juices all right thereafter.

Don't take smoked meats, fried foods, spiced foods, rich, buttery foods, raw fruits and vegetables for the first three weeks after attack; any egg or milk fillings, such as custards.

The less you eat, and the more water you drink through your waking hours, the sooner you'll feel relief and lose all your discomforts.

Your doctor may order some antacids in pill, powder or liquid form which can give repeated relief.

Eat from the listings preceding, less than 500 calories daily, for quick weight loss. As you reduce rapidly, the liver, stomach, gall bladder and intestines lose their bloat. Your health, vigor and overall feeling and look of well-being will return. Many pounds lighter, you'll feel and look better than before becoming ill.

Typical Day—440 calories

Make up your own daily menus, keeping under a 500-calorie total per day, from foods permitted, making sure to leave out those listed as "don't take."

Breakfast: 1 slice of protein bread, toasted, eaten in very small bites, 2 cups of weak tea.

10 A.M.—4 tbsp. cottage cheese, 2 cups of weak tea.

12:30 P.M.—1 poached egg, 2 cups of weak tea.

3 P.M.—2 tbsp. farina or soft rice, with ½ cup skim milk.

6 P.M.—1 soft-scrambled egg in no-fat pan, 2 cups of weak tea.

8 P.M.—1 banana, small bites or mashed:

10 P.M.—1 slice protein bread toasted, small bites, weak tea.

Follow this kind of daily eating for a week, juggling the permitted foods around as you please. Keep servings small, fewer than 500 calories daily. You will be losing pounds rapidly and feeling better quickly. If any heartburn is still present, take an antacid.

After one week, you may add some fish, then later some raw fruits and vegetables, as in the previous listing. You may also eat less frequently if you like, but keep portions small at each feeding, never eating a large meal.

When you are down to ideal weight, you may increase the number of calories daily to the total that will keep you at that desired weight. When you are well again, you may add some other foods, but never again should you stuff yourself or eat spicy, fried, rich foods. Watch the scale, and if you go 3 or more pounds over your desired weight, cut back to 500 calories a day of the bland foods until you are at ideal weight again. Or you can take off those excess pounds in a hurry on the basic Quick Weight Loss Diet.

ANTI-DIVERTICULITIS QWL DIET

To review this too-common large-bowel trouble, especially for those who are overweight, a diverticulum of the stomach or intestines forms a small or large round pocket anywhere along the intestinal tract. If there is more than one, the covering term is "diverticula"; if bulges are present in a great number, particularly in the descending tract of the colon, this is called "diverticulosis." If any of the out-pockets, or pouches, become inflamed, the condition is known as "diverticulitis."

If pains are felt, it is vital to see a physician for diagnosis and treatment, also to calm unnecessary alarms, as the pain may seem like appendicitis. I have found that the overweights are more likely to have the weak points associated with the problem than patients of normal weight. The first step is to take off excess weight, using a diet that is bland and leaves little residue.

If inflammation is present, one should fast for at least 24 hours, then go on liquid-formula dieting, and gradually work up to soft, mushy and puréed foods. With further improvement, protein foods may be added, some bananas and potatoes, then fruits and vegetables from which all skin, pits and fibres have been removed. All fruits and vegetables should be stewed, not raw.

No spices or sharp, irritating foods and flavorings are allowed. Cottage cheese is good, but whole-milk and milk products should be avoided as too high in calories. No jellies, jams or other high-calorie products made with sugar (a little artificially sweetened jelly is permitted). No butter, margarine, mayonnaise or oils. No catsup, mustard, other spicy items. For flavoring, use salt sparingly, a little vinegar or lemon juice.

Drink plenty of liquids, including plenty of low-calorie, artificially sweetened sodas except colas, and no coffee. If diarrhea accompanies the abdominal discomfort, relief may be obtained on the basic Quick Weight Loss Diet, avoiding spices. If constipation occurs, take a teaspoon of mineral oil once or twice a day, as required.

Foods Permitted

To lose weight rapidly, a prime requisite with this condition if you are overweight, keep daily intake of calories below 500, selecting from the following foods. It is best to break up the daily food intake into at least six feedings a day for the first few weeks at least—never eat a large meal.

* Eggs in any style except fried in any kind of fat.
* All lean meats—baked, boiled or broiled—chopped into small pieces.
* Fish or shellfish—baked, boiled or broiled—cut into small, soft pieces.
* Dairy products—all bland cheeses, cottage cheese, farmer cheese, pot cheese, skim milk sparingly. It is better to avoid whole milk and cream because of high calories. If allergic to milk, boil before drinking.
* Vegetables—puréed or strained, mashed potatoes.
* Fruits—applesauce, softened banana, soft-stewed fruit, no raw fruit or pits or skin in early weeks of diet.
* Cereals—only cooked cereals, such as farina, very fine oatmeal, soft rice.
* Macaroni products, soft, spaghetti, egg noodles (not "protein-type" or egg-rich noodles).
* Bread—any style with the least amount of vegetable or other fats or shortening, not seeded, refined.
* Soups—bland types only, consommé, bouillon, broth, with any fat removed; pastina or rice may be added.
* Desserts—only low-calorie, artificially sweetened gelatin, artificially sweetened, soft, skim-milk rice pudding,

soft-baked apple with skin and pits and fibres removed, baked with artificial sweetening.

* Beverages—skim milk, weak tea, low-calorie artificially sweetened sodas but no colas.

Take a vitamin-mineral tablet every day. Keep intake below 500 calories daily. If you feel at all weak, eat a half-banana softened.

Foods Not Allowed

No whole-wheat products, no nuts, no mayonnaise (you may use low-calorie dressings sparingly), no fatty, fried, or greasy foods, no gravies or sauces, no fatty or heavy soups, no strong spices (flavor with salt sparingly or a little vinegar or lemon juice), no smoked meats or fish (water-packed tuna and salmon are permitted), no raw fruits except bananas (later an apple, pear or peach may be eaten after skin is removed), no dried fruits unless well stewed and sweetened with artificial sweetening—not sugar—no pastries, éclairs, salads or candies.

No coffee, no ginger ale or cola drinks even if non-caloric (you may drink other no-calorie artificially sweetened sodas, weak tea, lots of water, plain soda).

Typical Day—455 Calories

Make up your own menus from the permitted foods, spreading out in three to six feedings per day, no large meal at any time. Stay on the diet until you are down to your ideal weight, then increase calories to stay at that weight, never getting heavy again. This kind of eating must be followed for the rest of your life for maximum health, energy and well-being (especially if you are prone to occasional flare-ups of pain). Keep watching the scale every morning—if you go 3 pounds or more over your desired weight, go back on the 500-calorie-per-day regime, or on the basic Quick Weight Loss Diet.

Breakfast:

4 tbsp. creamed cottage cheese
1 slice of protein bread, small bites, toasted if desired

3 cups of weak tea, adding a little skim milk and artificial sweetener if desired.

Lunch:

1 slice of processed American cheese, bland
1 slice of protein bread with a bit of artificially sweetened jelly if wanted
3 cups of weak tea

Dinner:

2 oz. chopped meat, well broiled
1 slice of protein bread
3 cups of weak tea

If you wish, you may have a mid-afternoon or evening snack of a banana or 4 tablespoons of cottage cheese.

Drink plenty of water, weak tea (but no coffee) and the other non-caloric, non-irritating drinks allowed.

Check your doctor for approval of all these suggestions as aids for your condition. I am sure that he will agree.

ANTI-ACNE AND SKIN PROBLEMS QWL DIET

Acne is often but not necessarily associated with overweight. The condition, and many skin problems in adult years, is due primarily in most cases to a disorder in which the oil glands of the skin are overactive. Taking off excess pounds of fat may be helpful, along with other treatment. I strongly recommend that young people particularly see the family doctor or a dermatologist in cases of acne rather than waiting "to grow out of it." Without proper treatment, serious psychological problems as well as unhappiness may arise for the youngster (as well as for the young or older adult).

By taking off overweight, maintaining slim, attractive, ideal weight and obtaining any other indicated medical treatment acne can now be relieved and controlled in over 75 percent of cases. Certainly that makes it worth taking proper steps immediately, rather than letting the condition go on and on, perhaps worsening with delay.

As an important part of the treatment of acne, I recommend low-fat, low-sugar eating. The basic Quick Weight Loss Diet and the Inches-Off Diet are both excellent to get excess pounds off in a hurry and to help relieve and clear up the acne condition. The aim of dieting is to reduce the tissue fat, which is lodged under the skin in the face, chin, shoulders, chest and back, abdominal area, hips, thighs and legs.

Another aim of the diet along with taking off overweight rapidly, is to diminish the amount of fat and perspiration, and secretions from the oil glands of the skin. While a low-fat diet is not always completely successful in eliminating the oily shine of the skin, in my experience it is generally very beneficial.

Along with dieting instructions, I have found that these general directions are usually helpful:

* Wash your face with any mild antiseptic soap at least three times daily.
* Shampoo the hair several times a week to help get the oiliness out of the hair and scalp.
* When combing hair, be sure to comb away from the face, and keep it from lying across the brow where oily contact with the skin may be harmful. When combing hair back, throw a towel over your bare shoulders, as dandruff and oily particles that fall on the skin are great irritants to the acne-prone person.
* Keep your hands and fingers away from your hair and face, avoiding touching frequently. This alone is a big help usually in avoiding the development of acne pustules.
* Use fat-free lotions and creams, if any, on your face.
* Don't plaster your face with cover-up or heavy creams.
* While dieting, take a Vitamin-A and Vitamin-C pill daily.
* Keep active; if you sweat easily, bathe or shower at least twice a day.
* Keep your hands clean; wash hands as often as necessary, five to eight times daily.

* Whatever you eat, avoid too much salt and any *iodized* salt.
* Avoid iodized foods, such as shellfish, which contain a great deal of iodine. It appears that iodine seems to act in some way to aggravate facial skin disturbances, although seafood is generally excellent in a reducing diet. In my experience, iodized foods tend to slow the metabolism of the body, worth consideration for acne-prone patients but not for most overweights.
* Take a brisk walk for 15 minutes or more at least once each day unless harsh weather prohibits, then get some indoor exercise, such as mild, not strenuous, calisthenics.
* If you like to drink milk, make it skim milk, not whole milk or milk with any cream content, and *boil* the milk (then refrigerate it if desired) before drinking. There is some medical opinion that acne-prone patients may be allergic to certain foods, of which milk is often one, and that boiling the milk changes its chemistry and makes it hypoallergenic.

Foods to Avoid

A good many foods seem to cause flare-ups of worsened acne and should always be avoided. It is best *not* to eat any chocolate, rich or fatty cheeses (you may have creamed cottage cheese), peanuts or peanut butter, nuts, milk, especially whole milk and cream, any greasy or fried foods, no rich dressings, no butter, oils, fats of any kind, rich desserts, cakes, candies, no cola drinks (not even artificially sweetened cola), no coffee or coffee drinks, no spices, catsup, mustard, other sharp ingredients, no ice cream, fatty meats, such as ham, pork, bacon, no spiced or smoked meats or fish, no beer, wine, whiskey or other alcoholic beverages.

ANTI-ACNE QWL DIETING

Your best bet to get excess pounds of fat and flabby inches off rapidly, a primary step in combating acne, is to go on the basic Quick Weight Loss Diet, or one of the Quick Weight Loss Variety Diets, or the Inches-Off QWL Diet. They will all reduce you quickly while providing the desirable low-fat foods to help clear up an acne condition and to help prevent recurrence.

After you are at your ideal weight, limit your calories to the amount that will keep you at that desired weight, according to the weight and calorie table in the first chapter. Enjoy lean meats, poultry, fish (but not seafood), loads of fresh raw and cooked vegetables and fruits, lots of fruit and vegetable juices, limited amounts (to keep calories low) of bread, cereals, macaroni products, rice. Stay away from all the foods in the "avoid" listing and use only a minimum of any sugar and sugary foods (use artificial sweetening). Drink loads of water, weak tea (no coffee, cocoa, colas or chocolate drinks), and all low-calorie, artificially sweetened sodas except cola, coffee and chocolate flavoring.

While taking off pounds, keep your daily calorie intake below a 700 total. Make up your own menus of the permitted foods, like this *typical day's eating:*

Breakfast:

> 4 tbsp. cottage cheese, or 1 hard-boiled egg
> 1 slice toast, or 2 plain crackers.
> 3 cups weak tea, or 1 glass pre-boiled skim milk

Lunch:

> Vegetable salad with low-calorie, no-cheese dressing
> 2 oz. lean hamburger, well broiled.
> 3-4 cups weak tea, artificially sweetened.

Dinner:

> Baked potato, no butter, margarine or sour cream or any
>   other dressing
> Tossed green salad with low-calorie, no-cheese dressing
> 3 oz. of lean meat, poultry or fish—baked, boiled or
>   broiled, never fried
> 3 cups of weak tea, artificially sweetened

9-10 P.M.:

> Piece of fruit—apple or pear or melon or water-packed
>   pineapple

Between Meals:

You may have two servings of fat-free consommé, broth or bouillon during the day; also, low-calorie artificially sweetened gelatin dessert twice a day.

In addition to proper dieting and weight loss, your doctor will prescribe further treatment. Doctors sometimes prescribe anti-biotic medication to be taken internally where indicated, pills if the pulse is slow and may be a contributor to an acne condition, a diuretic if hands and legs are swollen. Above all, get that excess weight off now, and see a physician for treatment—never put it off!

ANTI-LIVER AND GALL BLADDER PROBLEMS

As in so many other ailments, many individuals with liver and gall bladder problems are overweight. A primary step is to get those excess pounds of burdensome fat off promptly. Certain foods should be eaten and others avoided, with further restrictions imposed by the physician in relation to the condition of the individual patient.

Foods to Avoid

* No meats high in fat, such as pork, ham, bacon (trim off fat from any meats).
* No fatty fish, such as mackerel, salmon, sardines.
* No fats, such as shortening, butter, margarine, cream.
* No raw fruits and vegetables.
* No cheese other than cottage cheese, pot cheese, farmer cheese.
* No coarse breads or cereals.
* No desserts rich in fats.
* No catsup, mustard, spices, sharp sauces, condiments of any kind, or seasonings other than a little salt.
* No alcoholic beverages.

Foods Permitted

* Cereals that are finely milled, cooked or ready-cooked.

* Cottage cheese, pot cheese, farmer cheese (no other cheeses).

* Lean meat, fish, poultry (fat and skin removed), liver, sweetbreads, seafood in small portions.

* Vegetables (not gas-forming types), finely chopped or puréed, potatoes mashed, boiled or baked (don't eat skin).

* Fruits, cooked or canned, all seeds, skins and fibres removed, ripe bananas.

* Eggs in all forms, but never fried in butter, oils or any fats.

* Macaroni products, spaghetti, vermicelli, noodles.

* Rice, cooked soft and bland.

* Breads, rolls, crackers, made with white or finely milled flour, no seeds.

* Desserts—artificially sweetened gelatin desserts, fruit tapioca puddings, artificially sweetened jellies, jams, marmalades, whips, other bland desserts without butter, cream or egg yolks; no candy, honey or sweets.

* Beverages—skim milk, buttermilk, fruit juices, tomato and vegetable juices, tea, coffee and cocoa in limited amounts (if your doctor permits).

Typical Day

Make up your daily menus from the listing of permitted foods, but for quick weight loss results limit to under 600 calories per day until you are at ideal weight. Then stay at that weight by increasing calories to the maximum allowed according to the weight and calories table in the first chapter. Keep watching your scale; if you exceed your desired weight by 3 pounds any morning, go back on the 600-calorie permitted foods daily until you are again at desired weight.

Breakfast:

1 egg (no butter or fats used in preparation).
1 slice toast with low-calorie jelly.
1 glass skim milk, tea or coffee.

Lunch:

> 4 oz. tomato juice.
> 4 tbsp. cottage cheese.
> 1 boiled potato.
> Skim milk, or tea or coffee.

Dinner:

> Strained vegetable soup.
> 4 oz. lean chicken, meat or fish.
> 1 medium-size baked potato (no skin)
> Half-cup vegetable cooked and finely chopped or puréed.
> Small slice angel cake.
> Tea or coffee.

Between meals:

> Bland consommé, broth or bouillon permitted twice a day. Serving of low-calorie, artificially sweetened gelatin twice a day.

Since there are some high-calorie foods in the "permitted" listing, be sure to limit your intake to the 600-calories maximum per day to take off excess pounds of fat.

ANTI-LOW BLOOD-SUGAR DIETING (HYPOGLYCEMIA, HYPERINSULINISM)

These recommendations are only for those who are obese and have no apparent directed-organic cause for their low blood-sugar condition. You should be checked regularly by your physician, of course.

Such people are usually tense and nervous. They overeat with tremendous amounts of sweets—cakes, ice cream, sugar, desserts, jams, jellies. After a few hours on a "sweet binge," they develop a secondary reaction to the initial rise of a high blood sugar. Now they suffer from too much insulin, with resultant burning up of the sugars producing a low blood sugar. This in turn causes weakness, trembling, sweating, extreme hunger.

The best food treatment for such individuals is a high-protein or all-protein diet such as my basic Quick Weight Loss Diet—no sugars, jellies, syrups, cakes, desserts, sweets of any kind. Basic foods are meat, fish, poultry, cheese, eggs. To lose weight, keep daily calorie count between 750 and 900 calories total. Spread the food over five to eight meals through the day instead of three meals a day. Drink lots of water, coffee, tea (without sugar), no-calorie beverages. Stay away from butter, margarine, fats and oils because of high-calorie content.

If you insist on following a "balanced" reducing diet, eat fruits, vegetables and high-protein foods; omit all sweets.

If an occasional weak spell occurs, take a small mint or hard candy or two, or a small lump of sugar.

ANTI-FRACTURES DIETING

When individuals, especially overweights in their adult years, suffer a fractured hip or leg and are confined to bed, special caution must be taken to avoid having the pounds pile on, as happens much too often. The patient tries to make up for her (or his) frustrations by overeating. The weight gain adds to her troubles, for she may develop diabetes, high blood pressure, gallstones, kidney stones, arteriosclerosis, other problems.

Eating is certainly not the answer, and too much rest in bed or on a chair, whether forced or voluntary, spurs muscle breakdown, increased calcium absorption, is harmful to kidneys and bladder. The person becomes heavier, bringing on more complications, finds it harder than ever to get about and may become almost completely dependent on relatives and friends.

Such increasingly dangerous weight gain must be fought constantly. All my low-calorie quick weight loss diets are excellent reducers, and one or more of the diets should be used at once if weight goes above normal.

Cravings for food can be met with low-calorie, diluted broths, a piece of raw fruit such as a medium-size apple, moderate portions of raw or cooked vegetables. No indulgences in sweets and rich foods can be permitted, as this only increases weight, brings on greater discomforts and sicknesses. Feeding the bedridden patient such forbidden foods can be the greatest harm you could do to him.

ANTI-CONSTIPATION DIETING

As excess pounds tend to inhibit the body from functioning most efficiently, a number of overweight individuals have diffi-culty, sometimes quite constantly, with constipation. If this con-tinues for any extended time, a physician should certainly be consulted. A first step, as with any undesirable condition, is to get down to ideal weight so that the burdens brought on by excess fat are removed. To help prevent and relieve constipation, and lead the system to normal bowel functioning, here are some basic factors involved. The diet should contain foods of increased bulk. Sizable quantities of water should be taken all during the waking hours. Lubricants are helpful. A vitamin-mineral pill, especially heavy in thiamin, should be taken daily. Certain sugars and organic acids may be helpful. Protein and caloric values in relation to body intake are the same as with normal functioning.

Foods That Are To Be Eaten

* Fruits, raw and cooked, especially figs, prunes, raisins, dates, apples, grapes.
* Fruit juices of all kinds, particularly orange and prune.
* Salads with mineral-oil dressing, once daily.
* Vegetables, especially those high in fibre.
* Dark breads, including whole wheat, rye, pumper-nickel, bran bread, bran muffins.
* Cereals, dry and cooked, including rolled oats, whole-wheat cereals, prepared bran when combined with other cereals.
* Buttermilk.
* Wheat germ or yeast preparation.

Typical Day

For quick weight loss results, limit your daily menu to a maxi-mum of 600 calories, selecting from the foods listed. Avoid all fats, rich foods, anything not listed here as permitted. When you are down to your ideal weight, you can raise the number of calories daily to maintain desired weight, referring to the weight and calorie tables in the first chapter, and to your scale each morning upon rising.

Breakfast:

> Whole-wheat cereal with a little skim milk.
> Coffee.

Lunch:

> Vegetable soup.
> 3 oz. lean roast beef.
> Medium-size baked potato with skin.
> Cup of carrots.
> Large portion lettuce with fresh lemon juice.
> Coffee.

Dinner:

> Corn soup.
> Omelet made in no-fat, no-stick pan.
> Cup fresh spinach.
> Tomato salad with a little vinegar.
> Ripe banana.
> Tea or coffee.

To help keep down your calorie intake, avoid sugar and use artificial sweetening instead. You may have servings twice a day between meals of fat-free consommé, broth or bouillon. Twice a day you may have a portion of low-calorie, artificially sweetened gelatin dessert. This kind of eating, with daily calories kept to a 600 maximum until you are at ideal weight, will slim you down quickly and should soon relieve any constipation condition and help you to normal functioning.

Such dieting should "bring you back alive"—feeling alert and with a zest for daily activities, as well as causing you to look more attractive and happy.

ANTI-CHOLESTEROL DIETING

Overweights are definitely more prone to high-cholesterol troubles than the slender person of normal weight. It is generally acknowledged in medical science today that low-cholesterol, low-fat eating, is more healthful. Rather than telling you what to eat, it is simpler for you to have a list of *prohibited* foods as a guide to low-cholesterol eating.

Foods to Omit

* No butter, cream, fats, gravies, pork (other than a few slices of crisp bacon), shellfish.
* No fried foods.
* No inner organs, such as brain, liver, kidneys, sweetbreads.
* No rich and highly seasoned foods, or foods prepared with cream or butter or eggs.
* Eggs, if eaten at all, should be limited to four a week.
* No oils, including olive oil and salad dressings.
* No heavy cheeses, nuts, olives, spicy foods.
* No candies, cakes, pies, pastries, chocolate.
* No pickled or smoked foods.
* No alcoholic drinks.
* No smoking.
* No bran and coarse whole-wheat products.
* In the case of digestive disturbances, omit salads, raw vegetables and raw fruits; also, all vegetables should be served chopped fine or puréed.

For quick weight loss, keep calories down to a limit of 600 or fewer per day until you attain your ideal weight.

You may switch from diet to diet in order to get down to your ideal weight, unless you require a diet for a particular condition, such as some of those listed in this chapter. You may normally go on one diet for a week, then another diet, and so on. Your goal is *ideal weight*, which inevitably means better health and increased attractiveness. Quick weight loss is the key to built-in will power that helps you attain your goal surely, swiftly. Don't delude yourself like the tubby young lady who ate constantly and when asked whether she was sticking to her diet admitted, "Yes . . . but only at mealtime!"

9

Exercises To Help Take Inches Off Problem Spots

The old stories insist that the best exercise you can get is "to push yourself away from the table three times a day" and, when someone suggests a second helping, "to move your head firmly from side to side." There is much truth in these worn gags, but they are not entirely valid. Moderate exercise *can* be helpful in taking inches off and keeping them off, especially at problem spots on the figure—*but only when combined with effective dieting.*

Centuries ago, Cicero said, "Exercise can preserve something of our early strength even in old age." In the 1700's an essayist affirmed, "Exercise thy lasting youth defends." Shakespeare wrote of "the rich advantage of good exercise." It is unfortunate that while the advantages of exercise may be well known, few take advantage of the health benefits in moderate activity. I urge that you will for the sake of your improved appearance and well-being.

However, don't let anyone convince you that exercise without effective dieting will reduce either your dimensions or your total weight significantly. Relying on exercise alone is a most inefficient way to lose pounds and inches. For example, to work off the calories in a small glass of orange juice requires a brisk walk of one mile. To get rid of the calories in one average cocktail or other alcoholic drink, you would have to take a brisk walk of about two miles or more.

To help tone up your muscles and firm the areas as an aid in trimming off inches, a moderate amount of exercising twice a day for about three to five minutes at each session is sufficient. Before breakfast and at bedtime are good periods for exercising— or whenever you find it convenient. The times can vary. The choice is yours.

You can easily take 4 to 5 inches off your waistline, for example, if you go on a quick weight loss diet. Then you remove additional inches through Inches-Off dieting plus moderate activity and/or exercising, but never through very strenuous exertion. But without proper dieting, exercise is almost useless in reducing weight and dimensions notably.

Beware of the dangers of overexercise. Those who recommend exercise often overdo it. It's vital not to overtax your system. With my suggestions you will exercise just enough to firm and reduce your muscle-mass areas. If you overexercise, you will *add* muscle mass and increase rather than reduce your dimensions.

Sensible limits in dimension reducing . . .

There is no question that practically everyone can make many slimming improvements in the figure, taking inches off the muscle-mass areas of the body, most commonly at the shoulders, back, arms, midsection, legs. You cannot, however, change your bone structure or the basic proportions of your build. You can reduce the dimensions of heavy thighs, calves and ankles to some extent, a definitely helpful degree, by Inches-Off dieting and moderate exercising. But no one can assure you that you will have model-slim legs from dieting and exercising if your legs are not built in such slender proportions basically. You can enjoy improvement without expecting ultimate perfection.

I disagree thoroughly with those who say that the ideal weight for a certain height—let's say 5'4"—can vary as much as 30 pounds depending on body "proportions," that is, whether you have a "small, medium or large frame." This has been disproved in my medical practice in examining and reducing thousands of overweights.

Don't let "large frame" or "basic large proportions" become an excuse for allowing yourself to remain 20 to 30 pounds over the figures given for your height in my ideal weight chart in the first chapter.

You will find here a variety of activities and exercises from which you can select to concentrate on combating your personal figure problems. All these exercises and activity recommendations are for men as well as women. If you enjoy sports such as tennis, squash, badminton, I suggest that you engage in them moderately. Here, too, overexertion can not only act to build up your muscle masses rather than to slim them, but can also be dangerous to the health of the adult.

Healthful, muscle-firming activities . . .

An article in *Today's Health*, a publication of the American Medical Association, recommends that "bicycling and brisk walking are excellent activities. Combined with sensible dietary practices, these may result in better muscle tone, firmer muscles and, to some degree, reduction of fat deposits." The American Heart Association states, "Studies show that men who are physically inactive run a higher risk of heart attack than those who get *regular, moderate* exercise." This applies increasingly to women, too.

Walking: Maintaining ideal weight and being active through daily walking and/or moderate exercising not only helps trim your dimensions to attractive slimness but also adds up to what is called "optimum fitness" through the maximum number of years of vigorous, productive living. A child is more likely to be active and energetic but, as individuals grow older, many tend to slow up and give the body less exercise than it should have.

In my opinion, there is no activity better for the adult than at least a mile a day, preferably more, of fairly brisk walking. This is in addition to the walking you do in going about the house, climbing stairs, and so on. Walking in the outdoors can be a lift to the spirits as well as good for the body and firming of muscles and problem spots. Walk properly (as shown in the drawing), head erect, chest high, buttocks tucked in, never slumping, never shuffling. I tend to agree, and I believe that you will also, with Thomas Jefferson, who advised, "Walking is the best possible

Walking Properly
for
Slimming and Posture

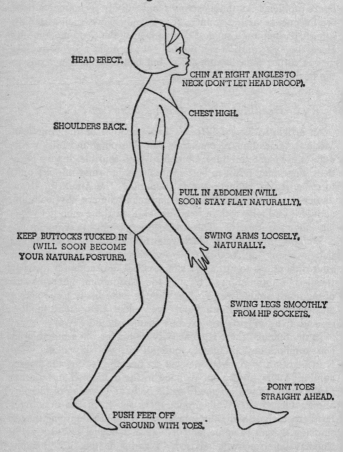

HEAD ERECT.

CHIN AT RIGHT ANGLES TO
NECK (DON'T LET HEAD DROOP).

CHEST HIGH.

SHOULDERS BACK.

PULL IN ABDOMEN (WILL
SOON STAY FLAT NATURALLY).

KEEP BUTTOCKS TUCKED IN
(WILL SOON BECOME
YOUR NATURAL POSTURE).

SWING ARMS LOOSELY,
NATURALLY.

SWING LEGS SMOOTHLY
FROM HIP SOCKETS.

POINT TOES
STRAIGHT AHEAD.

PUSH FEET OFF
GROUND WITH TOES.

exercise." Brisk walking daily will firm your derriere, whereas de-
positing it repeatedly on a car seat promotes the spread you are
trying to reduce.

Bicycling: Becoming increasingly popular for adults in parks
and on suburban streets, bicycling properly helps tone up the
system and firm the muscles. If you choose this activity, try to
get in about fifteen minutes of moderate, not strenuous, bicycling
daily. Coasting does you very little good except as pleasant
recreation, so keep your legs moving as much as possible in a
slow, steady rhythm. Don't slump, but maintain a fairly erect,
active posture as you roll, roll, roll along.

Swimming: This is an excellent activity for all ages, even into
the seventies and beyond for the alert, active individual. Steady
swimming each day is recommended if you have a pool or access
to one. You'll get desirable, figure-firming exercise if you swim
steadily for a length or two rather than plunging in, churning
down the pool and emerging breathless, with chest heaving.

It's excellent exercise to swim at moderate or even slow speed
for a length, then hold onto the side of the pool, flex your arms,
pulling your body forward and backward six times. Then swim
another length or two, go through the arm-flexing routine, repeating this procedure for ten or fifteen minutes. First, of course, you
should learn to swim properly, which is worth doing at any age;
don't despair, as in the story of the stubborn man who went on an
all-fish diet for three months and still couldn't swim (but he did
lose weight!).

Jogging: I don't recommend jogging for most adults. This is
really quite a strenuous form of exercise and may ultimately
increase some muscular dimensions rather than reduce them.
While jogging can be a worthwhile activity when learned properly, it requires gradual conditioning of the body over a long
period of time, for months, or even a year, until full jogging
ability is achieved. It can be a dangerous, too-strenuous activity
for the heart, particularly if done for any length of consecutive
time without proper preparation and build-up of the body. Brisk
walking for about fifteen minutes daily, moderate bicycling and
swimming, as recommended, are better for your health and as an
aid to trimming your dimensions, in my observation.

A medical report summarizes:

Optimum fitness permits a person to enjoy life to the fullest . . . the extent to which the individual develops his own potential for fitness depends on his daily living practices and exercise habits. Protracted exercise improves the work of the lungs by increasing their ability to expand more fully, take in more air, and utilize a greater proportion of oxygen in the inspired air.

Activities involving leg muscles also help to maintain good circulation against gravity through a "milking" or "squeezing" action of the muscles on the veins. . . . Prolonged inactivity, on the other hand, results in a decline in circulatory and pulmonary (heart muscle) efficiency. One must continue to exercise in order to maintain fitness.

Bear in mind that each person's capacity for exertion and exercise varies. Whatever the activity you undertake, if you feel a sense of exhaustion coming on, or any strain or pain—*stop*. Don't ever overtax your system either in exercising or working. Overexercising can be injurious and, instead of trimming off extra inches from arms and legs and other areas, can build up muscle masses and increase your dimensions if you overdo it. A clear proof is in the bulging thighs and calves of some dancers, who have slim, hard figures otherwise.

It must be repeated again that dieting is still at least 85 percent of the essential in taking pounds and inches off your figure. You *can* reduce without much exercising, although I advise exercising as a beneficial aid. You cannot reduce if you overeat and pile more calories into your system than you are using up, no matter how much you exercise. Always keep in mind that the purpose in exercising for figure-trimming purposes is primarily to firm and tone up muscles, not to transform you into a muscle-bulging athlete.

"Problem-Spot" Inches-Off Exercises . . .

Following is a sampling of exercises which many of my patients have found helpful, when *combined with my quick weight loss and Inches-Off dieting procedures,* to smooth out problem areas and promote a more beautiful, slimmer overall figure. There are many other exercises that may also be effective for trimming the bulging areas that concern you most. I find that instructions in exercise books and most other such sources suggest what I consider to be *over*exercising for the slimming purpose. In most cases, when others recommend doing a certain exercise "10 times," I suggest that 3 to 5 times is preferable for helping to trim off dimensions smoothly.

Make your own selection of exercises according to your personal figure problems and desires. Combine exercises for continuous exercising three to five minutes, twice a day. Don't expect overnight "miracles," but you will see your problem spots smoothing out after you are on the Inches-Off Diet for a while, along with your daily exercising. Your goal is a most desirable one— not only to look better, to look more attractive in a bathing suit or in clothes, but also to feel better all over.

Exercises for Overall Slimming Posture

1. Here is a simple, effective exercise for helping to smooth out problem areas all over the body. Take this position on the floor, pull in your abdomen, hold in for a slow count of 5, release abdomen. Repeat 6 times.

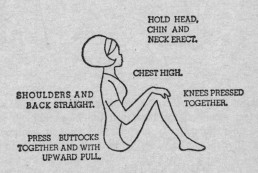

HOLD HEAD, CHIN AND NECK ERECT.

CHEST HIGH.

SHOULDERS AND BACK STRAIGHT.

KNEES PRESSED TOGETHER.

PRESS BUTTOCKS TOGETHER AND WITH UPWARD PULL.

2. This exercise will aid your allover slimming posture. Stand erect, legs together, head up, chest raised, back straight, hands on hips. Slowly rise on toes and raise arms straight out to shoulder height, taking a count of 5 . . . then hold to complete slow count to 8 . . . then lower arms and feet slowly to the beginning, hands-on-hips position. Repeat 6 times, resting as long as you wish with hands on hips between arm and body lifts. Keep your abdomen in during entire time.

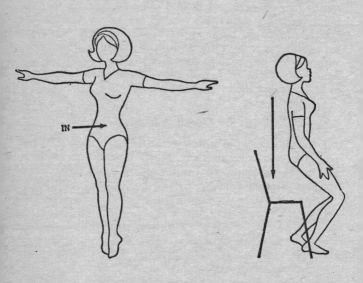

3. Stand in front of a straight-back chair, your back to chair, head erect, shoulders and back straight, chest high, legs together, arms at sides. Bend slowly, keeping back straight, head and chest high, as illustrated above, and sit in chair. Rise slowly to original position. Repeat 6 times. (Keep abdomen in while exercising, and as much as possible always; it will become your natural posture.)

Exercises To Firm Neck and Chin Area

For greatest beauty it is desirable to firm the neck and chin areas. You can do these exercises when you think of it, up to a half-dozen times a day.

1. Sit straight in the recommended seated posture in a straight-back hard chair. Very slowly, drop the head back as far as possible, opening the mouth wide as though screaming. Straighten neck slowly, closing mouth. Repeat 6 times.

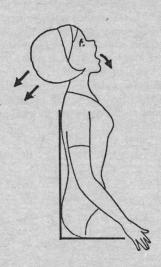

2. Seated, clasp both hands across top of head. Push down with hands and upward with head, opening mouth a little, to slow count of 3. Relax. Repeat 6 times.

3. Place both hands under chin, with bottoms of palms cradling the chin. Opening mouth a little, press palms upward and chin down hard against palms for count of 3. Relax. Repeat 6 times.

4. Clasp both hands at lower back of head against back of neck. Opening mouth a little, press forward with hands and backward with head and neck for slow count of 3. Relax. Repeat 6 times.

5. Place palms of both hands against forehead, side by side. Opening mouth a little, press hands against forehead as you press head and neck forward for slow count of 3. Repeat 6 times.

These are good exercises to firm tops of shoulders and upper arms as well. If you are becoming fatigued at any point, stop.

To Help Firm Bosom and Chest Area

1. Stand erect, legs together, facing wall at a distance just right for placing palms of hands against wall. Now push forward with your whole body. Keeping arms straight, putting pressure on palms for a slow count of 3. Relax. Repeat 6 times.

2. Standing erect, legs together, bring arms up straight, in front of you, thumbs touching each other. Keeping arms straight, separate arms and swing out to sides at same shoulder height as far as comfortably possible (as in the swimming breaststroke). Hold for slow count of 3. Bring arms forward again and repeat exercise 6 times.

3. Stand erect, legs together, arms at sides. Place right hand on left forearm and press hard backward with right arm, resisting by pressing forward with left arm, for a slow count of 3. Straighten arms, relax, then repeat exercise 3 times. Then do the same with the left hand pressing on the right forearm and repeat 3 times.

4. Sitting on a backless low stool, keep legs together, back straight. Raise your arms straight overhead so that the palms are flat against each other. Now press palms as hard as you can together for a slow count of three, then relax the pressure but keep palms together. Repeat the palm-pressure routine 3 times.

To Help Firm Upper and Lower Back

1. To help firm upper back areas, to counteract and correct "dowager's hump," this is an effective exercise. Place the palm of your left hand against the back of your neck, clasping firmly. Press forward with your hand and backward with your neck for a slow count of 3. Relax, then repeat 3 times. Now do the same exercise 3 times with your right hand (rather than left) clasped across the back of your neck.

2. To help firm the lower back, straddle a hard straight-back chair so that you face the back of the chair. Grasp the chair back with both hands, elbows bent. Now straighten your arms stiffly, thrusting your body back, then bending arms at elbows again and pressing your body forward until it touches the chair back. Repeat the exercise 6 times, pressing your body forward and backward slowly from the hips, with tension, as your arms bend.

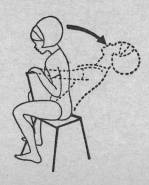

3. For firming upper back muscles, place your right hand across the top of your left shoulder, gripping firmly. Now push your right hand back and your left shoulder forward and hold pressure for a slow count of 3. Relax, then repeat 3 times. Do the same exercise 3 times with your left hand gripping your right shoulder, and going through the push-pull action similarly.

To Help Firm Shoulders and Upper Arms

1. Stand erect, legs together, back straight, arms at side, head up. Now slowly stretch both arms sideways straight upward and hold straight up for a slow count of 3, then lower arms to sides slowly, keeping tension in arms. Repeat this exercise 5 times.

2. Stand erect with arms straight out in front of you, not touching, palms facing down. Rotate arms to a slow count of 3, holding arms stiffly under tension, until palms face up. Then rotate stiff arms back until palms face down for a slow count of 3. Repeat the 6-count exercise five times.

3. Sitting in a hard, straight-back chair, hold your back straight and head erect, legs together. Bend your elbows in front of you

so that your palms are flat against each other. Now press your palms together as hard as you can for a slow count of 3. Relax. Repeat this pressure exercise 5 times.

Exercises to Help Firm Flabby Upper Arms

1. Stand erect, legs together, back straight, head up. Place your hands on your shoulders with fingertips touching shoulders, elbows up, arms at right angles to body. Now stretch both arms straight out to the sides slowly at shoulder height, as far as possible. Hold taut and outstretched for a slow count of 3. Slowly return fingertips to shoulders. Repeat this exercise six times.

2. Sitting, holding your body erect, back straight, head up, stretch both arms out stiffly at shoulder height in front of you. Place stiff left arm over stiff right arm, crossing at the wrists. Now

press your left arm downward and your right arm upward, holding pressure against each other for a slow count of 3. Relax. Repeat the pressure exercise 3 times in this way. Now repeat the exercise three times with the arms crossed so that right arm presses downward on the left arm pressing upward.

3. Stretch out on your back in bed (when awakening and at bedtime are good periods) or on the carpeted floor. With legs together, touching at the toes, and arms straight down at your sides, spread your fingers and bend them slightly to form claws with palms facing downward. Now press down with your hands as if you were trying to push your fingers right through the mattress or carpet, and hold pressure for a slow count of 3. Relax. Repeat the exercise 3 times.

Exercises To Help Firm and Flatten the Abdomen

1. This is an excellent, very simple, completely non-strenuous exercise to help firm and flatten your abdomen—that abominable problem for so many women and men—a bulging front midsection. First, of course, you must get down to your ideal weight and go on my Inches-Off Diet, which pulls extra fat out from between the muscles.

Now, a half dozen times a day, whenever you think of it, whether you are lying down, sitting, standing or walking (even sitting in your car and parked or waiting for a traffic light), do this: *Roll your abdomen in an up-and-down motion to a slow count of 10.*

′ Also, always try to keep your abdomen pulled in as if you were trying to make the front of your midsection touch your spine. The exercising and the constant conscious pull-in will strengthen your muscles in the area, and a flattened middle-front appearance will soon become your natural posture, improving your flatness up front and enhancing your appearance.

Those frontal muscles are very important in helping to support the contents of the entire abdominal cavity and as an aid to many vital body functions. Firming those muscles can be a great aid in reducing and eliminating bodily weakness and fatigue.

As people grow older and muscles become flabbier, some fat may be deposited in the lower abdomen of even slim persons.

The abdomen-flattening exercises help tone up muscles in this area and dissolve some of the fat.

2. Stand erect, feet about 2 inches apart, arms extended straight out to the sides at shoulder height. Now, not moving your feet, turn your body from hips as far as you can to the right without straining and hold there for a count of 3. Then return facing front, and pause for a second or two. Now swivel your hips to the left and hold for a slow count of 3, returning to face front. Alternate swiveling right and then left, 3 times in each direction. Like some of the other exercises, this one will help firm and tone up your hips, buttocks, back muscles, legs and arms—in fact, much of your muscular system.

3. Lie flat on your back on a carpeted floor with legs stretched out close together and arms at sides a few inches from body with palms pressing flat against the floor. Now bend your knees and bring legs up slowly so knees press as closely as possible to your

abdomen, but without straining at any time. Hold position for a slow count of 3. Now straighten out legs so that feet point straight up, with legs at right angles to your body, and hold straight up for a slow count of three. Then, keeping knees stiff and legs straight, lower legs slowly to the floor (bend knees some if you feel strained at all). Relax. Repeat entire exercise 3 times. If you feel any strain in trying this exercise, skip it until you become slimmer and more limber.

4. Lie flat on your back on carpeted floor with hands on your hips. Curl up both legs, bending knees, so that your knees are close to your abdomen. Now "pedal" with your legs revolving in the air as if you were riding a bicycle at a moderate pace. Keep "pedaling" for a slow count of 10, but stop at any point before 10 if you begin to feel strained in any part of your body.

To Help Firm the Buttocks and Hips

1. Sit on carpeted floor with your legs straight out and touching at the feet, with your upper body raised, supported comfortably by your arms with palms against the carpet. Now pull up your right leg, bending at knee, foot pointed, bringing knee as close to your chest as possible without straining. Hold there for a slow count of 3, then return leg slowly to starting position. Now repeat the exercise with the left leg. Alternating right and left, repeat exercise with each leg three times.

2. Lie flat on your stomach on carpeted floor or bed with a pillow under your midsection. Bend your arms so that your crossed hands cradle your head under your chin. Stretch out legs comfortably so that they touch at the feet. Now raise your right leg, keeping it stiff, as high as possible without straining, foot pointing out, and then revolve the leg in 3 slow outward circles in the air. Keep leg stiff, return slowly to original position. Do the same exercise with your left leg. Alternating right and left, repeat exercise 3 times with each leg.

3. Standing erect, legs a few inches apart, back straight, head up, chest forward, place your hands behind you with right hand against your right buttock and left hand against your left buttock, both palms cradling the buttocks. Now walk slowly backward in

a wide circle while pushing forward against buttocks with your hands to resist the movement backward. Keep walking backward in a circle slowly to a slow count of 10.

4. Lie on your back on carpeted floor or bed. Keep your arms straight down in comfortable position at your sides, with hands relaxed about a foot away from your body. Bring up both legs, keeping knees tight together and bending knees into position as close to your chest as possible without straining. Now, keeping your arms tight against the floor, roll your hips to the left until your left knee touches the floor, knees still bent and tight together. Hold that position for a slow count of 3. Now slowly roll your body so that your right knee touches the floor, knees still bent and tight together. Repeat exercise, touching floor at the left and right 3 times on each side.

5. Sit in a hard, straight-back chair, sitting forward on the seat so that your back is straight, not supported by the chair back. Sit head up, chest forward, arms hanging loosely at sides. Now lift your right leg slowly, bending knee, pointing toes down, lifting leg as high as possible without straining. Hold in that position for a slow count of 3, then return leg slowly to original position. Do the same exercise with the left leg. Then, alternating right and left, finish 5 times with each leg.

6. Keep same position on the chair as in the preceding exercise. Lift your right leg up, keeping it straight, toes pointing forward, as high as you can without straining. Hold in that top position for a slow count of 3, then return leg slowly to starting position. Do the same exercise with the left leg. Alternating right and left, repeat the exercise 5 times with each leg.

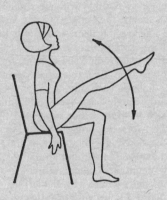

Exercises To Help Firm Your Thighs

1. Stand erect behind a chair, facing the chair, in position so that you can grasp the back of the chair to keep your balance, yet so that your right leg can swing freely past the chair. Now, keeping your right leg stiff, foot pointed forward, swing your right leg in a slow arc, as high forward and then like a pendulum as far backward as you can go without bending your knee and without straining. Complete 4 slow pendulum swings. Now shift position to the left, grasping the chair back, and do 5 slow, complete pendulum swings with your left leg.

2. Sit erect on a hard, straight-back chair with your knees about 12 inches apart, your arms stiff, with left hand cupped over your

left knee, and right hand cupped over your right knee. Now pull your knees together to a slow count of 5 while resisting the inward movement with outward pressure against knees with your hands. Now pull your knees apart to a slow count of 5 to their original separated position while you resist with inward pressure on knees with your hands. Repeat the closing and then separating exercise 3 times. Try to do this thigh-slimming exercising 3 to 5 times a day, whenever it's convenient and you think of it.

3. Stand erect, back straight, chin up, chest forward, arms stiff at sides with palms of your hands resting against *outside* of each nearest thigh. Now slowly move your left leg as far out to the left side as possible so that your pointed foot rests on the floor, all the while resisting the *outward* movement of your leg by pressing *inward* with your palm. Hold leg out, pointed foot resting on floor, keeping the pressure on for a slow count of 3, then return to original position. Do the same exercise with your right leg and hand, exerting counter-pressures. Repeat 3 times with each leg.

To Help Firm and Slim Knees, Calves and Ankles

1. Stand erect, holding on to chair back with right hand, your left arm and hand at shoulder height straight out at side. Now keeping your left leg as stiff as possible, knee stiff, foot pointed straight out, lift leg as high as possible to left side without straining. Hold in that outstretched position for a slow count of 3, then return leg slowly to original position. Repeat exercise 3 times. Then, grasping the chair back with your left hand, go through the same exercise 3 times swinging your right leg.

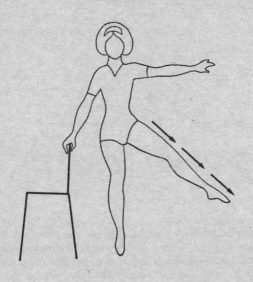

2. Stand erect, head up, back straight, feet touching, on the bottom step of stairs so that your toes are out *over* the edge, the

balls of your feet resting on the edge of the step. Now curl your toes slowly *down* as far as possible while pulling upward with your calves, knees and body. Hold in that pressure position for a slow count of 3, then relax to original position with toes straight out. Repeat exercise 5 times.

3. Sit in a hard, straight-back chair with your hands grasping the sides of the seat for support, your legs straight out at an angle so that your body is slanted, your buttocks resting at the front of the chair seat and your shoulders pressing against the top back of the chair. Your feet, resting on the floor, should hold a heavy book about 2 inches thick between them. Now, gripping the sides of the chair seat, lift your legs, knees stiff, toes pointing forward, as high as you can without straining, your feet lifting the book between them. Hold this in-the-air position for a slow count of 3, then slowly lower stiff legs to the floor. Relax for a slow count of 3. Repeat the exercise 3 times.

Massage After Exercise and Activity

After an exercise or activity session, if you have the time, it is desirable (and it feels so good) but not essential, to help keep the muscles relaxed and pliant. Of course, with the *moderate*, never strenuous, exercising I recommend, your muscles aren't likely to stiffen up.

A warm shower or bath is soothing and cleansing, helping to remove any perspiration. After the warm relaxing effect, dry yourself all over, rubbing with a Turkish towel. Rub briskly but not severely, never enough pressure to roughen the skin, helping to stimulate the surface of the skin. This acts on the skin blood vessels as an aid in tightening and contracting the elastic fibers in the skin and underlying tissue.

If you have the time, sit on a stool or on the floor with your legs out straight in a relaxed condition. With your hands, using a little witch hazel, stroke up your legs from toes to tops of the thighs lightly with your fingertips. Then knead the legs firmly but not roughly with light cold cream or mineral oil, from toes to knees to thighs, up to hips, for an all-over massaging effect.

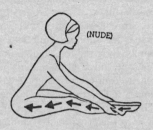

(NUDE)

Go through the same massaging routine with your arms, working from fingers up to the shoulder, if time permits. In fact, a light self-massage (or one done by a masseur) all over your body helps stimulate the blood vessels and gives you an enjoyable "glow."

However, keep in mind that the *exercise, along with Inches-Off dieting, is the essential,* with exercise only a supplement to your dieting—and that the massaging is just a pleasant "plus." Don't substitute the massaging for exercising, nor either one for dieting. In fact, the way to get the increasing and lasting effects from exercising is to *do it* every day or at least four or five days a week if you can't find the few minutes every day.

Don't figure on any unique shortcuts, such as the very energetic sleepwalker who claimed that he got his rest and exercise at the same time. Excuses don't help, not even the one dreamed up by the flabby wit who said that his favorite exercise was watching TV horror movies and letting his flesh creep.

You get allover benefits . . .

All the preceding exercises, I must again emphasize, can be beneficial for men and overweight youngsters as well as for women. While each exercise is specified for a particular area of the body for special purposes, the movements also often help to firm and flatten other parts of the body. You are actually getting all-over benefits from most of the exercising. Go to it with a sense of enjoyment, not as a chore, in order to get the greatest value from putting various parts of your body in motion for corrective effects and a more beautiful figure.

10

Stay-Slim Eating To Keep You Slender

One diet "expert" suggested a simple three-word way to avoid gaining weight: *"No more, thanks."* This is another one of those amusing gimmicks offered to concerned people who tend to gain weight—it's entertaining, but it just doesn't work. There's a lot more to staying slim than just staying away from extra portions.

Once you are down to your ideal weight, you can stay that way *only* if you don't consume more calories daily than your body uses up. So, actually or in effect you must count calories. It has been said that most people are poor mathematicians when it comes to counting calories—and they have the figures to prove it.

You don't have to be a mathematician to keep track of your calories. Once you go over the calorie tables in this chapter, and count calories of the food you eat for a few days or a week, the knowledge becomes second nature to you. You don't need will power so much as common sense—and the aids I provide for you in keeping you slim, as follows.

BASIC RULES FOR STAYING SLIM

1. Find out how many calories you should eat daily.

You are down to the weight you want to be, along with the minimum dimensions that are your goal, and you want to stay that way. First, determine the maximum number of calories you should average in your daily eating in order to keep your weight at the desired figure. Here is your weight/calorie guide:

WOMEN		MEN	
Weight	Calories	Weight	Calories
100	1100	110	1350
105	1200	115	1400
110	1250	120	1450
115	1300	125	1500
120	1350	130	1550
125	1400	135	1600
130	1470	140	1650
135	1520	145	1700
140	1600	150	1750
145	1650	155	1800
150	1680	160	1850
155	1700	165	1900
160	1750	170	1950
		175	2000
		180	2100

These calorie totals are certainly lower than the amounts you ate when you were overweight, but they allow you plenty of food. The lower the calories in each item, the more volume you are permitted to eat. For example, the average 3-inch round cookie—110 calories—doesn't give you nearly as much in the physical amount of food that you eat in one whole medium apple plus one-half canteloupe—same total, 110 calories. Take your choice. It may strike you as strange but true that one cookie is as fattening as a whole apple plus one-half canteloupe, since there is so much more bulk in the apple-canteloupe serving.

It's up to your personal choice what you eat on Stay-Slim Eating, just as long as you don't go any higher than your daily calorie allotment according to the chart.

2. *Refer to the calorie charts until you know the numbers.*

You can refer to one calorie chart or to one hundred—they all add up to the same numbers if they have been figured out correctly. The calories in the items listed on the charts don't change, they are as constant as that 12 inches make 1 foot, and 16 ounces make 1 pound. Calories are a measurement like inches or ounces. Minor, unimportant variations in charts occur in something like "1 tsp. sugar," for example, depending on how "rounded" the sugar may be in the spoon.

For the first few days or a week or so, make a mental or paper listing of the number of calories you eat at each meal and throughout the day. If you go over your calorie maximum one day, cut back the next in order to average out the two days. If you keep exceeding your maximum day after day, it's inevitable that you will gain weight.

Don't think of calorie-counting as a chore; it can be kind of a game. As with everything else, like learning the alphabet, in a week or less you should know the approximate calorie count of most of the foods you eat commonly. If you're not sure of the count of a food, look it up in the calorie charts in this book, or any other. Carry a chart around with you if it will help you to keep within your daily maximum.

3. *Weigh yourself daily—and watch the 3-plus danger signal.*

Get on your bathroom scale unclothed first thing each morning. If you find that you have gained 3 or more pounds above your desired weight, consider that your *3-plus danger signal.* You are consuming more calories than your body is using up! If you continue eating the same way, you'll soon be bulging again, burdened by all the problems that go with overweight.

Take action immediately at that 3-plus danger signal—don't wait another day. The simplest and most successful action is to go back on my basic Quick Weight Loss Diet, my Inches-Off Diet, or any other of my quick weight loss diets. Or, cut calories from then on to a figure below that daily allowance to return to desired weight.

4. *Take advantage of Combination Dieting/Eating from now on.*

By the time you are down to your desired weight on one of my quick weight loss diets, you know that you can lose pounds in a hurry the quick weight loss way. Use my Quick Weight Loss or Inches-Off diets for the rest of your life in this way:

If you have a big weekend of eating and find that you have gained weight by Monday morning, go back on a quick weight loss diet that day. If you put on 3 more pounds over the weekend, you can take it off in two or three days, and then switch again to Stay-Slim Eating.

If you go off on a vacation and have an eating spree (which I don't recommend), and come back 10 or more pounds over your desired weight, go on my Quick Weight Loss or Inches-Off diets the day you get back. In a week or so, you'll be back to your desired weight and dimensions again—but if you keep putting it off, you'll keep carrying around that 10 or more extra pounds of dangerous overweight.

Whenever you gain 3 or more pounds over your desired weight, go right back to quick weight loss dieting. Will you be doing this off-and-on routine for the rest of your life? It's quite possible. Thousands of my patients do this and live happier, more healthful lives than when constantly overweight. The only harm in such an up-and-down way of gaining and losing weight is if you permit yourself to stay UP.

5. *Get the benefits of low-calorie shortcuts.*

There are many ways that you can help yourself eat plenty of food on Stay-Slim Eating, and yet hold your weight down to the desired figure. For example, a glance at this listing of some of the foods readily available, and the calories you can save by using the low-calorie shortcuts, should convince you and lead you to keep a slim, attractive figure.

High-Calorie	SIMILAR FOODS	Low-Calorie
6 oz. regular —80 cals.	Carbonated Soda	artificially sweetened, 6 oz.—1 cal.
Coffee, milk, 2 tsp. sugar—50 cals.		Coffee, black —0 cals.
8 oz. milk, whole —165 cals.		8 oz. milk, skim —90 cals.
3½ oz. wine, sweet 150 cals.		3½ oz. wine, dry —80 cals.
½ cup, reg—60 cals.	Gelatin Dessert	artificially sweetened ½ cup —12 cals.
1 tbsp. reg.—60 cals.	Jams, Jellies	artificially sweetened 1 tbsp. —3 cals.

1 cup clam chowder, with milk —200 cals.	1 cup Instant Broth —10 cals.
1 tbsp.—60 cals. Salad Dressing	1 tbsp.—6 cals

These are just a few shortcuts, and the enormous differences that exist in calories by choosing a low-calorie type for the same high-calorie food. There are many other shortcuts you can figure out that can become second nature to you. For instance, if you have a thin slice of bread toasted at breakfast (figured within your daily calorie allotment) and spread it liberally with butter, you add about 100 calories. But spreading that same thin slice of toast with the same amount of artificially sweetened jam adds only 3 calories—that saves you and your weight close to *100 calories just on one thin piece of toast!*

Facts on artificial sweeteners . .

Fat people who like to indulge themselves and who avoid change of any kind, no matter how promising, look for excuses, such as claiming that artificial sweeteners are harmful to the health. I have checked on this point for years and, of course, one must continue to do so on anything new in food and medicine. At this writing, artificial sweeteners have been in use for over ten years. Here is the current statement about them from the Food and Drug Administration, U.S. Department of Health, Education, and Welfare, Washington, D.C.:

> *Are artificial sweeteners safe?* There is no scientific evidence available now that shows the artificial sweeteners are a hazard to the health of man. The safety of artificial sweeteners—saccharins and cyclamates—has been reviewed periodically for more than a decade. As is true of a wide array of other food additives developed by industry, the artificial sweeteners have undergone extensive toxicity testing in past years. They are listed among the additives "generally recognized as safe" by scientists in and out of the Food and Drug Administration.

As stated, Government departments are constantly checking the additives in foods, particularly the artificial sweeteners. They must be considered safe, after ten years of testing have proved them safe, unless future tests reveal otherwise, at which time you would be informed immediately and the use of such additives would be stopped at once. A report by a committee of the National Academy of Sciences–Research Council suggests maximum daily intake by adults of ten 6-ounce glasses of artificially sweetened sodas, and about half that as maximum for youngsters.

Discover fresh, natural flavors . . .

As you by-pass the calorie-rich, heavy-tasting foods, you'll find that you not only stay slim but also feel lots better and even enjoy the fresh natural flavors much more. A nationally known woman in politics, noted in Washington for her beautifully slim figure and unflagging energy, gives you a few tips in this area: "I don't like salad dressings, preferring fresh lemon and mineral oil. And when I have baked potato it's not fattening, simply because I don't ruin its delicious taste by putting butter or margarine on it."

WARNING: DON'T BE FOOLED!

Keep reading about dietary shortcuts in foods in order to save calories in your daily menus—but don't be fooled by what are known as "permissible lies"—that is, when a food-maker misleads you to think that his food has many fewer calories when it's not true. Look for the number of calories printed on the package.

As a common instance, most people, when I've questioned them, reply that ice milk and sherbet have much less than half the calories in ice cream. Here are the facts for one leading brand: A half-cup (4 fl. oz., ¼ pint) of this ice cream has 225 calories, ice milk 135 calories, sherbet 135 calories, their "dietetic sugar-free ice cream" 145 calories. The figures may vary some by brands due to the amount of fat the maker uses, but to be called "ice cream" (dietetic or otherwise), the product must legally contain a minimum amount of butterfat and 20 percent or more of milk solids. So don't let terms such as "dietetic" on any foods fool you; *always check calorie counts* and realize that if calories aren't printed on the package, it may be because they are high.

I'm going into this category in some detail just as an example of how you must be on the lookout lest you be fooled by not knowing the facts and taking in many calories that you would otherwise take pains to avoid. Regulations for *ice milk* vary, but most states require 2 to 7 percent milk fat, and 11 percent or more of milk solids, which add up to many calories. Milk products are also used in *fruit sherbets*, along with a good deal of sweetening, so that calories are still quite high. Watch out, too, for the high calories in *"water ice,"* which doesn't contain any milk solids but has so much sweetening that it's just about the same calorie count as sherbet.

6. *Live an active life . . . move your body around.*

"The only exercise I ever get," boasts an overweight acquaintance of mine, "is pushing my arms into my overcoat sleeves." All the time he is bragging about this, he is wheezing and puffing as though about to take his last breath. While you cannot stay slim through activity and exercise if you overeat, the ideal way to remain slim and healthy through your life is to combine Stay-Slim Eating with moderate activity. Walk plenty, go bicycling if you enjoy the sport, swim for exercise as I recommend in the preceding chapter in detail, and do a moderate amount of exercising daily. The specific exercises recommended in this book will help women and men stay more attractive and vigorous at most any age. Robert Browning wrote this good advice: "What's a man's age? He must hurry more, that's all. Cram in a day what his youth took a year to hold." The poet was referring mostly to mental exercise, but women and men in their seventies and beyond should try to be as physically active as possible within their personal physical limitations.

Figure Out Daily Menus To Your Taste

Once you are down to your ideal weight through my quick weight loss methods, you don't have any desire to gorge yourself. You can have plenty of food on Stay-Slim eating and still retain your attractive new weight and dimensions. It's a good idea for the first week, or at least the first few days, to figure out your daily eating the day before for the following day so you can plan your shopping and meals. As you'll see in the following, on Stay-Slim Eating you go right along with what the rest of the family (if you're feeding a family) eats at regular meals. You watch your personal calorie intake with moderate portions, leaving out high-calorie foods, using the tips given to you throughout this book.

Here's one day's menu, a generous amount of tasteful foods, listed by one of my patients, a very attractive woman, 5′ 4″ tall, who had used the basic Quick Weight Loss Diet and then my Inches-Off Diet to get down to the slim dimensions she wanted so much, and to her ideal weight of 115 pounds. At her weight (see chart in Chapter 1), her maximum daily calorie allotment was 1300 calories. She listed her Monday eating as follows:

Breakfast—200 calories

Half-grapefruit	50 cals.
Oatmeal, skim milk	100
Thin slice toast, thinly spread with artificially sweetened jelly	50
Black coffee	0
	200

Lunch—260 calories

1 cup vegetable soup	80
Salad—two hard-boiled eggs on lettuce, medium sliced tomato, low-calorie dressing	170
Gelatin dessert, artificially sweetened	10
Tea, artificially sweetened	0
	260

Dinner—740 calories

Martini cocktail, dry	150
6 oz. roast chicken	300
Asparagus	20
Carrots	40

Mixed green salad, low-calorie dressing   30
Sherbet with 3″ round cookie   200
Coffee, black   0
                                                        ———
                                                         740

1 large apple as snack   100
Day's total calories 1300

You can see clearly that there's a good deal of delicious food on
this "limited" allotment of 1300 calories for the day. The slim
lady who made up her daily diet said that most of the time it was
too much food for her. She found no interference with her
family's eating, as she could partake of most of what they ate at
regular family meals.

The main pitfall to watch out for is the old habit of snacking,
and of piling on lots of butter, rich dressings, cream in the coffee,
and so on. It's all a matter of becoming accustomed to being careful. Practice this and it will soon be second nature. Doing without certain rich, calorie-heavy foods is a small sacrifice when you
get the marvelous benefits of a slim, attractive, far more healthy
body—and a more active, happier life. As your weight drops your
spirit lifts, as is generally true with the many thousands of overweights I've seen transformed into better-looking, brighter individuals.

It was about 400 years ago that John Heywood wrote:
"Enough is as good as a feast." That's still a worthy guideline for
your Stay-Slim Eating.

BREAKFAST FOODS

To help you make up your daily menus more quickly, according to the calorie count you find that you are allotted for the
day to maintain your desired weight, here's a briefer list of most
common breakfast foods, and calories for each. Since sizes of
fruits vary, figure that the calorie count on each, as on bread
depending on thickness of each slice, may vary by 5, 10, or a few
more. A few calories one way or another won't make much
difference in weight gain or loss. When the increase in calories
is 100 or more, then the pounds start piling on. Here's your par-

ial guide for breakfast foods (if you like a small steak for break-
ast, for instance, enjoy it—but write down that you're using 235
calories of your day's total for a 4-oz. lean, well-broiled steak).
Do the same with the condensed lunch/dinner listing that follows this one—if you like dry cereal with a sliced half-banana
and skim milk as your main luncheon dish, go to it, figuring it at
200 calories (cereal 110, half-banana 45, 4 oz. skim milk 45).

Juices (all unsweetened)

Orange juice, 4 oz., 55

Grapefruit juice, 4 oz., 50

Prune juice, 4 oz., 85

Tomato juice, 8 oz., 50

Vegetable juice, 8 oz., 50

Fruits

Apple, med., 70

Banana, med., 85

Canteloupe, med., half, 40

Grapefruit, med., half, 55

Orange, med., 65

Prunes, cooked, no sugar, 5, 85

Strawberries, fresh, 1 cup, 70

Cereals

Cooked, 1 cup, average, 105

Dry, no sugar, average, 1 oz.,
110

Eggs

Average-size egg, boiled, or cooked in no-fat pan, 75

Miscellaneous Foods

Bread, average slice, 60

Roll, average, 125

Bagel, 150.

English muffin, 140

Melba toast, 1 pc., 25

Danish pastry, med., 250

Donut, med. plain, 135

Waffle, 1, 215

Sugar, 1 tsp., 16

Jam, jelly, 1 tbsp., 55

Butter, marg., 1 pat, 50

Cottage cheese, ¼ lb., 100

Cream cheese, 1 oz., 100

Cream, heavy, 1 tbsp., 50

Bacon, crisp, 2 slices, 95

Ham, smoked, 3 oz., 290

Pancakes, 4", each 55   Smoked salmon, 1 oz., 100
Syrup, 1 tbsp., 55   Sausage, 4 oz., 340
                               Yogurt, plain, 8 oz., 120

LUNCH/DINNER

Here is a selection of the foods most commonly used for lunch and dinner, or dinner and lunch—whichever you eat at noon o evening. Again, calories may vary according to size of portions but if you have any doubt whether a food is "small, medium, o large," better figure on the highest calorie count so that the cal ories in the food you eat don't in actuality exceed the number o calories you write on your listing for the day. You can't fool you body—if your figures on paper add up to fewer calories than yo actually eat per day, the difference, *unwanted weight gain*, wil show up in the unhappy enlargement of your figure on the scal and in the mirror. If you deceive yourself, you'll learn the trutl of the old saying "To deceive a deceiver is no deceit."

Remember that according to nature's mathematics, two meal plus too many calories equal a 5-by-5 figure. If you exceed you calorie allotment for lunch, cut down the surplus by the sam number of calories saved at dinner. Calorie-counting is as simpl as that, and as effective as you make it yourself.

Juices

Tomato juice, 8 oz., 50   Orange, 4 oz., 55
Vegetable juice, 8 oz., 50   Grapefruit, 4 oz., 50

Fruits

Orange, med., sliced, 65   Strawberries, fresh, 1 cup, 70
Grapefruit, med., half, 55   Fruit cup, no sugar, 1 cup, 100
Canteloupe, med., half, 40   Canned fruit, average, 1 cup,
                                   200

Soups

Bouillon, broth, consommé, 1 cup, 10
Chicken, tomato, veg., 1 cup, 80
Creamed soups, 1 cup, 200

Meats, Poultry

Beef roast, lean, 4 oz., 210
Bologna, 4″ slice, 85
Hamburger, lean, br., 4 oz., 245
Steak, lean, br., 4 oz., 235
Chicken, turkey, lean, 3 oz., 180
Frankfurter, med., 155
Ham, canned, lean, 3 oz., 255

Lamb roast, lean, 3 oz., 155
Lamb chop, br., lean, 3 oz., 165
Pork roast, lean, 3 oz., 210
Tongue beef, 3 oz., 205
Veal roast, lean, 3 oz., 280
Veal cutlet, br., 3 oz., 185
Potpie, 8 oz., average, 460

Fish, Shellfish

Lean fish, average, not fried, 3 oz., 135
Salmon, canned, drained, 3 oz., 120
Sardines, canned, drained, 3 oz., 180
Tuna, canned, drained, 3 oz., 170

Oysters, med., 5, 60
Clams, med., 5, 45
Crabmeat, 3 oz., 90
Shrimps, med., 5, 50

Vegetables, Salads

Average serving, green vegs., 1 cup, 40-50
Beans, baked, 1 cup, 320
Lima beans, 1 cup, 150
Peas, 1 cup, 80
Potato, med., baked, 105
Potato, med, boiled, 90
Potato, fr.-fried, med., each 15

Sweet potato, med., baked, 155
Tomato, med., raw, 30
Cucumber, 7½″, 25
Carrot, raw, 5½″, 20
Celery, 8″ stalk, 5
Lettuce, ½ med. head, 35
Onion, raw, med., 50

Desserts, Misc. Foods

Apple, med., raw, 70
Grapefruit, med., half, 55
Mixed fruit cup, fresh, 100
Strawberries, fresh, cup, 70
Angel cake, 2″, pc., 110
Chocolate layer, 2″ pc., 420
Plain cake, med. pc., 180
Cookie, plain, 3″ round, 110

Gelatin dessert, ½ cup, 80
Gelatin dessert, sugar-free, ½ cup, 10
Ice cream, ½ cup, 200
Sherbet, ½ cup, 120-150
Chocolate syrup, tbsp., 20
Pies, fruit, 4″ pc., 330
Puddings, average, cup, 275

Beverages

Coffee, Tea, plain, 0
Cocktail, average, 150
Scotch, whiskey, gin, vodka,
   average, 1 oz., 75
Sodas, average, 8 oz., 100

Sodas, sugar-free, 8 oz., 1
Beer, 8 oz., 100
Wine, dry, 3 oz., 75
Wine, sweet, 3 oz., 125

SNACKS

Between-meals snacking is the downfall of many overweights.
Note that the difference between a snack of a raw carrot (20
calories) and a half-cup of shelled peanuts (420 calories) is *400
calories*. You can ruin a whole day's sensible dieting by one
quick, thoughtless and certainly needless moment of snacking,
stopping while out for an ice cream soda or pie and coffee, or
munching potato chips while watching TV. A snack at a time
adds pounds a day. Don't snack unless you deduct the true number of calories you ate in snacking from your daily total allotment.

The choice of what to eat and what to snack (if at all) in order
to keep your weight down is yours. If you prefer to skip a hamburger (245 calories without roll) at lunch and instead have a
mid-afternoon or mid-evening snack of a half-cup of ice cream
with 2 tablespoons of chocolate syrup (240 calories total), that's
up to you.

Carrot, raw, 5½", 20
Candy, caramel, fudge, 1 oz.
   120
Chocolate, 1 oz., 145
Cookie, average, plain, 3"
   round, 110
Fig bar, small, 55
Donut, med., plain, 135
Sponge cake, 2" pc., 115
Cream layer cake, 2" pc., 420
Gelatin dessert, reg., ½ cup, 80
Gelatin dessert, sugar-free,
   ½ cup, 10
Ice cream, ½ cup, 200

Ice milk, ½ cup, 150
Ice cream soda, average, 350
Pie, fruit, average pc., 330
Lemon meringue pie, 4" pc.,
   300
Nuts, shelled, ½ cup, 420
Peanut butter, 1 tbsp., 90
Potato chips, med., 10, 115
Pizza, 6" wedge, 200
Figs, dried, large, 60
Dates, pitted, ½ cup, 250
Apple, med., 70
Cherries, cup, 65
Grapes, cup, 85

Peach, med., 35   Plum, med., 30
Pear, med., 100   Tangerine, med., 40
Pineapple, fresh, diced, cup, 75

CALORIE TABLES

As noted before, calorie-count is basically a dependable measurement, such as ounces per pound. You may find some variations in calorie-table numbers due to differences in sizes (fruits, for instance), portions, the amount of an item on a teaspoon, and so on. However, variations of a few calories one way or another are not significant. It's the grand total that counts—and the grander the total the higher your weight will rise. If you cheat in counting, your mistakes will show up where it hurts most, in the flab on your figure.

MEATS AND POULTRY

(Most meats and poultry figured here as lean, all visible fat trimmed off, about 60 calories per ounce.)

	cals.
Bacon, fried crisp, 2 slices	95
Beef roast, lean, 4 oz.	210
Hamburger, lean, broiled, 4 oz.	245
Potpie, 8 oz.	460
Steak, lean, broiled, 4 oz.	235
Bologna, 4" slice	85
Chicken, turkey, broiled, 3 oz.	180
Drumstick and thigh with bone, fried, 5 oz.	275
Frankfurter, medium	155
Ham, smoked, 3 oz.	290
Canned, all lean, 2 oz.	170
Lamb chop, broiled, lean only, 2.5 oz.	140
Leg, lean, 2.5 oz.	130
Pork roast, lean only, 2.5 oz.	175
Sausage, 4 oz.	340
Tongue, beef, 3 oz.	205

Veal cutlet, broiled, 3 oz.	185
Roast, lean, 3 oz.	280

FISH AND SHELLFISH

Bluefish, baked, broiled, 3 oz.	135
Clams, medium, each	9
Crabmeat, 3 oz.	90
Haddock, fried, 3 oz.	135
Mackerel, broiled, 3 oz.	200
Oysters, medium, each	12
Salmon, canned, drained, 3 oz.	120
Sardines, canned, drained, 3 oz.	180
Shad, baked, 3 oz.	170
Shrimps, medium, each	10
Swordfish, broiled with butter, 3 oz.	150
Tuna, canned, drained, 3 oz.	170

VEGETABLES

Asparagus, medium	3.5
Avocado, medium, half	185
Beans, baked and canned types, 1 cup	320
Beets, 1 cup	70

Broccoli, 1 cup	45
Brussels sprouts, 1 cup	60
Cabbage, raw, shredded, 1 cup	25
Cooked, 1 cup	45
Carrots, raw, 5½", each	20
Cooked, 1 cup	45
Cauliflower, cooked, 1 cup	30
Celery, 8" stalk, raw	5
Corn, cooked, 5" ear	65
Canned, 1 cup	170
Cucumbers, 7½", each	25
Lettuce, 5" compact head, 1 lb.	70
2 large leaves	5
Lima beans, 1 cup	150
Mushrooms, 1 cup	30
Onions, raw, 2½", each	50
Cooked, 1 cup	80
Parsley, raw, chopped, 1 tbsp.	1
Peas, fresh, cooked, 1 cup	110
Canned, frozen, drained, 1 cup	80
Potatoes, medium, baked, with peel, each	105
without peel, each	90
Boiled, medium, each	90
French-fried, 2" x ½", each	15
Mashed, milk, no butter, 1 cup	145
Chips, 2", medium, each	11
Radishes, raw, medum, each	3
Sauerkraut, drained, 1 cup	30
Spinach and other greens, 1 cup	45
Squash, summer type, 1 cup	35
Winter type, 1 cup	95
String beans, 1 cup	35
Sweet potatoes, medium, baked	155
Candied	295

Tomatoes, raw, medium	3
Canned, 1 cup	4
Juice, 1 cup (8 oz.)	5

FRUITS

Apples, raw, medium	7
Juice, 1 cup	12
Applesauce, canned, sweetened, 1 cup	18
Apricots, raw, each	2
Canned in syrup, 1 cup	220
Bananas, medium, each	8
Blueberries, blackberries, 1 cup	8
Cantaloupe, 5", medium, half	4
Cherries, 1 cup	6
Cranberry sauce, canned, 1 cup	55
Dates, pitted, 1 cup	50
Figs, dried, large 2" x 1", each	6
Fruit Cocktail, canned, in syrup, 1 cup	19
Grapefruit, 5" medium, half	5
Juice, fresh, 1 cup	9
Grapes, 1 cup	8
Grape juice, bottled, 1 cup	16
Lemons, medium, each	2
Oranges, medium, each	6
Juice, fresh, 1 cup	11
Peaches, 2" medium, each	3
Canned in syrup, pitted, 1 cup	20
Pears, 3" medium, each	10
Pineapple, fresh, diced, 1 cup	7
Canned in syrup, 1 cup	20
Plums, 2" medium, each	3
Prunes, cooked, unsweetened, each	1
Juice, canned, 1 cup	17
Raisins, dried, 1 cup	46
1 level tablespoon	3

Strawberries, fresh, 1 cup 70
Tangerines, med. 2½", each... 40
Watermelon, 4" x 8" wedge... 120

DAIRY PRODUCTS, EGGS, FATS, OILS, DRESSINGS

Butter, 1 8-oz. cup (2 ¼-lb.
    sticks) 1,605
    1 pat or square 50
Cheese, American, 1-inch
    cube 70
    American, process, 1 oz. 105
    Cottage cheese, creamed,
        1 oz. 30
    Farmer cheese, pot cheese,
        1 oz. 25
    Cream cheese, 1 oz. 105
    Roquefort-type, 1 oz. 105
    Swiss, 1 oz. 105
Eggs, large, cooked without
    fat, each 80
    Scrambled, fried with
        butter, each 115
    White only, raw, each 20
    Yolk only, raw, each 60
Milk (cow's), whole, 1 cup
    (8 oz.) 165
    Skim, nonfat, 1 cup 90
    Buttermilk, cultured, 1 cup... 90
    Cream, light, 1 cup 525
    "   1 tablespoon 35
    "   heavy   " 50
Margarine, 1 cup
    (2 ¼-lb. sticks) 1,615
    1 pat or square 50
Oils, cooking and salad—
    corn, cottonseed, olive,
    soybean, 1 tbsp. 125
Salad dressings—French,
    1 tbsp. 60
    Mayonnaise, 1 tbsp. 110
    Mayonnaise-type, 1 tbsp. ... 60

Russian, 1 tbsp. 75
Yogurt, plain, 1 cup 120

BREADS AND GRAIN PRODUCTS

Bread, all types, average
    slice, plain, toasted 60
Cereals, cooked, average
    type, 1 cup 105
    Dry cereals, unsweetened,
    average, 1 oz. 110
Crackers, Graham, medium,
    each 28
    Rye wafers, 2" x 3½", each 25
    Saltines, 2" square, each ... 23
Macaroni, spaghetti, cooked,
    1 cup 155
Muffins, 3" size, average,
    each 140
Noodles, egg, cooked, 1 cup... 200
Pancakes, 4", each 55
Rice, cooked, 1 cup 200
Rolls, medium size, average,
    each 130
Waffles, average size, each ... 240

DESSERTS, SWEETS

Cakes, Angel food, 2" sector... 110
    Chocolate layer, 2" sector ... 420
    Cupcake, 2¾", with icing,
        each 160
    Plain cake, 3" x 2" x 1½",
        piece 180
    Sponge cake, 2" sector 115
Candy, Caramels, fudge,
    1 oz. 120
    Chocolate, milk or dark,
        1 oz. 145
Cookies, Average type,
    3" round, each 110
    Fig bar, small, each 55
Chocolate syrup, 1 tbsp. 20
Doughnuts, medium, plain,
    each 135

Gelatin dessert, ½ cup	80	Cocktail, average	150
sugar-free	10	Gin, Scotch, vodka,	
Honey, 1 tbsp.	60	whiskey, average, 1 oz.	75
Ice cream, ½ cup	200	Carbonated beverages,	
Ice cream soda,		ginger ale, 8 oz.	80
average size	350	Cola-type, 8 oz.	105
Ice milk, 1 cup	285	Cocoa, cup	235
Jams, jellies, preserves,		Ketchup, chili sauce, 2 tbsp.	15
1 tbsp.	55	Olives, green and ripe, large,	
Pies, apple, other fruits,		each, average	9
4" sector	330	Nuts, Peanuts, roasted,	
Custard, pumpkin,		shelled, ½ cup	420
4" sector	265	Peanut butter, 1 tbsp.	90
Lemon meringue, 4" sector	300	Cashews, pecans, walnuts,	
Puddings, custard,		½ cup	375
cornstarch, 1 cup	275	Pickles, dill 4", sweet 3", each	18
Sherbet, ices, ½ cup	120	Pizza, cheese, 6" wedge	200
Sugar, granulated, 1 tsp.	16	Soups, Bouillon, broth,	
"　　　" 1 cup	770	consommé, 1 cup	10
Syrup, 1 tbsp.	55	Chicken, tomato, vegetable	80
MISCELLANEOUS		Creamed, asparagus,	
Beverages, Coffee, tea, plain	0	mushroom, 1 cup	200
Beer, 8 oz.	110	Rice, noodle, barley, 1 cup	115

SEEK OUT LOW-CALORIE RECIPES

The magazines, newspapers and books are filled these days with low-calorie recipes and food-preparation tips that can help you and your family enjoy more slimming, healthier meals from now on. You can keep your figure lovelier (and the same for other members of the family and guests) by taking the extra time and trouble (which can really be fun) finding, reading and keeping the low-calorie recipes, shortcuts and tips—and using them beneficially in all the years ahead.

Just as an indication, a few ideas follow.

EGGPLANT STUFFED WITH MEAT

1 medium eggplant
2 hamburgers
skim-milk mozzarella cheese

Cut a medium eggplant in half lengthwise.

Boil halves in salted water until centers are very soft (about twenty minutes). Remove pulp from skin, chop up pulp.

Add the equivalent of 2 medium hamburgers of very lean meat from which all fat has been removed by butcher before grinding.

Salt meat to taste, spoon back into eggplant shells after mixing with chopped eggplant center. Top with thin strips of mozzarella.

Bake in 375° oven until meat is cooked through (about half-hour).

Serves 2; for 3 portions, make with 3 hamburgers. In preparing dish, you may add herbs and spices to suit your taste.

OIL-LESS TUNA-DELIGHT

can of regular tuna, 7 oz.	1 onion
1 egg	½ lemon

Place can of tuna in sieve, run cold water through it briskly to remove the oil (or you may use tuna packed in water and skip this step). Drain thoroughly, stir up with fork.

Add to tuna juice of half-lemon, 1 chopped hard-boiled egg, a chopped raw onion.

Serve on lettuce with sliced tomatoes, cucumbers, celery, raw carrot strips, radishes.

Similar low-calorie oil-less dishes may be made with canned salmon or sardines, drained in sieve under cold water.

COTTAGE CHEESE AND TOMATO SALAD

creamed cottage cheese, 8 oz.	minced scallion, 1 tbsp.
3 large tomatoes	lettuce
1 cucumber	

Mix the cottage cheese, using a fork, with a finely diced cucumber and about a tablespoon of minced scallion or onion.

On a bed of lettuce, spread 3 tomatoes cut in wedges to form a circle. Place the cheese mixture in the middle. Sprinkle with paprika. Serves 3.

SHRIMPS AND EGGS

6 eggs
2 large scallions or 2 medium onions
¼ pound shrimp, cut into bite-size pieces

Beat the eggs very lightly and combine with the finely chopped scallions or onions. Salt lightly.

Using a no-fat, no-stick skillet, pour in the pieces of shrimp and heat for only a few seconds, then pour in the egg mixture. Keep mixing the eggs and shrimps lightly with a fork until the eggs are at the thickness you like.

Serves 3 or 4.

LOW-CALORIE CRABMEAT SALAD

1 can crabmeat
6 tbsp. low-calorie mayon-
    naise-type dressing
½ tsp. Dijon mustard

12 capers
half-lemon
2 stalks celery, chopped
1 tsp. cut-up chives.

Mix the salad dressing and the mustard.

Add juice of half-lemon, capers, chopped celery, chives, crabmeat and mix gently with a fork.

Serve on lettuce with no other dressing, sprinkle with paprika.
Serves 4.

Stay-Slim Sample Meals

Lunch

Medium-size shrimp cocktail.
Tossed green salad with low-calorie dressing.
2 slices Melba toast.
2 tbsp. creamed cottage cheese in the salad.
Half-grapefruit.
Coffee, tea, sugar-free soda.

Dinner

Clear soup, not creamed.
Roast chicken (no butter used in cooking).

Two low-calorie vegetables (spinach, asparagus).
Lettuce and tomatoes, low-calorie dressing.
Fresh strawberries or sliced orange.
Coffee, tea.

"A few kind words . . ."

You can enjoy stay-slim eating, and the good health that generally goes with it, along with a much lovelier figure, if you approach it optimistically and with a sense of humor. This can sustain you in stay-slim eating at home, in restaurants, and at parties. A very attractive lady patient who succeeded in going from mammoth to sylph on quick weight loss dieting, and has stayed beautifully slim for over ten years now, says that when a hostess offers her dessert she says, "No, thanks. All I want is black coffee, and a few kind words."

STAY-SLIM QUICKIE-TIPS

Since you probably know too well that "great pounds from little ounces grow," you may find these quickie-tips, reminders and shortcuts helpful in preventing an accumulation of those little ounces that eventually and inevitably add up to unwanted pounds and inches on your figure. These simple aids will prove to you that a calorie saved is a calorie not gained—thank goodness.

Get the spread-it-thin habit. When you spread jam or jelly, even the no-sugar kind, don't heap it on but spread it thin. You get flavor without excess calories. Do the same with butter, margarine, soft cheese, other spreads.

Keep washed lettuce handy in a damp towel in the refrigerator. You can whip up an "instant salad" with a little low-calorie salad dressing for a low-calorie snack or meal.

Keep many low-calorie snacks cool and ready in the refrigerator—carrot sticks, cauliflower buds, celery stalks, raw mushroom caps, tomato juice, fat-free consommé, no-calorie sodas in many flavors. They can save you hundreds of calories in daily snacks.

Clean your breath with water, drinking many glasses during the day. Especially when you're dieting, but actually at any time, plenty of water not only washes out waste matter from your system but also helps clean away unpleasant breath.

Don't gulp your food. By cutting up food in small pieces and chewing slowly, you make a little seem like more, and you'll be satisfied with less.

Become aware of every bite you take. Don't pick at snacks or appetizers without even realizing that you're eating—the calories amount to just as many whether you're really savoring the snack or gobbling it. Often you see a fat man finish a dish of nuts alongside his chair, and then exclaim, "My God, I didn't even know I was eating them!"

Drink coffee before meals. Two to 3 cups of coffee, tea or other no-calorie beverage *before* the meal will blunt your appetite and keep you from consuming as much food. Keep drinking during and after the meal, too, if you wish.

Realize that there are "hidden fats" in the foods you eat, even lean foods, so don't think your body *needs* butter or other added fats in the diet. You are best off skipping the butter and other fatty spreads entirely, enjoying the natural flavors of the other foods.

Reach for artificial sweeteners instead of sugar, and you can save well over 100 calories a day. Don't believe the myth that you need sugar's "energy"—your other foods give you plenty of that "energy" with fewer calories.

Get a little postal scale as a help in weighing out portions if your calorie table permits you "4 ounces of lean meat," for example. Soon you'll recognize weights by the size of portions, but check yourself with the scale until you know. You can even use it for weighing mail.

Never, never drink whole milk when you can get skim or fat-free milk instead. You don't lose any vital nutrients but you save 75 calories per glassful.

Cut your food intake weekdays drastically if social activities tend to boost your weekend eating. If you put on pounds over a weekend, a "starvation Monday" or a couple of days on one of my quick weight loss diets will trim off that extra weight rapidly —but if you keep eating heavily, you'll keep growing around the hips and elsewhere.

Don't pamper yourself when ill with a constant flow of snacks or bigger meals. In other words, don't "feed a cold" or any other sickness. The body will usually get well sooner if it doesn't have to handle too much food. And you won't look fat and flabby when you get on your feet again.

Use no-stick pots and pans for cooking without any butter, margarine, fats or grease. Foods taste remarkably good without the heavy added richness. Use cooking tips such as adding a little skim milk in scrambling eggs to fluff them up.

Use little tricks to check your figure growth so that inches don't sneak up on you. One lady marks her seatbelt in the car, and when the buckle goes beyond that line she knows her girth is expanding. Another keeps a tight dress handy, and if she can't get into it, that's a dire warning. A man marks his belt buckle, and he buckles down to dieting when he passes the "stay-slim hole" in the belt.

Try using wine in many recipes instead of the usual fats, shortening or oils. Much of the high-calorie alcohol is cooked away by heat, yet flavor and juices remain to improve the dish. Any alcoholic flavor tells you that some alcohol calories still remain, so a little more cooking is needed. Calories disappear fast from white or dry wines, stay longer with heavier wines such as port or sherry, or brandy.

Keep trying new low-calorie recipes all the time. A new taste sensation tends to be more inviting for the family than eating the same old dish, whether high or low in calories.

Keep making up new low-calorie dishes yourself, just as you do with most recipes that call for an ingredient you don't have handy. For example, plain tomato sauce is low in calories and goes deliciously with many foods and combinations. Also, the powdered broths, that are low in calories (as marked on the label) help add flavor and juiciness to many recipes, substituted for oils.

Add naturally low-calorie foods that bulk out recipes, as filling quantities help produce satisfactory eating for the dieter, and you still keep the calories very low. Chopped fresh tomatoes, onions, celery, cabbage, are some of the recipe-extenders that help stay-slim eating.

Use pure apple butter, unsugared, spread thin on rye wafers for an occasional snack. Also very tasty with cottage cheese.

Use chestnuts for snacking lightly. They are low·in calories—about 50 calories for 10 average-size chestnuts—and 2 or 3 hot-roasted chestnuts make a satisfying snack.

Treat yourself to popcorn, low in calories when you don't use melted butter or margarine. Season well with salt and spices.

Keep 'em out of sight. Keep high-calorie foods and snacks, such as cookies, cakes, other desserts, candies, and so on, out of sight, out of easy reach—and thus more surely out of your stomach.

Remove fat before serving. Best way to be sure that all possible fat is removed from meats and poultry is to cut out every reachable speck of fat *before* serving. That way there's less chance of eating fat as an oversight when the food is on your plate and you're busy chatting.

How to remove the most fat: To skim off all possible fat from a natural beef gravy, pour it into a bowl, spoon off all the fat you can get. Drop in a few ice cubes, leave, and soon any remaining fat will rise to the top of the bowl, become solid and easy to remove.

Lift extra fat off soup by floating a lettuce leaf on top for one or two minutes, then lift it off and much of the fat will cling to the leaf.

Pep up the appetizing look of salads by combining various types of lettuce rather than one. For example, toss together Boston, Iceberg, and Romaine lettuce. Also combine lettuce with chicory, chives, spinach, water cress, parsley, raw cauliflower, scallions, other greens and herbs.

It's better to broil. Remember that roasting and broiling meats, poultry and fish remove more fat than other cooking methods, since the fat drips off the meat onto the pan below. In braising, boiling, simmering and frying, the fat settles on and around the meat, and while much can be skimmed off, some remains.

Use herbs and spices often, more important in low-calorie cooking than in any other. If a low-calorie salad dressing seems flat, sparkle it up with favorite spices, such as powdered mustard, curry, chili. You'll probably enjoy the home-flavored concoction more than the usual commercial salad dressing. If a low-calorie casserole or stew isn't satisfying in flavor, toss in some of your favorite herbs—rosemary, parsley, chives, sweet basil, whatever

—to your taste. You'll find that dishes don't have to be fattening to be tasty—in fact, even a hint of greasiness in a serving will be disagreeable to your taste.

Create your own herb-spice tricks. Add taste to vegetables and other servings in your own creative way. For instance, a little nutmeg with string beans gives them a different, zippy flavor. Basil sharpens the fresh taste of tomatoes. Try adding a bit of dill when cooking asparagus, cabbage, spinach, other green vegetables.

Combine two or more vegetables for variety and special appeal. Create your own combinations, such as these tasty duos: tomatoes and onions, mushrooms and green beans, bean sprouts and okra.

Use plenty of garnishes, such as parsley, watercress, carrot curls or sticks, cucumber slices and others along with meals as they're practically free of calories. At the same time, they add vitamins A and C to your intake.

Use wine vinegar as a salad dressing, with or without added herbs and spices. And, of course, fresh lemon juice always peps up a salad.

Make a low-calorie tasty soup by heating up plain tomato juice or combination vegetable juices, add some herbs and spices to your taste.

Freshly ground pepper gives more lively, satisfying flavor to low-calorie or any dishes than dried pepper. Keep peppercorns and a grinder handy for use in cooking and right on the table.

Adventure at breakfast. Enjoy lean meat, chicken, fish for breakfast—why not? It's all a matter of habit. If you shudder at the idea of steak for breakfast, or a slice of roast beef or lean lamb, then why not at the commonly approved breakfast meats such as bacon, ham, sausages? If chicken for breakfast appalls you, consider that eggs are among the most popular of breakfast foods, and eggs do come from chickens (don't know which came first). Many people react, "Lean fish, baked or broiled, for breakfast? Horrible thought." Yet smoked salmon (lox) and cream cheese is considered a gourmet breakfast treat, and how about smoked kippers? It's all in the mind of the eater.

Save calories with skim milk as a substitute for whole milk and cream not only for drinking and beverages but also for cooking.

If a condensed soup label calls for adding whole milk, use skim milk instead; you save calories and lose very little in flavor. In fact, some calorie-conscious cooks add a can of water instead of milk and make up for the flavor-loss by sprinkling in some herbs or spices.

Make a low-calorie shake of skim milk, low-calorie syrup or black coffee, artificial sweetening.

Make gelatin salad. To make a special treat and a bulkier main dish, mold the salad or other food in low-calorie gelatin. This adds very few calories yet gives the salad extra flavor, body, and the feeling of a big-meal serving.

Consider charcoal-broiling to add satisfying flavor to meats and poultry, also fish, so you don't miss butter or oils on the broiled food.

Vary the look of foods. Use cooking-aid gadgets—slicers, shredders, graters, choppers—to help satisfy the appetite by changing the texture of foods, thus subtly changing and usually enhancing the flavors.

Make stay-slim "Coffee Froth," an airy, low-calorie dessert. Make it in a few minutes. Combine skim milk, instant coffee, artificial sweetening and an egg white. Beat until thick and frothy. Place in a freezer compartment until thick and cold. Serve in dessert dishes.

Don't ever serve oversize portions of even the lowest-calorie foods. One of the first bad habits the overweight must break is that of stuffing himself. No diet that states "eat all you want" means that you should stuff yourself. Quite the opposite, never eat excessive portions or take second helpings. It's far better for you, and an actual aid in reducing, to spread portions over six feedings a day rather than stuff in three sizable meals.

Adopt a stay-slim posture, standing, walking, and sitting. Turn back to exercising in Chapter 9 and practice again how to walk and move properly so that you look and feel your slimmest. Check yourself in the mirror when standing correctly, and if you see any undesirable swellings, go back on one of my quick weight loss diets.

Leave food on your plate as soon as you feel at all full. Then put the plate out of sight, discarding the food or transferring it to a refrigerator dish. If it sits there on your plate in front of you, chances are you'll eat it even though you don't really need or want it. In other words, don't be a "pelican eater," as in the noted limerick:

> A wonderful bird is the pelican.
> His mouth can hold more than his belican.
> > He can take in his beak
> > Enough food for a week.
> I'm darned if I know how the helican.

11

Across the Doctor's Desk . . . Problems and Solutions

From the many letters and comments I've received from readers of my previous book, *The Doctor's Quick Weight Loss Diet*, a very popular and helpful feature was the relating of questions most often asked by overweight patients and my answers to them. Therefore, I'm covering more of these points here in the form of the problems that overweights most often present to me, and the solutions I offer them.

In all my writing, I try to "talk" with you as a reader the way I would talk and advise you as a patient sitting across my desk. This is in no way a substitute for the attentions of your personal physician but rather acts as a supplement in writing. Doctors I know tell me that they welcome this kind of sensible, professional corroboration and reminder, just as my patients have gained from the good advice of others.

In retelling the most common problems of overweight patients and my solutions, I cannot report the precise wording, of course. Some people, it is claimed, have "photographic memories," which enable them to remember and repeat each syllable of each sentence of a long-ago conversation. I am not one of those geniuses. But I do here "speak" solutions to your problems as if we were face to face.

The problems are always "serious" in that the patient is concerned, but sometimes there are amusing facets. One overweight woman said to me, "Doctor, my problem is that I can't resist buttery foods. I gobble them up and I gain weight. There's nothing I can do about it." I asked, "Would you give up buttery foods if you had an allergy to them and they made you break out in hives?"

She answered quickly, "Of course I'd give up buttery foods if I were allergic to them, but I'm not." "Yes, you are," I insisted, "every time you eat buttery foods you break out in extra pounds!" She was amused, said that she would avoid buttery foods as though she *were* allergic to them. This humorous slant helped her to avoid the higher-calorie foods that were forbidden on her diet. She went on my basic Quick Weight Loss Diet and slimmed down beautifully so that she was hardly recognizable a few months later; there was no sign of the bulging overweight she had been. This "allergy" twist won't work for everyone, but perhaps it will be another extra help for you.

Each problem, silly as it may sound, or sensible, as most problems are, is a serious problem for the one burdened with it and must be answered effectively if at all possible. I suggest that you pretend you are sitting across my desk in my doctor's office (which is now non-existent, since I have "retired" for writing and consultation) and are presenting me with problems for which I will try to present solutions that will work effectively for you.

> *"I want to attend an important affair a week from today but can't get into my best dress because it's too tight. Can diet help me in time?"*

You can lose 5 to 10 pounds within the week and get into a too-tight dress (or suit) by doing this: Start fasting today for 24 to 48 hours as I suggest (taking water and vitamins). Then go on my basic Quick Weight Loss Diet. By the end of the week, your dimensions as well as your weight will be reduced remarkably so that you can fit into too-tight clothing (unless you were 20 or more pounds lighter when you bought the garment).

> *"I'm afraid to lose weight too quickly because friends and relatives tell me it's not healthy."*

It never ceases to amaze me that people will often take the word of a "friend or relative" who is totally ignorant about a subject rather than the advice of a doctor like myself who has put most of a lifetime into gathering information about overweight and to reducing thousands of men, women and youngsters. The fact is, proved beyond question in my lifetime experience, that the quicker an overweight can take off excess pounds, the better off she will be in good health and every other way.

The premise that quick weight loss is unhealthy is just as ridiculous as this: You are carrying a 25-pound iron ball and you tell me, "Doctor, I must put down this weight because it's breaking my back and tearing off my arms." I tell you to put it down immediately and you say, "No, that would be unhealthy. The best thing is to put down the weight a few pounds at a time over a long period of time—rather than to relieve my back and muscles and whole body, which is about to collapse." When you take off burdensome overweight rapidly, your whole body, your heart, circulation, all of you gets the speedy relief it needs badly lest your health break down completely.

> *"My husband insists that we eat in his favorite restaurant twice a week. The waiters get upset if I leave anything on my plate. How can I keep from stuffing myself and putting on weight?"*

You're hurting yourself most of all when you reach for this far-out kind of excuse for overeating. You probably started the meal wrong by ordering something creamy and loaded with calories rather than broiled steak, chicken, shrimp, or whatever is permitted on your diet. Nobody gets hurt in feelings, nor you in fattening up, if you simply explain, "I can't finish the delicious food because I want to look slim and attractive, and not fat." If a waiter or hostess can't understand that honest, sensible statement, better do your eating elsewhere. Don't be ashamed of dieting, speak up—it helps enormously.

> *"Oh, doctor, it's such a nuisance to count calories, I just can't bring myself to do it."*

Look at counting calories as a game instead of a bother. One patient told me that she's come to enjoy planning her Stay-Slim Eating for the next day by making up a listing in bed just before she goes to sleep. She keeps the calorie-count table and my book on her bedside table and refers to it, although by now she knows the figures well. She guesses at the figures, makes up her day's menu, then checks the figures in the book—"Better than doing a crossword puzzle," she says. It's all in your approach. It's much pleasanter to have a keen sense of enjoyment about maintaining a slim, healthful figure and buoyant good looks than to pity yourself for passing up some rich foods.

> *"Since the shock of an auto accident, I'm so shook-up and nervous that I keep eating and growing fatter."*

Many overweights blame small or large incidents for their overeating, from a car accident to an unpleasant phone conversation. You must break away from using all these excuses or excess fat will break your health. Instead of seeking blame, go on one of my quick weight loss diets, exercise and become interested in some social, school, political or other activities. Leaning on weak excuses rather than dieting can make the difference between an earlier, more painful death—and a longer, healthier, happier life. One very heavy man told me he had started overeating again because he believed a newspaper interview with a crackpot who foretold positively that the world was coming to an end soon. I asked this successful businessman whether he was also giving up his profitable business as long as the world was coming to an end. He grinned when he realized how foolish he was to use *any* alibi for overeating. He went back on his diet and lost weight rapidly. Are you indulging yourself in similar foolishness?

> *"I just can't break up eating habits that have gone on for years and have a psychiatric background."*

This lady told me that for years she had been going to a psychiatrist, who unearthed her primary problem. As a little girl, she said, she had adored her father and came upon him intimately embracing her mother. This so upset her that she started overeating. When the situation was revealed to her as an adult, she was still left with a twenty-year overeating habit she couldn't break, she claimed. I advised that all heavy people, whatever their original cause for overeating, had to come to grips with the problem. This can be solved by going on one of my quick weight loss diets, *making the start*. Once you begin, the rapid drop in weight is so encouraging that it drives you on to keep dieting until you're slim and radiant. Thus, the problem disappears.

> *"I have no pep, so I sleep a lot. I've gained weight, have no strength and don't know what to do."*

I told this woman to limit her sleeping to eight hours in every 24 as an absolute essential. By exercising and becoming involved in hospital-aide work, she didn't nap during the day. I advised her to drink loads of tea and coffee and convinced her that this would act as a helpful stimulant, with no harm at all. She soon found herself wide awake and able to stick to her diet, and she shed pounds in a hurry. She looks like a "new woman," which she is.

> *"I was never heavy before but my doctor gave me some shots for a European trip. The shots must have affected my system because I've been heavy ever since."*

I examined this gentleman thoroughly and found there was nothing wrong with his system, his problem was personal gluttony. He had overeaten in Europe, retained his health-shattering eating habits and blamed his doctor instead. Hundreds of patients have used this excuse (how about you?). When I convinced this man that his system wasn't off-kilter, that he was blaming a doctor for his own excesses, he started to diet realistically and became slim and handsome again. Now he tells all this as a joke on himself, but he didn't think his lame excuse was funny when he had an elephantine figure.

> *"I gained 50 pounds because I used The Pill, which you know is a hormone, and this type of hormone puts weight on women."*

I told her this was "a pilly-silly excuse," the same kind of empty alibi given by many women who get heavy after a pregnancy or a hysterectomy. None of these conditions need lead to overweight unless you have a special condition, which your doctor will know about. With The Pill, pregnancy, hysterectomy, menopause and some other "women's problems," the body may retain some water that can add 3 to 5 pounds, never 10 to 50 pounds. If your body acts that way, go on my basic Quick Weight Loss Diet at once. You'll lose the excess weight and water rapidly and will keep it off. If you think you're feeling a little weak and lethargic when dieting, walk, exercise, be active in body and mind. Take some deep breaths, a tall glass of cold water with a few drops of lemon juice and artificial sweetening—and any weakness will quickly disappear.

> *"I put on weight because my husband irritates me, and there's nothing I can do about that."*

Your husband's attitude (in so many cases) is due to your unattractive, overweight and therefore aging appearance. He becomes ashamed of you, and so do your children. Go on one of my diets and see how your husband and your life brightens up —it happens in most cases.

Too many of my patients have come to me *after* their homes were wrecked because the wife was fat, unappealing, leading to divorce. Many other overweights remain single and wonder why men (or women with fat men) don't want them. When I point out that their gluttonous appetites and bulging stomachs are the main obstacle to happiness and a good marriage, they start dieting and usually succeed in attaining an attractive figure and a new, more optimistic view on life.

> *"I gained weight soon after my marriage—why?"*

This is very common, especially among young men who put on 20 to 50 pounds and soon start feeling ill and old. This is due to a combination of causes. The newlywed eats as much as he did before marriage but is probably less active and energetic, so the calories turn to fat instead of being used up. He may gorge his wife's food to please her, and himself. He sits around eating snacks, drinking beer, watching TV. After age 25, the body requires 1 percent less food per year, partially due to lessened activity. By age 65, metabolism has usually slowed down about 40 percent and if the man is still eating as at age 25, he puts on weight. Since a woman's metabolism is 8 percent to 10 percent slower than a man's, she puts on even more weight and may become grotesquely fat. Quick weight loss dieting becomes essential if you put on pounds at any age, and then Stay-Slim Eating to remain slim, healthy and "young."

> *"I lost an average of 8 pounds a week for a total of 24 pounds lost in three weeks, then only lost 2 pounds the next week. Am I doing something wrong?"*

It sometimes happens on a quick weight loss or fasting diet that you lose weight quickly for a number of weeks, then find that one week the scale shows only a few pounds loss. *Stay on the diet,* since you are still losing weight that will show on the scale the following week or two. What is happening is that your fat is being pulled out of the fat depots in your body and being transformed into free fatty acids, which in turn are being burnt up for energy. While this process is going on, some of the fat is being turned into water. Furthermore, a good deal of the water you are drinking may be retained. Eventually the body must release this water. When it does, the loss may be tremendous; one patient dropped 16 pounds suddenly after one of these slow water-retention periods.

While your dimensions are changing that week, loss of actual pounds doesn't show on the scale. Other bodily processes are going on that hold up loss of weight in *pounds* for a brief period. Be patient and keep dieting faithfully and you will be rewarded in *a sudden drop in pounds,* which will be most heartening. The important point is not to become discouraged but to stay on the diet. Don't cheat, and you'll be more than amply rewarded for your patience.

> *"Why can't I have lettuce on your basic Quick Weight Loss Diet?"*

It will help you to understand why lettuce, which is a carbo-hydrate food, interferes with my all-protein basic diet (and is permitted liberally on my Inches-Off Diet). Everything that grows in the ground, above the ground and on trees is a carbo-hydrate. That includes all vegetables, fruits, grains, beans, and so on. Some of the low-calorie 5 percent carbohydrate vegetables, such as lettuce, celery, broccoli, asparagus and others, contain so little food value and so few calories that a person could eat 14 pounds of them a day and still be under 900 calories for the day.

However, regardless of their food value, if you are on my all-protein, basic Quick Weight Loss Diet, as little as a half-cup of spinach, lettuce, celery or the others will greatly diminish the process of pulling fat out of the fat depots in your body. Instead, the vegetables stimulate certain other internal functions that rapidly turn some of the carbohydrate into fat. (Carbohydrate stimulates the pancreas to produce extra insulin, and this in turn converts the carbohydrate into fat, immediately stopping the extraction of fat from the fat [adipose] storage compartments.)

If you "simply must have" some tossed salad and low-calorie dressing while on my basic Quick Weight Loss Diet, you'll have to settle for losing weight about half as rapidly (perhaps 4 pounds of weight lost per week instead of 8); or go on my Inches-Off Diet or another of the quick weight loss diets in this book.

"Can I have sugarless chewing gum, and the sugarless-powder drink mixes that make flavored drinks?"

While low-calorie, you should not use the gum or drink mixes on my basic Quick Weight Loss Diet or you may reduce the speed of weight loss, as they have some carbohydrates in them. You may have these items on my other quick weight loss diets and on Stay-Slim Eating, in limited amounts, not in excess.

"Since childbirth I've weighed a lot more than before and can't seem to take it off."

This is not an uncommon complaint from women after child-birth, hysterectomy and other "female" operations. Some trau-matic experiences may produce emotional upsets for which some women compensate by overeating. They become fat, unattractive, bring on other physical troubles and only make matters worse by their gluttony. They probably disobeyed the obstetrician's usual advice not to gain over 15 pounds or so during pregnancy, then found it more difficult to take off the excess weight. Many people have unfairly blamed childbirth or an operation by saying that it caused their overweight. Such responsibility has not been scientifically proven. There is a slight possibility that some hormonal disturbance has taken place, but if so, your physician will tell you so and treat it.

The best way to attack the excess weight, and get back to your former slim figure (and even slimmer if you were too heavy at the start) is to be positive and take effective action. Stop being negative, pampering yourself, feeling sorry for yourself, stuffing yourself with rich foods as compensation for "what I've gone through." Go on my basic Quick Weight Loss Diet until you're at your desired weight, then go on my Inches-Off Diet and soon you'll probably have lovelier slim dimensions than before your pregnancy or operation. Look at the many slim women who have three or more children and still retain their beautiful figures if you need further affirmation that it can and should happen to you.

> *"As soon as I skip a meal or do without foods I like, I get a headache."*

I heard this common complaint from a favorite television star, a very fine gentleman. I told him that there are two basic reasons for this reaction. In his case, as with so many people, he skipped the meal because he was in a pressure situation, having difficulties in rehearsing a show, meeting exasperating mistakes and delays, all of which alone can bring on a tension headache. This pressure, rather than missing the food, brought on the headache, but the lack of food was blamed, as in so many comparable instances.

Second, in missing his meal, he broke an entrenched habit. His subconscious mind as well as his stomach rebelled. On came the headache—but the primary causes were frustration, denial, tension, mishaps. If you are one of the small percentage who gets upset because of any break in your habits, my advice is to wait it out, and you'll soon adjust to cutting down on food or skipping meals. You can get relief with aspirin, or see your doctor, who may prescribe a soothing, stabilizing tranquilizer. Just don't give up your diet due to this flimsy excuse. You'll be so delighted with your quick weight loss in a few days that your disturbing symptoms will disappear. Thousands of my successful patients will attest to this.

> *"My menstruation was delayed; was this caused by my dieting?"*

Start with the knowledge that reducing an overweight body is a change for the better. A change in habit is a slight or considerable emotional disturbance, and a change in food also involves some physiological change. We are all creatures of habit, and the internal, unconscious workings of the body can also be affected. The aim of reducing is *to start a new pattern*. The changes make for some mental, hormonal and bodily changes, all for the better when you're down to your ideal weight.

If you feel slightly giddy or headachy when starting the diet, or if your menstruation is different, this may be coincidental or a response to the challenge and change. This is quite common with other changes, such as going to a different country, climate, altitude. In a brief time the human readjusts, and irregular menstruation (and other functions) becomes regular again. In checking patients with this complaint, I usually found that in the past they had encountered times when their periods were either lacking, scanty, or irregular. With such a condition, always consult your physician.

> *"Are so-called health foods better for me on my Stay-Slim Eating?"*

Absolutely not; it is absurd to pay double and triple and more for "health foods" in so-called health stores when you can get all the essentials in your regular groceries. Such "extra supplement" or "natural" foods don't cure diseases, improve health, or promote longer life. Maintaining ideal weight, and living actively, moderately, optimistically, are your answers for a healthier, happier, longer life.

One benefit some "health-food addicts" get is that they may be vegetarians and are rarely overweight. If this is the price you wish to pay for staying slim, go to it—but don't delude yourself that you're getting special life-giving properties in the health foods and supplements. Some of the common myths disproved by science are that there are special benefits for "iron-poor blood" and other problems in foods such as yogurt, bacillus acidophilis milk, blackstrap molasses, grapes, figs, dates, wheat germ, sea kelp, sea salt and many other screwball foods and concoctions. By buying them, you enrich the sellers, not your own body. There are values in foods such as grapes, figs, dates and yogurt—but they have no magical health properties.

"Is there special benefit in steam or cabinet baths, and in massage, for reducing?"

There is little or no value for true, lasting weight reduction in any of these methods. You must eat fewer calories than you expend—that's the only real way to weight reduction. Massage or vibration by hand or by machine may be pleasant and stimulating, but doesn't take off weight. Steam or cabinet baths may be psychologically helpful to some, but perspiring isn't lasting weight reduction and can be very exhausting (in my early years of medical practice I was often called on to treat individuals who had fainted in steam rooms). I don't approve of exhausting procedures whether steam baths, violent exercise or sports, or jogging. You must be in top physical condition, pronounced so after a physical examination before you undertake any of these wearing activities, and then only *after reducing to ideal weight.*

"Why aren't the mathematics of calorie intake and output for all people as exact as mathematics should be?"

Individuals vary and so does their metabolic functioning, affecting calorie intake and output—no question about it. Some people use up calories quicker than others. However, that's no excuse for overweights who claim that they're fat due to faulty metabolism; the overwhelming majority, generally figured by science as 95 percent, are fat due to overeating. If your metabolism is faulty it will show up in a thorough medical examination. Your physician will prescribe corrective treatment accordingly. Except for very few persons, the calorie intake/output formula is sound. If you are overweight and insist on blaming an underactive thyroid or other organ instead of an overactive fork, you'll never be slim.

> *"I'm afraid to diet because I have a high blood-pressure condition."*

When overweights alibi to me that they don't want to diet, because of high blood pressure or some other sickness, I point out that this is like saying, "I don't want to take steps to get well —because it will interfere with my sickness." Overweight is a prime contributor to a high blood-pressure condition with many patients. As you lose excess pounds and relieve pressures of fat compressing and congesting your organs and blood flow, high blood pressure usually drops. So the sooner you get down to ideal weight, the better for your blood pressure and most any other illness. You certainly shouldn't fear that dropping fat will hurt you, as your present overweight condition is obviously harming you. If you have some malfunction, it should be treated by your physician, who will agree that one vital step is to take off burdensome extra pounds of fat. This is also true with diabetes and many other afflictions.

> *"My chubby husband wears out his shoes in no time; could that be connected to his overweight?"*

A very heavy man or woman can wear out a pair of shoes in a week if he moves around much. The weight, strains and pressure fat people exert upon their feet is tremendous. Can you imagine what those heavy extra pounds do to the arches, ankles, knees, hips and your poor aching back? All these horrors are minor compared to how overloading, congesting extra fat harms the heart, blood vessels, pancreas, gall bladder, lungs and other organs. The fat comedian wasn't joking when he said, "I swallowed a big square meal and the corners are cutting up my insides!"

"A friend said hypnosis would get rid of my overweight."

Realize that hypnosis is an *outside* influence, and once the suggestions wear off, which usually happens quickly, you're back where you started. All the motivations, patterns, habits and denials superimposed on you by hypnotic influence make no lasting impression on your original thoughts and actions, because the instructions have been inserted from the outside. Hypnosis ignores calorie values, quality and quantity of food, hunger and satiation. A temporary weight loss due to hypnosis may be helpful for emergency relief to a strained body, but after the hypnotic effect has worn off you still have to save yourself. In my experience with dieters, cases involving hypnosis have proved to be almost a total waste, with added frustration due to failure. Quick weight loss dieting involves the overweight's personal knowledge, understanding and control—it works remarkably to get excess weight off and *keep it off*.

"Doctor, I'm sure my overweight is due to being constantly constipated."

You're wrong—there is absolutely no relationship between overweight and the weight of dried bowel waste. Even large, bulky stools weigh very little. Digestion and absorption of food are practically completed by the time the food reaches the large colon or bowel. It is dangerous to take laxatives almost daily, as tried by some overweights who are misinformed. Most effective reducing diets, other than all-fruit and all-vegetable diets, result in sizable weight loss but minimal waste matter. An occasional laxative isn't harmful, but a suppository or warm water enema is preferable.

"Should I go to a psychiatrist for help in reducing?"

If you are emotionally disturbed, have wide and sudden swings of mood, are despondent, very irritable, hot-tempered, repressed, I would probably suggest consulting a psychiatrist. Your personal physician will refer you to a psychiatrist if he thinks it is indicated in your case. There is a good chance that you will be helped in respect to these symptoms. However, don't think that the psychiatrist will help you reduce or you'll be in for a shock. After all problems are aired by you, and the psychiatrist's advice given to you, realize that you will still be confronted with your overweight problem. This can be solved by following recommendations such as mine, which will reduce you speedily and effectively. (Two famous New York psychiatric clinics give copies of *The Doctor's Quick Weight Loss Diet* to the overweight patients they treat.)

> *"I was sick with a virus, gained weight, and have been overweight since because of it."*

Except with rare complications, which the physician diagnoses and treats, there is no scientific reason why a virus disease or most other sicknesses should cause weight gain. Quite the opposite, sickness often involves loss of appetite and a drop in weight. What happens too commonly is that the person recovering lies around too much, gets no exercise or activity, overeats, gorges on candies and other high-calorie sweets, feels sorry for herself, pampers himself, and puts on ugly and dangerous fat. As soon as possible, become active, move around, exercise, and if you're pronounced well and are overweight, *go on a quick weight loss diet immediately* to get down to ideal weight as rapidly as possible for the sake of your good health and good appearance.

> *"I failed on my diet because I missed rich foods too much."*

If you're more concerned about alibis than looking beautifully slim and radiantly healthy, you'll always be fat. Many people who "miss rich foods too much" don't give the right diet a chance. All I ask you to do is go on my basic Quick Weight Loss Diet for one week—one short week. When you're up to 10 pounds slimmer by the end of the week and see the wonderful difference in your mirror and hear friends say how lovely you look, you'll throw the alibis into the garbage can, where they belong, and you'll keep on with your better-health, better-looks reducing.

One such stubborn dieter who alibied at first, then really went at his reducing seriously, told me, "Envious friends who see my newly slim figure ask me, 'What do you miss most from the old days?'—one way of giving me the needle. I tell them I *don't* miss the indigestion, shortness of breath, discomfort, fatigue and all-over flabbiness I felt when I was fat. I also emphasize that when I try rich foods now they taste fatty, greasy, almost repulsive."

"I eat low-calorie foods and still gain weight."

Truly low-calorie foods are a boon to the dieter, but count the calories beforehand, and if you find it all adds up to more calories per day than you're expending, you'll gain weight. You must constantly beware of a percentage of deceitful manufacturers and advertisers who aim to fool you for their own profit. A drink or food that is normally 200 calories may be cut to 160 calories and is then advertised as "reduced in calories" or "lower in calories" by some makers. You suffer if you assume that the beverage or food actually contains few or no calories.

Here's a shocking example of what some advertisers consider a "permissible lie"; that is, a deception that they justify because they think it will increase their sales: A restaurant advertised a drink and called it "Skinny Shake . . . made with 88-calorie diet-approved skim milk." Many weight-conscious people flocked to drink "Skinny Shakes" because they considered it an 88-calorie meal. The Department of Consumer Affairs investigated and revealed that the creamy half-quart milkshake actually contained *almost 400 calories* . . . and consisted of additives other than skim milk. The advertiser contended that he didn't lie in saying that the drink was made with 88-calorie skim milk, he simply omitted the fact that there were other high-calorie ingredients in the drink. Meanwhile he was endangering the health of overweights who were getting fatter on "Skinny Shakes."

"I didn't lose on your diet, because you said not to stuff myself but I did stuff myself."

This comment sounds childish but you'd be surprised how often I've heard it from grown men and women, otherwise sensible, who act like idiots when approaching dieting. I purposely warn that you should eat as much as you want on my basic Quick Weight Loss Diet (or any other diet) but "don't stuff yourself." If you pile in enough of even the lowest-calorie foods, the total will be higher than you expend, and you'll gain weight, or at any rate, you won't lose. Again, I ask that you go on the diet one short week, and the remarkable weight loss will keep you dieting and stop you from trying to fool yourself.

I sometimes tell overweights about a true report from a humorist who visited a famous Viennese pastry shop: "I heard a low rumbling, groaning and moaning. Each afternoon the women come here and start moaning, 'Oh, I can't eat this—it's so fattening. Oh, I can't take another bite, I shouldn't! Tomorrow I will eat nothing all day. I swear this is the last Sacher Torte I will touch for a month.' They never stop eating while they're talking." Are you that kind of hypocrite?

> *"Most diets I've gone on in the past have involved so much detail that I've failed on them. I'm afraid the same will happen with your diets."*

Early in my medical practice when I first became concerned about reducing my overweight patients for the sake of their *total* health, I found this to be true in many prevailing diets, which still exist. Instructions tell the overweight to "weigh this, measure that, do this, don't do that," and so on. I felt that this built another roadblock to successful reducing. On my basic Quick Weight Loss Diet, Inches-Off Diet and others, you simply eat to satisfy yourself, without stuffing, from a list of foods. That, along with a few other simple instructions, is the basic guide. It's easy to do, you lose pounds immediately, no complicated procedures waiting for proof that the diet works. Those are the main reasons why overweights who have failed on countless other diets usually succeed on mine.

> *"Doctor, I'm a gymnast, loaded with muscle, little excess fat, yet you say I'm overweight and must take off 10 to 15 pounds. I don't get it."*

Being a muscle-ridden gymnast, "muscleman," or athlete doesn't necessarily mean being healthy. Overweight muscle is a drag on the heart and other organs, as is excess fat. Each muscle cell must have a capillary entering it, feeding it, and removing waste material. While overweight in muscle may not be quite as dangerous as excess fat, it still is a terrible strain which, I am convinced, shortens life. Just as a truck engine has to labor harder to carry an excessive load of scrap iron, the heart and system must strain harder to support extra pounds—fat, muscle, whatever. Your body functions most smoothly, most healthfully at ideal weight, all other things being equal.

> *"My husband says he was 'born to be fat' and that he's a 'happy, jolly fat man.' Yet he's about 30 pounds overweight and I worry about his health."*

"Born to be fat" is a common excuse that is scientifically baseless for the vast majority; overweights who emphasize that are too often "born to die young." The "jolly fat man" or woman is also a myth—through the years there has been a parade of moaning, groaning, weeping, despondent overweights waddling into my office depressed about their excess fat. Many have put on a "jolly face" for their friends in order to hide their personal embarrassment and shame for being unattractively heavy. When they slim down, the cheerfulness becomes free, natural, wonderfully refreshing for all about them. I suggest that you have your husband bet his best friend $25 that he'll lose 5 to 15 pounds in a week. He'll do it on my Quick Weight Loss Diet. That will prove to him that he was not "born to be fat."

> *"I've lost 24 pounds on your diet, Doctor. I'm down to my ideal weight, and I'm going to take off 10 pounds more so I can be real skinny."*

"Ideal" weight means just that, what I consider your perfect weight for health, beauty, vigor. Stop at your ideal weight and stay there, don't go more than a few pounds under it. Otherwise you might be like the "invisible man" in the famous limerick:

There once was a hermit named Green
Who grew so abnormally lean,
    And flat, and compressed,
    That his back touched his chest,
And sideways he couldn't be seen.

"You tell me to be active and to limit my sleep to eight hours, but I can't function unless I sleep at least ten hours a night."

A story in *The New York Times* is headlined "Sleep is Linked to Heart Attack." It goes on: "A person who sleeps ten or more hours a night may be snoozing his way into a heart attack or stroke, according to a six-year study of almost 800,000 men and women conducted by the American Cancer Society." The facts showed that men and women who slept ten or more hours a night were up to four times as likely to suffer a heart attack or stroke as people who slept seven hours a night. Of further significance: "Overweight men had three and a half times as many heart attacks and strokes than men of average weight for their group."

"Sure, I'm overweight, but I'm young, so it doesn't worry me."

Parents quoted to me that common statement from their son, who was 60 pounds overweight in his early twenties. He was a mass and a mess, unattractive, and about to lose his job, which he valued. His employer told him flatly to "shape up or ship out" because he was too much of a "monstrosity" to represent the company properly. At that crucial time of decision the young man learned about my basic Quick Weight Loss Diet (his parents gave him the book). He lost his 60 pounds of overweight on the diet in three months. His parents said that he has advanced remarkably in his business career, "is slim, straight, alert and very attractive," and is "about to marry a beautiful girl." They said that the weight loss provided *the psychological lift* that transformed his character, while the effectiveness of the diet transformed his appearance. That wonderful "psychological lift" is waiting for most every overweight in whom a happy, slim individual is hiding.

> *"My husband has arranged a seaside vacation trip three weeks from now, but I'm so fat that I'm ashamed to get into a bathing suit."*

I told this woman that she could lose 20 pounds on the QWL Diet in three weeks, and she was so determined that she did. It's a good idea to set a target date for a few weeks from now—a big party or dinner, a vacation beginning, a trip you're making, and determine that you will be many pounds slimmer by then. With my quick loss methods, you'll probably attain your goal and keep going down to your ideal weight—you'll feel so much healthier and happier. One smiling patient told me, "Diet cures more than doctors."

> *"I'm afraid to lose weight because I may go right up again, and I'm sure going up-and-down is unhealthy."*

This common fallacy makes no sense. Understand this clearly: When your weight goes down from an "up," and then back again, you still average less than when you were always "up." Consider that you're carrying two 15-pound bags of groceries in your arms. Your heart is strained, your muscles are aching, your back is breaking. If you put that load down and walk a block without the 30-pound weight, you're much better off than before—your heart, arms, back and other strained organs had a rest. The same is true of up-and-down weight loss: If you lost 30 pounds and gained it back over a period of six months, you still averaged 15 pounds less during the six months and were better off than being 30 pounds overweight continuously. Realize, too, that you're not "carrying" overweight in your arms like 30 pounds of groceries—it's much worse internally. The added fat includes small capillaries, which result in increased blood volume, making more work for your heart muscle.

> *"Doctor, I've had my heart attack, it's really too late for me to diet."*

I have the records of many heart patients as living proof that it's never too late to diet. A number have had severe heart attacks as long as 30 and more years ago, when they were very much overweight. I warned them that it was probably "diet or die" for them. They reduced with my quick weight loss methods and have been slim, healthy, vigorous ever since. Of course, it's best if you are overweight to slim down in your twenties and stay that way as the best chance for a longer, healthier life (the proof is clear and plain in insurance statistics and rates). But in reducing, the ancient proverb "Better late than never" (*potius sero, quam numquam*) was never truer than it is today.

> *"I couldn't resist loading in a big, heavy meal—and blooey, there went my diet!"*

You're lucky that others aren't saying about you, "Blooey, there went his life!" Each year I see more evidence of sudden deaths and serious internal destruction caused by stuffing in a big, heavy meal. This concentrated overloading of your system with a sudden mass of food intake is one of the most dangerous things you can do—*avoid it, without question!* Pass on this tip—it can save your life, and those you know. As for falling off your diet, you're not the first one. Instead of brooding, decide that you've gotten the overindulgence out of your system and go right back to losing weight quickly on a quick weight loss diet.

> *"Is it true that drinking lemon juice or grapefruit juice every morning makes one slim?"*

These juices have excellent properties but don't embody any magical slimming formula. Other reducing rages included goat's milk, vinegar, curious combinations of two or more foods—all resulting in eventual failure and sometimes (as in drinking vinegar three times a day) ruining the health.

> *"Is it all right to go on a liquid-formula diet?"*

Yes. If you can stay with the powdered formula diet it will take off weight quickly, which is the most important goal. Many people fail because this method requires too much discipline. For a quicker reducer in this category, drink 4 or 5 glasses of buttermilk each day, lots of water and take a vitamin-mineral pill.

> "I can't help gaining weight, my wife keeps forcing food on me, and she's a great cook."

More women have killed their husbands with the unkindness of forcing rich foods on them than deaths caused by auto or plane accidents each year. Think of this, madam, please: Even one large, rich meal a day is harmful because it takes the body six to ten hours to rid itself of the oversupply of fat-laden blood. The liver tries to get rid of the fat but cannot handle the overwhelming amount. Those extra fat particles in the blood are deposited in the arteries, too often producing arteriosclerosis (thickening and hardening of the walls of the arteries) in the heart, brain, kidneys and legs. As a good cook, you can certainly learn to prepare fine, healthy, low-calorie and moderate-size servings. Make that your cooking challenge!

> "I can't understand gaining weight. I eat moderately and only snack, on 'dietetic' candy."

Many dieters are ruined by snacks without realizing it. If you'll count up the calories in the snacks you consume—and keep an honest list and total—you'll find that you're adding hundreds, sometimes thousands, of calories to your daily eating. Don't let the word "dietetic" fool you. If the product package doesn't list the calories, don't touch it. And usually they're not listed because the calories are very high. For example, one checkup showed a regular chocolate candy with about 150 calories an ounce, while the "dietetic" chocolate ran from 100 to 150 calories per ounce, a really fattening "snack." A misleading TV commercial showed slim women gobbling up "dietetic" candies one after another, indicating that you could eat as many as you want without gaining weight. It isn't true.

> "Friends tell me I look better when I'm a few pounds heavier."

One reason some friends are friends is because they tell you what you want to hear. I urge you to believe the bathroom scale, believe your mirror, believe the tightness of your clothes, rather than well-meaning friends who assist you in your dangerous delusions. Such a "friend" met the poet Byron on the street and said, "You're putting on some weight, you're looking very well. . . ." Byron retorted angrily, "Do you call getting fat looking well, as if I were a hog?" The poet had a horror of gaining weight, for according to one report, "when he added to his weight, even standing was painful."

Fooling yourself about overweight can be tragic. Yet most overweight people say they weigh 10 to 20 pounds less than the scale shows. I've been tempted to say to such a woman, who was bulging yet told me, "I only weigh about 115"—"Madam, you must be hollow."

Overweights have argued with me: "I have an aunt of 78 and an uncle of 81, and both are overweight, so how can you say it's unhealthy to be fat?" These people are exceptions, as there are exceptions in everything medical. If you want to use this feeble excuse for staying fat, less vigorous and attractive than you can and should be, that's your personal responsibility. Just don't delude yourself that overweight is "better for you." Statistics prove overwhelmingly that *the fat die younger, and have many more serious illnesses* than people of average weight.

A quotation from an authority in the *Medical Tribune* sums up the revealing medical fact: "Obesity is our most common disease and is an epidemic problem."

12

Turning a Fat, Sad Youngster Into a Thin, Happy One

A fat youngster wrote home from summer camp to his parents: "Please rush food packages. All they serve here is breakfast, lunch and dinner."

Unfortunately there is a tendency for too many parents and other relatives to think of the pudgy youngster and fat teenager, girl or boy, as "funny" or "cute." When the young ones seem upset about their overweight, many adults counter that "It's nothing to worry about, you'll grow out of it." Then they usually add conclusively, "Some extra fat and meat on your bones is good for you."

Such a "forget it" attitude couldn't be more wrong on the part of the parent or other adult, winding up in a future of hopelessness for the concerned youngster. The worst thing you can do is to pass off most childhood "tragedies" in the youngster's view—and being fat is indeed tragic for many girls and boys—as being trifles. Please consider the few basic facts, not theories but *facts*, that follow.

You don't need any complicated tests to know whether a youngster is overweight. The doctor can tell you readily, as can the size of clothes, the comparative appearance of other youngsters of the same age—and, for the child or teenager, *a look in the mirror*. The reflection of the unclothed figure in the mirror doesn't lie.

A Serious, Perhaps Lifelong, Problem

Obese (considerably overweight) children and teenagers—going back to as early as age seven—are likely to grow into obese adults unless they are properly directed to lose weight early, before reaching the adult years. The longer they wait to reduce, the more difficult it becomes in later years to take off extra pounds and to stay slim.

Every possible way to reduce that might work for the particular overweight youngster should be explored and considered and, with the consent of the child's physician, tried and followed through with utmost attention and encouragement. As with adults, quick success in taking off pounds is the best motivation and surest way for the youngsters to continue and achieve the goal of attractive, active slenderness.

My recommendations to you are based on my 45 years of experience in helping to reduce youngsters and teenagers. Because of my special interest, liking and concern for the young (who are the future), I spent many summers as a camp doctor for girls and boys. Everything I convey to you includes what I have learned in treating all types of youngsters, and in working to reduce the overweights, unfortunately thousands.

In my own studies, I have found that about 50 percent of the youngsters of about seventeen years of age whom I examined were overweight. Admittedly, my standards and criteria for ideal weight are stricter than that of some others. Nationwide studies have revealed from 20 to 40 percent of sixteen-year-olds to be considerably overweight. A New York report of first-year students in college, averaging eighteen years of age, showed that about 30 percent of the young men were overweight, and 36 percent of the girls were too heavy.

The facts proved beyond question that the overweight child is likely to grow into an overweight adult. One study shows that 86 percent of men and 80 percent of women who were too fat as children became overweight adults. In other research covering fifty overweight girls aged ten to fourteen, all of them 20 percent or more overweight, forty of these pudgy youngsters (80 percent) were obese adults 21 years later. Of fifty other average-weight girls, only nine (less than 20 percent) were fat as adults in their thirties.

There is lots more clear proof that the time to start reducing the overweight is from age seven up, or chances are that he will grow into an overweight adult with far less chance for a long, healthy, happy life. Increasingly, medical findings warn that the "chubby baby," going right back to the crib, is not necessarily the most healthy baby. Fat appears to be a fearful impediment to maximum health for the individual at any age—from the cradle, and for the seriously overweight, to a too early grave.

Does fat "run in families"?

The parent of an overweight youngster must look at himself first to see whether he is to blame for his child's ungainly, uncomfortable, ugly fat. It has been found in extensive studies that in families, if one parent is overweight, chances are 40 percent that the child will be fat. If both parents are overweight, the chances are double, 80 percent, that the child will be overweight.

It has not yet been determined scientifically whether this may be related to some hitherto unrecognized form of mysterious metabolism in these children. It *is* generally agreed upon by science that only one out of twenty adults (including these overweight parents) has some metabolic disturbance that causes the overweight; with 95 percent of these fat parents, overweight is therefore due to overeating. The habit of excess eating, passed on to the child at every meal, is certainly a contributing factor in fattening the child excessively.

Furthermore, children are great imitators and are most likely to do what parents do (not what parents say they do, such as, "I can't understand my overweight, I eat like a bird"—to which one teenager retorted, "Yes, like a giant vulture!"). If you as a parent are too heavy, the least you are doing in respect to your overweight child is setting a bad example. A study at the University of Washington reported that when the children of the overweight families studied tried to reduce, they failed, due primarily to family eating habits.

It is significant that these fat children aged ten to seventeen were considered to be difficult, rebellious youngsters as a whole.

They had had troubles in school. They showed exceptional sexual anxiety. Most of the girls up to age sixteen said that they had no interest in ever getting married. This all adds up to the usual picture of the deeply unhappy overweight youngster, far from what many adults, including parents, try to smile off as "a jolly, fat kid."

Ills caused by overweight start young

Lessons learned during the Korean war about how overweight begins ruining the body at a very early age shocked many in the medical profession. Close examination of the arteries of the hearts of young men aged nineteen to 25 disclosed that many of them already had serious thickening and calcification, which slowed the blood flow. Most of these boys, it was learned, had been overweight for a good many years, and the results of excess fat already showed in the deterioration of their arteries. Other severe problems also showed up.

Many in medicine were shocked, and have been since, into doing something about preventing narrowing and hardening of the arteries, and other complications, in the very young. No longer was reducing just a matter of slimming and trimming women in their forties and men with "middle-age spread." The lesson was clear that the quantity and quality of food eaten affected the individual from babyhood, as never realized so vividly before.

The lessons seemed clear. It was wrong to overfeed our babies and young children. It was bad medical practice to tolerate permitting youngsters and teenagers to become overweight. It became more urgent than ever to teach parents of the dangers in excess weight for their youngsters as well as for themselves. It became even more necessary to destroy in parents the myth that fatness in a baby or child meant good health, that being thin exposed a youngster to many illnesses. It was clearly tragic rather than funny to allow mothers to go on stuffing their children, accompanied by "motherly," threatening exhortations to "Eat! Eat! Eat! It's good for you!"

Of course, eating properly is "good for you" at any age. But *overeating* is eating most improperly. It's true that youngsters and teenagers should be watched more closely than in later years for vitamin-mineral deficiencies (easily prevented and corrected now by taking a daily vitamin-mineral tablet), since they are growing and need more protein, calcium and iron than the adult. But moderate, planned food restrictions are often absolutely essential, along with planned activity and exercise.

More food than is needed, excess calories that put on pounds of fat, start a long, insidious drain and strain on the tissues of the body, right from the early years. That's why it is pathetic to see a mother still pushing food in front of and into her youngsters, who are already overweight and suffering the taunts of their friends as a "fatty."

These unhappy, heavy children are rarely asked to participate in sports, games, even social activities. They even resist involvement because they are not as agile, graceful or competent as their slim contemporaries. As a result, they get less exercise, become increasingly lazy, sedentary, inactive. Studies have shown that obese children watch television more, walk less, and that this lack of exercise is primarily due to lack of enjoyment in using their cumbersome, slow-moving bodies. They resist dancing, also, afraid that they'll be a laughingstock to their friends. Added to overeating, this inactivity often makes them swell up like balloons.

Study after study has shown that these obese youngsters are mostly miserable within, much as some try to conceal it. Usually their unthinking parents are heavy and don't seem to care that the child is following in their dragging footsteps. They lead the children into an overweight existence that not only incapacitates them, makes them unhappy, but will statistically shorten their lives and block their chances of the most healthful existence.

Both as youngsters and then as adults, these overweight children are prone to diabetes, high blood pressure, heart disease, hernias, skin diseases and arthritis. Statistics show that the overweights have many more and more serious accidents. Overweight among the young, as among adults, writes a sad story of progressive sickness and deterioration. And it is all so unnecessary!

Overweight youngsters psychologically impaired . . .

The psychological effect of considerable overweight on the young can be a major impairment. Heavy children tend to feel and act like members of a minority group. They feel discriminated against, ashamed of themselves because of fat handicaps and appearance, and because they seem to be denied many of the joys and opportunities normal youngsters have. Within they have contempt for "fatties," and admiration, perhaps excessive, for slim, graceful contemporaries. Because they are heavy, children tend to withdraw—"What's the use? I'm not accepted anyhow."

The situation worsens as the discouraged overweight child gives up, lets herself go completely, indulges in eating binges, becomes gross and ungainly. She tends to give way to boredom, become increasingly depressed, is more apt to sulk and burst into tears for seemingly no reason at all. From lying about the amount of food she eats, she is apt to lie and be evasive and ineffectual about other matters.

Above all, the overweight youngster must never be left to feel that he or she is ruined beyond salvage. An effective dieting routine coupled with more exercise and activity can work wonders. I have saved many hundreds of fat youngsters and helped them turn into slim, optimistic young people. *Quick weight loss dieting has proved to be the best weapon.*

Prevention, a desirable approach . . .

Of course, nothing is better than preventing excess pounds from overtaking the child, starting right from infancy. Under the care of a pediatrician, the baby should never be permitted to become too heavy. One must be particularly watchful and take preventive steps if (1) the parents, one or both, are heavy, and (2) if the child has small bone structure and is slow in growing taller.

It is vital to keep your youngster moving from the earliest years, opposing laziness, listlessness, stagnation; this is especially important if the child has any locomotion problems due to some illness or impairment. Particularly if the youngster shows any tendency to put on excess weight, lead him to become *Homo Sportius* rather than *Homo Sedentarius*—that goes for girls, too. If not, warn him that he'll become a *Homo Adiposius*, who soon may be lumbering around like the elephants in the zoo.

Impress upon your youngsters from the start that *thin* is far better in every way than *fat*. Teach them early about the calorie intake/output system as described in this book (by all means try to get a fat youngster to read this book). Emphasize the way *activity burns up more calories*, so that it's far better to run than to walk, to walk rather than sit, to walk briskly to school or the shopping center or any reasonable distance, or to go by bicycle, instead of always depending on the auto.

Get them to walk up stairs instead of taking the elevator. Point out how it burns up more calories (making room for more ice cream and cookies if they're slender) to shovel the snow, mow the lawn, to dance energetically rather than being a bystander. Inform them that exercise and activity generally do not increase the appetite. Above all, win your youngster's confidence and admiration *by staying slim and active and young yourself!*

Revealing study of 500 boys . . .

Because of the special research opportunities available to me as a camp doctor during many summers, I undertook a study of 500 teenage boys averaging seventeen to eighteen years old. Over a period of time of observation and examination, I divided the subjects statistically into two groups, which I designated as "tall and lanky" versus "stocky."

The *lanky* boys were between 5'11" and 6'3½" tall. Their average weight was 140 pounds each and average height 6 feet. Comparing this with a general "average weight" for this height, each should have weighed about 175 pounds; according to such calculations, these teenagers were 35 pounds underweight.

The *stocky* youngsters averaged 5'9½" tall, about 2½" shorter than the lanky boys. Their average weight was 190 pounds compared with an "average weight" for the height of 158 pounds; thus, they might be considered 32 pounds overweight.

From the first selection I had classified the stocky boys in my view as overweights. The findings differ from some other studies, which maintain that tall teenagers are more likely to be overweight than shorter boys of the same age.

A glance at the individual weights of the lanky youngsters showed the variation to run between 116 and 165 pounds, compared with weights ranging from 165 to 205 pounds for the stocky teenagers.

Among my general observations and conclusions, the following should be considered most seriously and personally by teenagers and their parents, facts that apply in large part to girls also, judging from the many youngsters I have treated over the years:

The tall and lanky boys were more energetic, athletic and moved about constantly in their work and play.

Exactly the opposite, the heavy, overweight teenagers were basically lazy, slow-moving, sluggish. They preferred to sit or lie around rather than engage in sports or other activities, or even to walk and run a lot during waking hours.

This again established a very specific relationship between weight and activity as a vital factor influencing whether the teenager of any sex is slim or fat (eating habits being equal, of course). The active teenager can, in most cases, definitely consume more food than the sluggish youngster and still maintain a comparatively slim figure.

Coupling my observations of thousands of teenagers and tens of thousands of adults, I could safely predict what would happen to most slim teenagers as they grew into adults. Cutting down drastically on their physically demanding activities, becoming sedentary at desk jobs and enduring the rituals of meetings, they would soon gain weight. Many of them would become overweight unless they compensated by *eating less* primarily, and also continuing some exercise and sports activities, as simple as plenty of brisk walking and stair-climbing. Teenage activity used up many calories that would now settle in fat depots and turn to flab.

Even greater health dangers faced the already stocky teenager. As his already limited activity as a youngster diminished further in adult pursuits, as he married and his wife stuffed him with food to show that she is a good cook, he would usually become fatter and fatter—unless he took steps to counteract this.

The lesson for you and for teenagers is to take that weight off quickly if the youngster is overweight, fat and flabby (or even too heavy with muscle), with quick weight loss methods that work. The next step is to establish Stay-Slim eating habits and an increase in exercise and activity to maintain ideal weight.

My aim is to reduce the overweight teenagers so that they will live healthier, longer lives—and will be able to live to see the

wonders of the world sixty to seventy years from now. I can assure you from my studies that being fat is *not* healthier, that contrary to popular notion the slim boys were not weaker but were
much stronger physically, and as a whole much more alert
mentally, as well as engaging in and enjoying social activities
more.

Teenage reducing methods that work

The old-fashioned, fallacious and dangerous practice of stuffing
food into youngsters of all ages is hopefully vanishing, and should
be banished entirely in order to produce healthier, more effective
youngsters and eventual adults. If you have a fat child, then it
follows almost automatically that you are overfeeding the youngster, and probably that the child isn't getting enough exercise
and activity. If your child has some abnormality in bodily functioning that causes him to be overweight, your physician will tell
you so and what to do about it for correction. *At any age, fat is
not healthy.*

My most successful methods for reducing youngsters and
teenagers are similar to what works for adults—quick weight loss
dieting. There is no danger in controlled strenuous dieting except
for the child under seven years of age. It has been shown that
lack of sufficient and proper food in the first year of life can
retard physical and mental growth, primarily if the diet is severely
deficient.

Once the child has reached seven years of age, the greatest
dangers of dietary insufficiency are over, within reason. Of course,
the youngster needs plenty of protein and minerals for growth,
but the lack is not as serious. As the child grows older, only
enough protein and minerals are required for proper growth and
bodily repair.

There is increasing evidence that too much fat in the diet is at
least as dangerous for the growing child as for adults. A notable
report states: "The degree of coronary sclerosis (involving hardening of the arteries of the heart) was found to increase propor-
tionately with age *from early childhood* through the seventh
decade at a nearly uniform rate." Thus, improper eating can increase the dangers of later heart attack right from early child-

hood. I recommend low-fat eating as best for humans of all ages.

I have learned this important fact in treating overweight youngsters: *The will to be thin is strong in the minds of youth.* In treating overweight youngsters, they throw questions like this at me with great seriousness and intensity:

"How did I get this way, am I built differently?"

"Is my fat due to something wrong with my glands, my hormones, my circulation?"

"Am I fat because of my age, my sex, my ancestry?"

"Should I blame my inactivity, my food, my nervousness?"

"Is my problem my blood sugar, or am I a water retainer, or do I function wrong in some way?"

"Do I metabolize my food differently from other kids?"

"Is my bone structure too heavy?"

My answers to youngsters' problems

In practically every case I can reassure the overweight child and teenager that the main problem is *the amount and quality of the foods you eat.* Exercise and activity are also essential to becoming and staying slim, but the points raised in the questions mostly play minor roles, if any, in obesity for you. Overwhelmingly the primary reasons for your overweight are overeating at meals, too much snacking and nibbling right through your waking hours.

Some of the points mentioned in the questions may make your personal ability to reduce a little more difficult but not crucially so. You can correct them surely, quickly, healthfully, safely— and only you can do it. *Any or all of the quick weight loss and inches-off diets listed in this book for adults can rid your body of excess weight and fat, can make you slim, healthier, more graceful, more attractive.* This has been proved by many hundreds of overweight youngsters who have trimmed and slimmed down with these methods. If they can do it, you can. Quick weight loss dieting works.

Rather than going around indulging yourself and blaming all the things mentioned, blaming everything but your own eating, understand this fact. It boils right down to the quantity and quality of the foods you consume, to your daily calorie intake.

There are no "all-fattening foods" as such—unless you should do something as crazy as drinking plain oils or eating pounds of butter and nothing else; you couldn't do that even for one day.

However, you could, and many overweights do, eat a stack of pancakes with mounds of melting butter, a cupful of sugary syrup, a glass of orange juice and a glass of milk, all in just one meal (probably breakfast). If you eat that quantity and quality of high-calorie foods, you will have in effect eaten as though you had consumed a pint of oil or one pound of butter.

If that kind of eating pattern is yours, my recommendations are to break with the past completely, abruptly, immediately. To get those ugly, excess pounds off, your eating habits now can be as "screwy" as you like, you can eat as little as possible, as long as you drink loads of water and no-calorie beverages all through your waking hours and take a vitamin-mineral pill daily. If you skip the normally nutritious foods, it's no catastrophe while you are overweight. Your body will compensate.

You should be checked by a doctor first and regularly. If you skip milk, cheese and other such foods, you can take calcium pills along with your daily vitamin-mineral tablet. You can take iron if it is lacking in what you eat. If you encounter minor body imbalances, such as girls having irregular periods for a short time, this is not disastrous—have your doctor check you. It takes much more than a few weeks of deprivation of "normal" eating to harm the body generally.

Let's face it, all dieting embodies some frustration, whether it's done slowly or quickly. Quick weight loss works because, as I point out repeatedly, your "built-in will power" comes from getting on that scale first thing every morning in your bathroom and seeing the number of pounds go down, down, down. In my experience, youngsters—even more than adults fail on slow "balanced" reducing methods, which become a drag with loss of only a pound or two a week. Patience isn't a common characteristic of the young, nor should parents expect it to be. I urge parents, especially mothers, to provide the youngster every possible cooperation in losing weight quickly.

I recommend to you young people that you read over the details of the diets in this book, and preferably read every page so that you learn all the vital why's and how's of dieting with my

methods, and why they lead to wonderfully gratifying success for
so many overweights. Pick out the diet that suits your personal
likes and temperament best. Don't be concerned about becoming
"too hungry." The appetite usually decreases after a day or two of
dieting.

If you like meat, poultry, fish, seafood—go on my basic Quick
Weight Loss Diet, the most rapid reducer of any dieting method
I've ever learned about in a lifetime of medical practice and
effectively reducing tens of thousands of overweights of all ages.

If you like vegetables and fruits, go on my quick Inches-Off
Diet, or on an all-vegetable or all-fruit diet.

Mix up the quick weight loss diets if that appeals to you most
and turns out to be your individual best way to lose pounds
quickly. Try the basic Quick Weight Loss Diet for a week, then
switch to the Inches-Off Diet for a week, back on the QWL Diet,
and so on. Or eat all vegetables for a day, all fruits the next day,
back on vegetables or on lean meats or whatever suits you that
day of the quick weight loss diets, but stay on the basic Quick
Weight Loss Diet for at least a week at a time.

Try one-dimensional dieting if you like, always remembering
to drink loads of glasses of water and no-calorie beverages, and to
take your daily vitamin-mineral tablet. Here are some of the
bizarre one-dimensional diets teenagers have concocted for themselves under my care, and which worked for them:

Cottage-cheese only—preparing a dish of 16 tablespoons of
creamed cottage cheese, mixed with cinnamon and artificial
sweetening—eating this dish three times a day. That totals only
720 calories and has high "Specific Dynamic Action," burning up
many more calories a day than the same number of calories eaten
in "normal" meals. You'll lose even quicker if you divide the total
48 tablespoons of cottage cheese into four, five or six meals a day,
burning up even more calories. Keep drinking water and other
no-calorie beverages, and keep watching your excess weight
vanish marvelously on the scale and in the mirror.

Hard-boiled eggs only—this is also a rapid reducer with high
"specific dynamic action" in burning up calories swiftly and more
efficiently than normal eating. You're getting all the vitamins except vitamin C (which you get in your vitamin-mineral tablet
daily), plenty of iron, a little essential fat. Just take that daily

vitamin-mineral tablet and drink many glassfuls of water and no-calorie beverages. For an effective egg diet like this, take 3 hard-boiled eggs, eliminating 2 of the yolks, cutting or crushing the balance of the eggs together. Add a little salt and pepper. The 3 eggs minus 2 yolks add up to 150 calories per meal. You can eat this three to five times a day and you'll lose pounds and inches swiftly.

Chicken-leg diet—cut off all visible skin and fat and a chicken leg averages about 75 calories. Eat a chicken leg five to six times daily, along with lots of water and no-calorie beverages, and a daily vitamin-mineral tablet. You'll lose lots of weight in a hurry.

Combine any of these one-dimensional diets, or those you make up for yourself, so that you have a chicken-leg day, then a day of lean broiled hamburgers only, a hard-boiled-egg day of eating, to your taste and pleasure. The quick way the pounds and inches come off will certainly be a pleasure.

Again, the basic Quick Weight Loss Diet is my prime recommendation for taking off pounds and inches of excess weight swiftly, surely, healthfully, safely. Read all the details in Chapter 5, then follow the instructions exactly. You don't count calories, but make up your selections daily from the permitted foods, eating as much as you want *but never stuffing yourself*. Here's a typical QWL day's eating prepared for herself by a teenager who was 32 pounds overweight. She lost 12 pounds the first week, and came down to her ideal weight in a hurry. Now she enjoys a slim, beautiful, admired figure, and is happier about it than she ever thought it was possible to be.

Breakfast

> 2 scrambled eggs (in no-fat pan).
> 2 tablespoons creamed cottage cheese.
> 2 cups decaffeinated coffee.

Mid-morning snack

> 1 glass skim milk (permitted 1 glass daily for youngsters and teenagers, not for adults)

Lunch

> 1 chicken leg (no skin or fat).
> 2 tablespoons creamed cottage cheese with cinnamon and artificial sweetening.
> 1 portion low-calorie gelatin dessert.
> 2 glasses no-calorie cherry soda.

Mid-afternoon snack

> 1 hard-boiled egg.
> 2 glasses no-calorie ginger ale.

Dinner

> 1 cup bouillon (from "instant" cube).
> 1 lean broiled hamburger.
> 1 tablespoon pickle relish.
> 1 portion low-calorie gelatin dessert.
> 2 cups weak tea, artificially sweetened.

Evening snack

> 3 tablespoons creamed cottage cheese with cinnamon and artificial sweetener.
> 1 glass no-calorie orange soda.

Miscellaneous

> 8 glasses of water.
> 1 vitamin-mineral tablet.
> 1 glass no-calorie cream soda.

From this selection for just one day, you can see that the QWL Diet offers you plenty of variety of foods to get you down to ideal weight and figure in a hurry. That's a goal worth working for, especially since your reducing won't drag on for months.

IMPORTANT QUICK WEIGHT LOSS TIPS

The kind of dieting described on the preceding pages applies only until you get down to ideal weight. From then on you switch to Stay-Slim Eating (be sure to read all the details in Chapter 10), which is balanced, more "normal" eating (but not the kind of eating that made you fat in the first place).

Get on the scale unclothed first thing every morning in your bathroom and see the weight drop if you're truly following my quick weight loss dieting instructions. You'll lose 5 to 10 percent of your weight the first week, the number of pounds depending on how much overweight you are. If the pounds don't go down, you're cheating on the diet in some way, and the tragedy here is that mostly you're cheating yourself.

Look in the mirror full length and unclothed every few days and you'll see the inches start to vanish, your contours start to taper down all over, your belly bulge begin to diminish remarkably—if you're sticking to your quick weight loss dieting properly.

Don't ever reach for food, unless you're hungry, even when not on a diet. At no time should you stuff yourself, or you'll ruin the effectiveness of whatever diet you're on. Again, you hurt yourself most of all.

Promise yourself and me one full week of quick weight loss dieting. I have great faith in your success, as very few youngsters in my care have failed to reduce beautifully once they have seen the remarkable loss in pounds and inches after just one short week. Think of your dieting as just one day at a time, then another day, then another, until the week has gone—along with a lot of your unwanted fat. Don't worry about next week until you get there.

A glass of skim milk daily is permitted on all my quick weight loss diets, including the basic QWL Diet, but for youngsters only, not for adults.

Enjoy low-calorie gelatin desserts a couple of times a day, in a variety of flavors, on any of the diets except the Inches-Off Diet.

Drink "instant" no-fat bouillon, broth, consommé, if you wish, on any of my diets, several cups a day.

Don't skip 8 glasses of water daily, and tea and coffee without real sugar, and lots of flavors of no-calorie beverages (up to 5 glassfuls a day). The liquid is essential to wash the waste matter out of your system, as your dieting method burns up calories much more rapidly than usual.

Low-calorie chewing gum, artificially sweetened, in reasonable quantity, is permitted, but not many packs a day.

Beware of misinformed friends and parents who think the little darling isn't eating enough and is wasting away and getting sick. Don't let anyone talk you into going on a binge of sweets or fattening foods "just this time." Tell them off as you stick to your personal convictions. A slim, lovely young actress who had been very chubby said angrily, "There is a vicious streak in some people that makes them want to make the fat fatter."

Don't worry about dieting "forever." Most everybody has to be careful throughout life about not putting on weight. Now with my quick weight loss methods, you can take off any pounds that creep up, and do it rapidly. One of our favorite girl singers went from a chubby 150 pounds to a slim, beautiful 115 pounds and has kept her weight down for years without trouble. One of our most beautiful young actresses dropped from very overweight to 117 pounds, her ideal weight, and has also stayed that way for years. Many actors, actresses, people in all branches of show business from teenagers up, swear by my quick weight loss dieting because it gives them swift, sure, healthful "fat removal."

If you insist on balanced dieting, your maximum daily intake in order to reduce should be 1200 calories, preferably much less. If you get discouraged by slow weight loss, don't quit—switch to one of my quick weight loss diets for at least a week.

Don't kick yourself around for a "binge" that puts on lost pounds after a weekend of heavy eating or a big party. Go right back on a quick weight loss diet the next day and the gained pounds will vanish along with more fat each day. Don't worry about ups-and-downs. They won't hurt you, as long as you have more "downs" than "ups."

Don't be concerned about missing meals—the idea that it's harmful to skip a meal is an old-fashioned, disproved notion. Skip as many meals as you want. Go on a fasting diet for a day if you wish, drinking loads of beverages and taking your daily vitamin-mineral tablet. Don't eat if you're not hungry, even if it is meal-time; your body is an extraordinary mechanism that self-adjusts readily and can feed on itself.

If you tend to have skin problems, reread "Anti-Acne Dieting" in Chapter 8. For example, avoid any kind of chocolate and cola drinks.

Once you're down to desired weight, switch to Stay-Slim Eating (reread Chapter 10). Keep exercising (Chapter 9). For further slimming of any problem spots on your figure, consider my Inches-Off Diet (chapters 3 and 4).

Read over the additional tips that help make dieting most effective, as given throughout the book, such as making food go further by cutting into small pieces, eating slowly, and so on.

EXERCISE! BE ACTIVE! USE YOUR BODY IN MOTION!

Movement uses up the most calories, sitting and lying around use up the fewest calories. As you know, excess calories that the body doesn't use up turn to fat and settle in the fat depots, gradually swelling your body and limbs more and more. Being less active generally, and with metabolic differences, girls need even fewer calories than boys. Stand instead of sitting, walk or bicycle instead of riding in a car whenever possible, walk up stairs instead of taking the elevator (within reason, of course, which applies to all advice). Engage in sports and dancing for exercise and fun. Don't sleep more than eight hours daily. Get up, move around, be more agile and alert in every way.

See your doctor if you're concerned about any unusual physical disturbances while dieting, or at any time. Don't put it off. A few minutes visit with your physician can help prevent troubles before they deepen and drag on.

Tip to Parents: I suggest that you let your teenager read this information rather than try to hammer in suggestions yourself. Otherwise you might find yourself in the position of the parent whose daughter wailed, "Oh, Daddy, how can I stop putting on weight?" The eager father poured out a stream of facts, stories and orders, finishing up with, "Are you going to take my advice?" The girl replied dazedly, "No ... I'm going to stop asking for it." Most young people, I find, respect and are far more likely to follow the recommendations of a professional with a proved record of success, especially with those of their own age group.

13

Your Slimmer, Healthier, Happier Future

My previous book, *The Doctor's Quick Weight Loss Diet,* took over a year to land on best-seller lists. Sales started rather slowly, then began building more and more, then the book suddenly spurted to the best-seller lists.

The significance is that remarkable *results* in reducing overweights who used the book, and their "word of mouth" to friends, are what caused the book to become so popular. It's as simple as that. The first few hundreds of people who bought the book followed my basic Quick Weight Loss Diet or one of the other quick-reducing diets and lost weight rapidly. They were so delighted and enthusiastic that they told other people with an overweight problem.

Now hundreds of thousands who had failed miserably before went on the Quick Weight Loss Diet. Friends, acquaintances, business or social associates saw their newly slimmed and beautiful figures and asked, "How did you do it?" Then *they* used my quick-loss dieting methods, succeeded, told others—and demand for the book snowballed. Apparently it's true that "nothing succeeds like success."

As I noted at the start of this book, additional information wanted by overweights, further insights, an expansion of some important phases of reducing and the desire of so many to further smooth out "problem spots" in the figure, all lead toward this new book. Read it and use it, and it will serve you well.

A few matters that should be emphasized and on which further details will be helpful, are covered in this "round-up" chapter.

Why "Balanced Dieting" Usually Fails . . .

It's worth while reviewing again why my quick weight loss and inches-off methods can succeed for you when the usual slow "balanced dieting" advice fails. One of the "balanced dieting" books admits the following about the slow-reducing methods:

The dieter, having to constantly make choices about foods, soon becomes irritated with himself . . . extreme irritation which will last at least two weeks. During these two irritating weeks the dieter will be suspicious and belligerent. Chances are that he will show no visible weight loss . . .

That sums up the reason for most dieting failures on "balanced diets." That record of failures is what led me to develop quick weight loss methods for my overweight patients—I had to *get that weight off actually*; I saw no point in giving those needful, distressed and unhealthy patients theoretical instructions that overwhelmingly failed to reduce other overweights year after year.

Quick weight loss dieting works because the dieter sees the pounds going down on the scale by the second day, and day after day. As the number drops for the overweight woman (or man) and her measurements decrease, as her clothing loosens on her figure, her delight increases—and her "will power" along with it.

No longer does her mirror reflect a bulging figure that says, "Too much food—too little woman." As she continues her quick weight loss dieting, her former large appetite also diminishes, another vital help. She soon becomes slim, usually in a matter of only weeks (or months if grossly overweight at the start). But—without the quick and rapidly continuing loss of pounds and inches, she never would have achieved the slim, attractive, youthful figure she wanted so much.

Reducing the Elderly

It is astonishing that many people, as they grow older, believe that they can eat as much food as in their younger years and still not gain weight. They keep putting on pounds and inches, and complain, "But I'm not eating any more than I used to for years. Something in my system must have changed." Something basic does change as you grow older, other than the general aging of the body, which affects your food intake and usage drastically.

As the years add up, the body's metabolism is *decreased* as noted previously. The individual at 65 years of age should be eating 25 percent to 40 percent less than he did at age 25, in order to maintain ideal weight, granted that he was slim at 25 as he should have been. Yet as the person grows older, he is likely to accumulate more money and to indulge himself more.

Many older people, like the young, enjoy filling up with sugary foods, rich desserts, cakes, candies, fatty meats and heavy gravies and alcoholic drinks. Such food habits have become so fixed, and now can be afforded, that it is difficult to get such older persons to change their eating habits, with a couple of exceptions. If the individual is bright, alert, youthful and very much wants to look slim and more attractive, he is a good subject for reducing successfully.

If the elderly person has a shocking illness, a breakdown of the body, a heart attack, specifically related to overweight—and has a real desire to live—he is likely to follow instructions and reduce, thereby often saving his life. Unfortunately, when the heart attack or other illness hits, it may be too late to save his life, due to the complications of excess weight all over the body and internal organs. It is clearly imperative as the years advance to stay slim in order to prevent complications and breakdowns due to the burdens of excess fat.

I'm often asked, "If overweight is such a killer, how come that my fat aunt is 78 years old, and my 225-pound uncle is 79? It seems to me that maybe they live so long because they're always eating what they want and are overweight." There are two sound answers to this. First, as proved conclusively by insurance statistics which involve simple arithmetic, people who stay slim generally live longer, no question about it; the overweight elderly are exceptions, the mathematically few who have survived, survived in spite of overweight, not because of it.

Second, examination shows that the vast majority of overweights past age 65 are ridden with various discomforts and illness. Their usual and most common afflictions are hernias, aches and pains in muscles and joints, moderate high blood pressure, mild diabetes, varicosities (swellings, especially in veins), excessive perspiration, some shortness of breath, fatigue, skin-lesion (especially fungus-infection) increases, slight vertigo, general slowness and clumsiness.

In the elderly, the ingesting of a large meal increases the workload of the heart about 25 percent. This can produce heart pain. (substernal pain), shortness of breath (dyspnea), shallow breathing and palpitations. Great discomfort is involved, along with danger. Those who stay overweight usually endure the discomforts, drag and pain because eating is the prime pleasure they get out of life.

On the other hand, with practically all my elderly patients, when I told them that they had to reduce in order to live comfortably, more healthfully and for more years, they cooperated and lost weight even more rapidly and surely than younger men and women. Again, as with others, *my quick weight loss methods were most successful with the elderly*. The older you are in years, the greater the necessity to take off burdensome pounds and inches in a hurry. The elderly haven't much time to wait for slow, dragging weight loss to lift the overload from aging organs.

Primarily I recommend my basic Quick Weight Loss Diet if you are in your later years and overweight. Check with your physician. Reread chapters 5 and 6. Start dieting now, and feel more alert, agile and youthful shortly.

The health benefits for my elderly overweights have been swift on quick weight loss dieting, and they suffered no ill effects from cutting down total calories intake. In fact, on the all-protein basic Quick Weight Loss Diet, the overweight (or anyone) can consume as much as 1500 calories a day compared with 1,000 calories of variety "balanced" eating and still lose weight—due to the Specific Dynamic Action of such protein intake, which burns up calories much faster and more efficiently, sometimes as high as 50 percent more efficiently.

Does reduced-calorie intake hurt the elderly patient? "No" is the definite answer based upon my experience with thousands of patients over 65 years old. In another study of elderly overweights afflicted with heart-disease problems, 42 patients were limited to eating as little as 600 to 800 calories a day for four weeks. Then the low calorie intake was increased only slightly, and continued for month after month, as long as twelve months, depending on the amount of overweight.

All the patients benefited from the very low-calorie eating, rather than being harmed by this drastic regime. Since this is true with sick patients, there is little reason to fear for the apparently healthy elderly overweight who undertakes low calorie or quick weight loss dieting. The sooner excess pounds and inches disappear, the better it is for you—at any age.

Overweight Accelerates Aging.

Four centuries ago an aged nobleman, Cornaro, gave as his rule for maintaining youthfulness: "Eat and drink little." Through the years scientists have considered, and increasingly, that overeating and overweight can act to bring on aging earlier than if you stay slim.

A past president of the American Geriatrics Society has emphasized that we would be better off, stay healthier and retain youthfulness longer, if the food intake in the nation would be cut on the average to about half what it is now for most people who can afford as much food as they want. He stresses that extra fat not only burdens the body and organs but is living tissue itself. As living tissue the fat must have its own blood supply.

For each ounce of excess fat you add, your heart must pump extra gallons of blood over long distances each minute, every hour of every day of life. No wonder excess pounds of fat are likely to accelerate aging.

Certainly to the eyes and minds of most people, as you know, slimness is generally associated with youthfulness, and vice versa. Listen next time to the description "She looks so slim and youthful," or the compliment "You're so much slimmer, you look years younger."

Do Women Lose Weight More Slowly Than Men?

Since men have about a 10 percent higher metabolism than women, they tend to burn up calories faster. This is important, as women—with a slower metabolism on the whole—must work harder in reducing. They must exert more will power to keep dieting and deny themselves the temptations of rich, high-calorie foods. In youngsters, too, girls generally have a lower metabolism than boys and are more likely to become overweight unless they are careful about their eating.

This may be the basic reason why, between ages 35 and seventy, there is a higher percentage of overweight women than men—as well as more women who are excessively fat. There still are more men whom I consider overweight than slim, but a smaller percentage who are enormously heavy (it's quite possible that a higher percentage of overweight men, being more prone to heart attacks than women, die much younger than the ladies).

The vital lesson, as a warning to the ladies, is that they must be more careful to avoid overweight and more persistent about fighting it, using every means that works for the individuals. An example is the plump woman who joined an exercise class and appeared in a very tight T-shirt and shorts. Told by the instructress to change to looser clothing, she snorted, "If I had any loose clothing, I wouldn't have joined this class."

A few weeks on one of my quick weight loss diets would provide her with plenty of loose clothing.

Plastic Surgery For Overweight?

For the vast majority of overweight women, plastic surgery after reducing is not indicated. In the case of a very few who permit themselves to become enormously obese, without any bodily malfunctions involved, plastic surgery may be needed after getting rid of a good deal of excess fat. This may involve face-lifting, removal of a pendulous abdominal "apron," or excessive skin anywhere on the body.

With the tiny percentage of women who become grossly overweight due to pituitary disorders ("pituitary obesity"), the first step usually is to correct the disorder and then place the patient on a special reducing program, usually under constant medical checking and supervision, often in the hospital. After reducing is achieved, plastic surgery is usually required for this type. Decision is made with the personal physician, of course.

Must The Former Smoker Become Overweight?

Whatever the reason may be, most individuals gain weight soon after they stop smoking. Cigarettes often act as a substitute for food in gratifying oral desire. A cigarette may function in a way as a weight-reducer on the human system in some cases. Since heavy smoking dulls the taste, foods usually have more flavor after smoking is stopped. Therefore the ex-smoker enjoys flavors more and accordingly eats more.

My recommendation to smokers who quit (which has worked with many patients) is that they try to keep their food intake down in the weeks following withdrawal from cigarettes, but that they postpone strict dieting until they have "kicked the habit." It takes an extremely strong-minded person to give up smoking and to take up dieting at the same time, doubly depriving himself.

After you have "kicked the habit" and stopped smoking cigarettes, and if you are overweight, I urge you to go on my basic Quick Weight Loss Diet. The sooner you take off the excess pounds, the better for your health and spirits—and the QWL way can help you do it better than any dieting method I know.

Should the Mental Patient Diet?

I must make it very clear again that my recommendations in this book are for reducing the great majority of overweights, not those with any serious illnesses, such as severe diabetes, severe gastric or intestinal ulcers, hyperthyroid, cirrhosis of the liver, Addison's disease, ulcerative colitis, severe tuberculosis, other severe diseases—*and not for neurotics.*

For the neurotic or near-neurotic individual, man or woman or youngster, dieting may create further problems which they cannot handle. They should undertake their reducing, which is often particularly needed, under the specific orders and constant supervision of a qualified physician.

It must be emphasized, too, that the fat person with some serious physical or mental disorder, especially physical, is more likely to need reducing as a matter of life or more imminent death.

Some psychiatric clinics, as previously mentioned, recommend my quick reducing methods to their overweight patients.

How Overweight Affects Sexuality.

There's a story about an angry husband who growled at his wife, "Where the devil is all the food-budget money going?" She snapped, "Look at yourself sideways in the mirror, Fatso, and you'll see." That doesn't sound like a very happy marriage or a fulfilling sexual relationship.

Overweight, particularly ponderous overweight, or obesity, may generally be called a deterrent to sex, in my professional experience, all other factors being equal. The unadorned truth is that a fat, flabby, ungainly body is not "a lovesome sight" to the other party leading up to or during the sexual act.

The fat woman (or man) may well be inhibited and deterred because she is openly or secretly ashamed of her body. The partner, again consciously or subconsciously, may find his wife's (or husband's) loose or bulging torso unexciting, uninviting, even repelling. Heavy, single patients, women and men, have told me that they are "not interested in the opposite sex or in marriage," yet the same individuals become very much interested when they slim down; obviously their "disinterest" was due to shame because of an ungraceful, overweight appearance.

Scientifically there are too many variables affecting sexual drive and potency versus sexual lassitude and impotence to relate them directly to overweight. Mental, temperamental and psychological factors are extremely important. However, I have often found in treating overweights that when a fat, ungainly woman reduces and achieves a slim, lovely, limber figure, her sexual desire and ability usually improve. The same is true for the majority of men I've had as patients when they changed from a roly-poly fat man to a compact, firm, youthful figure, which is more the masculine ideal.

There is no question also that massive overweight not only tends to slow up the individual and make him more sluggish in all activities, but rolls or bulges of fat and flab may impede as well as inhibit the sexual act. From the standpoints of attractiveness, more vigorous health and agility, the slim human body has a better chance in respect to sexual potency and ability than an ungainly overweight figure. Nevertheless, it is also a fact that being a muscular Adonis, athlete or model of either sex doesn't necessarily indicate greater sexual interest and ability.

In my experience, many marriages that were approaching unhappiness and even breakup were saved, and the interest and affection of both man and wife renewed, when one or both reduced and transformed a massive, fat, flabby figure into a slim, attractive shape. Often I've heard the comment from a newly slim woman, "I feel like a bride again, we're having our second honeymoon."

Gratifying bodily transformation often brings on improved health and energy, along with a change in the mental state from sluggishness and depression to a bright, optimistic, more loving outlook not only for the partner but for life and living in general. A sexual transformation for the better at the same time is not unusual.

While the wonderful change from ugly, impeding fat to slimness and improved health has saved some marriages, and led to marriage, there is no guarantee that reducing from considerable overweight to ideal weight and a more attractive figure will assure improved sexual potency, desire and ability. There are too many imponderables involved for any such all-out assurance.

The answer boils down to this: guarantee of improved sexuality—*no;* possibility of improvement—*yes.*

Should Reducing Drugs Be Used?

The only time "reducing drugs" should be used is when they are prescribed and recommended, with full details on usage, by a qualified physician. "Reducing drugs" sold over-the-counter in stores, without a prescription, should *never* be used; some such "reducing pills" are nothing but vitamins sold at an exhorbitant price, others may contain elements that may be very harmful over the long run.

If he thinks that such medication is necessary in your case, the doctor has many good drugs to choose from for your particular aid. The giving of drugs of any kind, for reducing or other purposes, is a very skillful art, trustworthy only when coming from a doctor who knows exactly what he is doing for you. Nurses, druggists, dieticians and other such professionals are not qualified to recommend or distribute drugs—and certainly a friend, neighbor or any other lay person endangers your health in giving or suggesting any drugs to you.

I have prescribed drugs where necessary—appetite depressants, and suppressants; drugs to counteract mental depression and physical lethargy; others to increase mental interest and physical activity; drugs that help rid the body of excess salts and liquids; the right drugs for other purposes. However, most overweights can reduce successfully without drugs, using my quick weight loss methods.

Keep in mind always that for reducing or any other purpose, drugs can be a good thing when prescribed by the physician who knows their functions well, *but a dangerous and even deadly thing otherwise.*

Why You Must Diet or Die Younger.

Some of the primary negative effects of overweight are (1) changes in body functions; (2) increased risk of developing certain diseases and malfunctions; (3) increased harmful effects and complications from existing diseases and problems; (4) detrimental psychological effects.

The vast majority of overweights have harmful and discomforting symptoms. I earnestly believe that all fat people are not as healthy as thin ones, aside from special diseases and defects. Fat people have many respiratory complaints and function more poorly in heat, work and exercise. Their poor breathing ventilation is due to heaviness of fat deposits on the chest wall, and a high diaphragm due to an enlarged liver, a ballooned stomach and fat deposits in the abdomen.

All these changes lessen the breathing capacity of the lungs. The heart may be completely surrounded by fat, impeding its functions badly. Fat people often have excessive water retention and excessive amounts of blood in their vessels; this also fills the lungs, diminishing the breathing space. With the obese, breathing tends to be rapid, shallow, stertorous (sounds like snoring) and difficult. Due to poor ventilation in their systems, they have greater accumulations of carbon dioxide, producing lethargy and sleepiness. The oxygen exchange is poor.

It is known that rich, fatty blood and poorly oxygenated blood clots more readily to produce thrombosis (clotting in the brain and heart blood vessels). The heart functions poorly, and high blood pressure is common among the obese. This in turn may produce atherosclerosis (hardened arteries), strokes, heart attacks, gangrene.

These conditions directly or indirectly produce a half-million deaths a year.

Excess fat is the bane of the surgeon and anesthetist, causing marked difficulties in operations. Breathing is very capricious, fluctuations in blood pressure are more common and dangerous. The surgeon has to wade through inches of excess fat, making operating and sewing more difficult. Separation of wounds is more frequent with the obese, along with greater incidence of infection.

I could go on for pages telling of the specific medical dangers in overweight. Statistics show that the risk of disease in the fat over the slim is increased 50 percent; when high blood pressure and diabetes accompanies overweight, sickness and death may increase 150 to 1,000 percent!

I couldn't agree more thoroughly, from personal examination and treatment of thousands upon thousands of overweight women, men and youngsters with the warning statement of a president of the American Medical Association: "... *the greatest danger to the health of the American people is obesity.*" I am certain that excess weight, especially to a pronounced degree, directly or indirectly kills—yes, *kills*—more people than any other disease or affliction.

The statistics of death by overweight are hidden. Many a death certificate that lists cause of death as "heart disease" or any of dozens of other malfunctions should add "caused by excess weight" or "involving excess weight." For these reasons alone, putting aside all considerations of vanity and wanting to look your attractive best, *you should and must get those excess pounds and inches off, starting today—or tomorrow at the latest.* One of the best things you can resolve is to start with a "starve-in" tomorrow, and then go on to quick weight loss dieting.

Don't Believe False Fears About Dieting.

The three most common fears expressed to me by overweights who resist dieting are these:

    1. "If I reduce rapidly, won't I gain it back just as quickly?"

    2. "Isn't quick weight loss harmful?"

    3. "Isn't it more dangerous to keep going down and up, losing weight and gaining it back again, than staying fat?"

Here are the definitive, dependable answers:

1. No, when you lose weight quickly, it doesn't follow that you soon gain it all back. On the contrary, most of my thousands of overweight patients took pounds off quickly and kept them off for a number of reasons. They felt so good about their quick new slimness that they were motivated to stay slim. They now had a method by which they could take off a few pounds quickly instead of letting the fat and weight accumulate and grow. Quick weight loss dieting soon reduces your appetite rather than increasing it.

2. No, quick weight loss is most healthful, not harmful. That's just as true as it being more "healthful" (and comfortable) to drop a red-hot plate quickly than to put it down gradually and let the heat burn your fingers badly. A load of excess fat slows up, burdens and threatens your body's functions, may cause a breakdown any day, any hour—so the sooner you relieve your body of the load imposed by the excess fat, the better off you are in every way.

3. Even if your weight goes down-and-up, down-and-up, you're better off than having your weight at a constant *up*, weighing down your body's functions without even the temporary relief of lifting off 5, 10, 20, or more pounds. If a man drops from 180 pounds to 150 pounds (ideal weight) then back up to 180 pounds, over a period of six months, his body has been relieved and his heart, too, of pumping blood for an average of 15 pounds of excess fat instead of supporting 30 excess pounds over the six-month period.

These answers are all sound common sense as well as good

medical sense. Yet fears continue to beset the overweights who are looking for any excuse not to deprive themselves of the fat and flab that is aging and killing them quicker. My quick weight loss methods have proved conclusively over and over again that they are healthful, pleasant, safe—*and that they work.*

I'm particularly pleased that many physicians, doctors' wives, nurses, dieticians and others affiliated with the medical professions have written to me or told me in person that they lost weight on my diets. The most repeated sentence is, "I look and feel wonderful."

I urge *you*, also, to put your fears aside, whether you are fearful of feeling unwell or of failing to lose weight. Start quick weight loss dieting as instructed here and chances are excellent that you, too, will soon lose those unwanted, unhealthy, unattractive excess pounds and inches.

The instructions in this book apply to every race and nationality all over the world. Color of skin is simply an unimportant physical actuality. Environment makes no significant difference. People are people, and overweight is a danger to all.

Quickie Weight Loss
Questions & Answers

Quickie Weight Loss Questions & Answers

You may wish to refresh your memory of some of the facts in this book by referring now and then to these quickie answers to some of the most-asked questions about dieting. Most of these points are discussed in more detail on other pages.

1. Do I count calories on the Inches-Off and other quick weight loss diets?

> No—by eating only the specified foods, your calorie intake is controlled "automatically," and there's no need to count calories.

2. What do I do about my diet when eating out?

> It's simple to stick to your diet by ordering only the foods in the diet listing.

3. Can I have "coffee breaks" during the day and evening on quick weight loss diets?

> Yes—enjoy as many "coffee breaks" as you want, within reason, of coffee, tea or artificially sweetened sodas with a snack of something on the diet listing, but no sugar, cream or milk, or other forbidden items.

4. Can I go off a quick weight loss diet, then go back again?

> Yes—if you put on unwanted weight when off the diet,

go back on a quick weight loss diet for a few days, a week, or longer, and that will start taking off pounds immediately.

5. Is it dangerous to drop weight rapidly on a quick weight loss diet?

Absolutely not; If you're overweight, it's dangerous not to get rid of the excess pounds quickly.

6. How can I develop the will power to diet?

When you go on a quick weight loss diet and see the figures on the scale dropping every day, and your figure in the mirror slimming down, that's likely to supply the "will power" to keep dieting.

7. Isn't "balanced dieting" the healthiest way to lose weight?

"Balanced dieting" is fine in theory but it just doesn't work for most overweights because they become discouraged and stop dieting when they lose only about a pound a week.

8. Over how long a period should I plan to diet—weeks? months?

Start a quick weight loss diet and each day tell yourself to keep dieting just "one more day" until you're at your ideal weight instead of counting in weeks or months, which can be disheartening.

9. Why do I gain weight too rapidly—could something be wrong with my metabolism?

It's not likely, since only one out of twenty (the consensus among physicians is one out of fifty) persons has been estimated to have some metabolic disorder that interferes with losing weight. If your metabolism is faulty your doctor will tell you so and act to correct it.

10. What is the greatest danger to health for most people?

Most medical opinion agrees that although cancer is generally the most dreaded disease, overweight is the greatest national menace to good health.

11. *Isn't quick weight loss usually followed by quick weight gain?*

Not at all—the person is most likely to stay slim who takes off weight quickly, sees the wonderful difference it makes in health and appearance and is thus inspired to stay slim.

12. *If I'm allowed all the food I want from a quick weight loss diet list, am I not likely to stuff myself and gain weight instead of losing?*

No, the foods on the lists soon make you feel full, and even if you start by eating a lot, you'll soon lose the desire.

13. *On a diet where I'm not instructed to count calories, won't I naturally be consuming too many calories a day?*

On my quick weight loss diets, patients I've checked have generally consumed only 400 to 900 calories a day without craving more food—and they've lost weight rapidly.

14. *Is it advisable for an overweight family to go on a quick weight loss diet?*

If parents and teenagers are all overweight, it usually works out excellently when all eat the wholesome foods and lose pounds day after day on one of my quick weight loss diets, each person encouraging the others.

15. *Are the "average weight tables" good guides?*

Since "average weight" includes too many overweights, thus bringing the averaged figures higher than they should be, I prefer that my patients, and all who wish to reduce to their most healthful weight, be guided by my "ideal" weight tables according to height.

16. *Shouldn't I reduce according to "large, medium, or small frame" figures?*

I don't believe in "frame size" figures because people vary so much according to sizes of shoulders, chest, pel-

vis, legs, and so on—and also because most overweights
of any size frame choose "large frame" numbers even
though very few belong in that category.

**17. Isn't it best to reduce simply by eating smaller portions of
foods recommended for "balanced eating"?**

This sounds fine theoretically but it just doesn't work so
it's quite useless—my goal for my patients and for you
is actual visible weight loss as quickly as possible.

18. How can I satisfy a desire for sweets?

Drink as many non-caloric carbonated beverages as you
wish, in a variety of flavors, to satisfy any craving for
sweets and to help keep liquids flowing through your
system: maximum 10 glasses a day for adults, 5 glasses
for youngsters.

19. Are seasonings permitted on quick weight loss diets?

Don't use mayonnaise, salad dressings, oils or fats, but
it's fine to use salt, pepper, herbs and spices, cocktail
and Tabasco sauce, horseradish and catsup—in moderation.

20. Are vitamins desirable when dieting?

I recommend a vitamin and mineral tablet be taken
daily, a combination such as vitamins A, B1, B2, C, D
and other vitamins and minerals.

**21. Is it necessary to limit calorie intake to under 1,000 calories a
day in order to lose weight?**

No—on some of my quick weight loss diets you can lose
pounds rapidly yet eat 1,300 to 2,500 calories daily (depending on your height) of permitted protein foods.

**22. Where does the system get fats and carbohydrates for energy
when there are none in the diet?**

Your body uses stored excess fat and carbohydrates for
energy, and also converts the proteins permitted on the
diet into starches for energy. It is estimated that 10 per-

cent of fat and 58 percent of proteins can be turned into sugar.

23. *Are the pounds lost through quick reducing mostly water loss?*

Not with my quick weight loss methods, which take off many pounds week after week—some of the first weight loss is water, but most of it is excess body fat.

24. *Can't I allow myself a little leeway in adding foods not on the list of permitted foods on a diet?*

A little leeway is a dangerous thing when dieting—as soon as you permit yourself to add "a little something," you're likely to continue adding more and more excess calories; you should stick to the permitted foods rigidly and save the leeway for Stay-Slim Eating later.

25. *Can I have a few small sweets on your high protein Quick Weight Loss Diet?*

No sweets at all—even the seemingly small amount of carbohydrates in a few candies, cookies, and so on seem to be converted into fat in the body rather than burned up for heat and energy, and this interferes with the most efficient functioning of the diet in burning up fat.

26. *Can't I ever look forward to enjoying sweets if I want to become slim and stay that way?*

Of course! You won't stay on my quick weight loss diets "forever"—soon you learn to control your intake and can enjoy some higher-calorie foods on Stay-Slim Eating without overdoing it.

27. *Won't I feel weak from losing pounds quickly?*

Quite the opposite—with pounds of burdensome fat removed, you'll feel more vigorous and probably in higher spirits from feeling and looking more attractive.

28. *Isn't vitamin C lacking in a high-protein diet?*

The vitamin C is provided by fresh fish, seafood and

meat, plus a vitamin-mineral tablet daily as an extra assurance, also adding other vitamins.

29. Won't it be bad for my system to lose 10 to 20 pounds in a few weeks?

I've examined many overweights who have lost far more than 20 pounds in a few weeks and never found any undesirable physical or neurological problems.

30. Should I be checked by a doctor when dieting?

It's good medical practice to be checked by a physician when going on any diet, and at least annually in any case.

31. Should I go off my diet if I don't have a bowel movement for a few days?

Stay on the diet, as nature adjusts bowel habits; if you're concerned, take some mineral oil or milk of magnesia, a suppository, or an enema.

32. Is a bloated feeling in my stomach a bad sign?

It's usually a sign that you're badly overweight; the bloated feeling should disappear quickly as the pounds come off.

33. Is it undesirable to urinate a lot more when dieting?

The extra urination is desirable, as this removes the unburnt fats and waste as well as water from your body.

34. What should I do if I retain water when dieting?

Eliminate salt and catsup from the diet and check with your physician, who may prescribe a diuretic drug to increase the flow.

35. Don't eggs on a diet add too much cholesterol?

If your doctor has told you that your cholesterol count is high, or has given you specific instructions about eating eggs, don't eat more than 4 eggs a week.

36. Isn't "creamed" cottage cheese too high in calories?

No, but if you have a high cholesterol count, use pot cheese or farmer cheese instead of creamed cottage cheese, which doesn't contain any cream but has been "creamed" by the addition of a little milk.

37. Do I need more sleep when dieting?

Limit your sleep to no more than eight hours daily, as you lose weight more rapidly when you're active than when you're lying about and sleeping.

38. What should I do if I get tired and sleepy when dieting?

Take a short rest, then get up and get active again; if you keep getting tired, drink 2 ounces of orange juice for quick energy, and if the tired feeling drags on, have a medical checkup, as this shouldn't happen and rarely does.

39. Won't dieting increase my hunger considerably?

The diets in this book soon decrease the desire for rich foods and oversize portions.

40. How often should I weigh myself?

Get on the bathroom scale unclothed the first thing each morning; if you see a gain of 3 pounds or more over your ideal weight, go back on a quick weight loss diet immediately to lose the extra pounds rapidly.

41. Is it all right to go back on a quick weight loss diet for a few days, time after time?

Certainly, go back on the diet any time pounds creep up on you, and as often as you wish, to keep from becoming overweight again.

42. After I reach my ideal weight, is it necessary to count calories in order to stay slim?

Your weight is controlled by the number of calories you take in and use up, so it's advisable to learn the calorie

counts of foods to keep from adding too many calories
daily and thus putting on weight.

43. How do I know how many calories I should have daily to stay at ideal weight?

Refer to the ideal weight and calorie table in Chapter 1,
then judge and abide by your own desirable calorie intake according to your height and ideal weight.

44. Can I average my calorie intake over a two-day period?

Yes, if you go over your calorie count one day, subtract
the overage from your next day's intake—but don't permit an excess often or you'll never catch up until you go
back on a quick weight loss diet for a few days.

45. What should I do if I gain weight again, just keep deducting from my calorie total permitted each day?

The best plan is to go off Stay-Slim Eating and go back
on a quick weight loss diet until you're at ideal weight
again, then switch back to calorie-counting—and don't
let yourself get behind day after day.

46. Isn't it harmful to go up and down in weight—gaining, losing, gaining, losing?

It's best, of course, to *stay* at ideal weight, but it won't
hurt you to go up and down—what is dangerous to your
health is to go up and up and stay up over your ideal
weight.

47. How can I judge whether a portion is "small, medium or large" to check the calorie count.

Use your good judgment and don't delude yourself by
saying that a "large" portion, as you recognize very well,
is "small"—you're only fooling yourself and endangering
your health and good looks.

48. Is there any way I can cut down my hunger before meals?

To help fill you up before a meal, have a tall glass of

water, club soda, non-caloric soda, or 1 or 2 cups of black coffee or tea without cream, milk or sugar.

49. *Can I have a cocktail while on Stay-Slim Eating?*

Certainly, as long as you count the calories in your daily total—for example, you could have a 150-calorie martini and skip a 155-calorie frankfurter that you were going to eat.

50. *Isn't there an easier way of staying slim than learning to count calories?*

Counting calories is very easy and can be an interesting game if you approach it in that spirit; after about a week you'll be counting calories automatically as you learn the count of each food—if you don't remember, take a few seconds to look up the figures, there's nothing difficult about that.

51. *Is it all right to switch from one diet to another?*

The important point is to get those excess pounds off so that if you get tired of one diet, such as all-protein, and go on another, like all-fruit, you'll still be taking weight off and there's no harm done—only good.

52. *Is fasting or semi-starvation dieting harmful?*

If you're overweight, going without food won't be harmful as long as you drink lots of water and non-caloric liquids every waking hour, take one to two therapeutic vitamin-mineral tablets daily and are checked by a physician.

53. *Won't fasting increase the appetite so I'll pile in loads of food after a few days and be fatter than ever?*

After a day or two of fasting, the body becomes satisfied with less, and the desire for food usually decreases.

54. *How long can a person continue fasting without harm?*

As I say repeatedly, it should be done under medical

supervision. Fasting has lasted from eight to over 100 days (more often 26 days).

55. *Is there any special way to be successful at fasting?*

Fasting is more likely to succeed when two or more people undertake it together as a spur to each other; also, it helps to keep consuming huge quantities of water and non-caloric liquids every waking hour.

56. *After supervised fasting, won't I become a bigger eater than ever from then on?*

No, the general result is that the body is satisfied with smaller meals due to altered bodily metabolic action and breaking the habit of overeating.

57. *Does overweight slow up the mental as well as physical reflexes?*

A report by the United States Air Force Medical Corps blames overweight as one contributing cause of aircraft incidents, accidents and deaths. It's likely that this also applies to automobile accidents.

58. *Can I reduce quicker by spreading daily food intake over six meals instead of three meals daily?*

This is true. In tests, people who ate 1200 calories spread over six meals a day lost as much as others who took in 900 calories in three meals a day.

59. *Are six small meals a day more healthful than three larger meals a day?*

Yes, especially vital for heart patients, since small meals tend to shrink the stomach and help prevent pressure on the heart.

60. *What happens in the body from a heavy meal?*

The blood vessels are flooded with emulsified fat, which slows the blood, may deposit fat particles on the inner linings and may clog and choke some of the narrowed, fatty blood channels.

61. Is there any special tip on starting a six-meals-a-day routine?

Go on a 48-hour fasting diet (with lots of water and no-calorie liquids), then it's easy to switch to a six-meals-a-day eating habit.

62. Is there a special diet for the six-meal-a-day eater?

Any good diet will reduce you even faster if the food and calorie intake is spread over six meals a day instead of three, without increasing the total that you eat.

63. Are meat-only, vegetables-only, fruit-only diets harmful?

No, unless (possibly) extended over a long period of time, but for a matter of weeks such diets take off weight quickly and have not proved harmful to people who have no particular health disorder.

64. Won't I lose weight just by having smaller portions of food?

Most people fail on a smaller-portions diet because they can't resist eating larger quantities; the best chance for success is to eat smaller portions and omit completely high-calorie foods, such as butter, cream, ice cream, pies, and so on.

65. Is it dangerous to skip a meal a day?

Not at all—you can skip breakfast or lunch or dinner without any harm, but you'll fail to reduce if you add the food from the skipped meal to the other two meals.

66. Do you recommend liquid formula diets?

The problem with liquid formula diets is that most people don't lose pounds quickly enough, become discouraged and start adding foods that put on weight.

67. Can I satisfy a craving for something like an ice cream soda, for example, without ruining my diet?

I sometimes advise a patient with such a persistent craving to switch for a few days to a diet of 3 ice cream sodas a day—that still amounts to only 1,050 calories a day and soon kills the craving as nausea sets in.

68. Are rice diets advisable?

Rice diets are monotonous but take off weight quickly and are particularly good for overweights who have a tendency toward high blood pressure.

69. Can a quick-reducing diet also help an acne condition?

Proper eating—such as plenty of lean meat, poultry with skin removed, fish, seafood, fresh fruits and vegetables; NO fats, oils, sweets, alcohol, sugar-content beverages, iodized salt—can be a big help to having a clear, clean, attractive skin and to taking off weight quickly.

70. Does quick weight loss dieting help against allergies?

The question of allergies is complicated, as many causes may be involved, but taking off overweight and staying away from fats and sweets often relieves some allergic conditions remarkably.

71. Does weight loss affect an arthritic condition beneficially?

Getting down to ideal weight doesn't necessarily control an arthritic condition, but overweight may aggravate it and is extremely undesirable; diets high in vitamin-B complex and acid ash foods have proved helpful in many cases.

72. Is excessive perspiration related to overweight?

Definitely, in many cases. I recommend getting excess weight off rapidly with a one- or two-day fasting diet, then switching to a quick weight loss diet and staying on it until down to ideal weight.

73. Is quick weight loss desirable with an ulcer?

Your doctor will give you instructions if you have an ulcer. If you're overweight, it's generally very desirable to lose pounds rapidly, spreading the eating out over the day so that you eat only a few mouthfuls every couple of hours. (See anti-ulcer dieting, page 158.)

74. Can I enjoy some wine and still reduce quickly?

Yes, by sticking to light wines only, no sherry or port, you can have a 4-ounce glass of wine at lunch and another at dinner, with limited amounts of cheese, bread, and lots of coffee and tea—for a few days or a week.

75. How long can I stay on a stringent diet?

Generally you stay on a "lopsided" diet for a few weeks or months, then go on Stay-Slim Eating, then back on the diet, and so on until you're at ideal weight—although I've had patients thrive on a quick weight loss diet for as long as a year.

76. Isn't it necessary to have three good meals a day to be healthy?

Positively not! A slim, trim career woman near seventy has lunched for years on powdered milk and cereal; a beauty-contest winner, glowing with health and beauty, often skips breakfast and lunch entirely and has a moderate dinner. You need enough nutrition to maintain your slim, vigorous ideal weight—the rest is burdensome excess baggage. A famous, energetic beauty, Mary Garden, thrived on only one meal daily; and a light one at that.

77. I was told that it's harmful to lose 30 pounds of overweight in six months and then put it back on again in another six months. Is that true?

False. Over the year your system had to support an average of only 15 pounds of overweight instead of 30 pounds.

78. Won't it hurt me to go suddenly from eating a lot to cutting calories in half or even less?

Quite the contrary. The sudden drop in intake will relieve your system and you'll start feeling wonderful quickly.

79. *Isn't it bad to change from the kinds of food my body is accustomed to?*

> It's bad to keep eating the kinds of food that have made you overweight. A sudden change is a change for the better.

80. *Should I start dieting now when I'm in a highly nervous condition?*

> See your doctor and get his help in relieving your nervousness and mental anxiety before you undertake dieting.

81. *Since I'm naturally heavy, isn't it bad for me to slim down?*

> Telling yourself that you're "naturally heavy" is just fooling yourself. I've never yet had a patient of normal health (that is, without a specific medical disorder) who wasn't much better off when down to ideal weight.

82. *Won't I have more colds and illness after I take off weight?*

> It's absolutely untrue that a fat person is healthier—exactly the opposite: Overweights are more likely to have more colds and other illnesses than when at ideal weight.

83. *Don't I need some extra fat as a reserve against illness?*

> Extra, burdensome fat impairs the body in fighting illness rather than helping you.

84. *Won't I risk vitamin deficiency on a restricted diet?*

> You won't develop vitamin deficiency on any of my diets —but as an added assurance, I suggest a vitamin and mineral tablet daily when dieting, and a stronger "therapeutic" vitamin tablet if you're on a fasting type of diet of 300-400 calories a day.

85. *Isn't it true that my skin will sag and I'll look scrawny from losing weight rapidly?*

> Mostly it's your clothing that will sag when you lose

weight. If your skin sags at all, it will soon firm again and you'll look far better than before in every way.

86. *I'm afraid I'll fail. How can I gain the confidence that I'll succeed in dieting this time when I've failed so often before?*

Your best assurance is when you see your weight dropping rapidly on one of my quick weight loss diets. That will give you confidence.

87. *Why is it bad for me to sleep more than eight hours a night when reducing?*

The average person uses up 2½ times more calories when awake and moving around actively on his feet than when sleeping. Thus, when lying down, you fail to use up the calories consumed during the day.

88. *I'm a very fast eater. Is that bad when dieting?*

Yes, because you're satisfied with less food when you take small mouthfuls and chew slowly and thoroughly, and when you stretch out a beverage by sipping slowly.

89. *How can I keep from snacking between meals?*

Most people snack from habit rather than from hunger, so ask yourself whether you're really hungry before reaching—and you'll usually find that the answer is no.

90. *Does the amount of food on my plate make any difference?*

It helps when you put *less* food on your plate than you think you want, then you won't be tempted to eat more after your appetite is appeased.

91. *Does the amount of salt in foods make any difference?*

Use salt sparingly and even omit it, if possible, since salted foods tend to retain more water and make you weigh more; also, salted foods are more tempting, and you eat more.

92. *Is sugar so fattening that I should really skip it?*

With each teaspoonful of sugar totaling 16 calories, you

can easily add well over 100 calories a day with suga
in beverages alone—and you get plenty of carbohydrate.
from the other foods you eat.

93. I love butter. Can't I keep it in my diet?

Not if you want to lose weight quickly (and perhaps a
all), since a couple of pats of butter per meal total abou
300 calories per day without any other food.

94. Can't I let go on just a few rich foods when on a diet?

Figure it out for yourself: a half cup of shelled peanut
adds 420 calories; a fairly small piece of chocolate layer
cake 400 calories; a medium portion of candied swee
potatoes about 300 calories; 4 tablespoons of hollan-
daise sauce 200 calories, and so on. Just check the calorie-count list.

95. How about my enjoying a sample of a forbidden food?

That's fine if just one moderate bite of layer cake will
satisfy you, or a spoonful of ice cream, just one small
hors d'oeuvres—but make sure you *can* stop with a small
sample. Stay away from any such sampling if on my
basic Quick Weight Loss Diet.

96. On a diet, can I really eat "as much as I want" of a food when it's permitted?

"As much as you want" means eating only as much of
the food as will appease your hunger, and then stopping
—certainly not stuffing yourself.

97. How can I refuse portions when I'm out dining?

It's very simple, just tell your hostess that you're dieting for the sake of your health and must limit yourself
to small quantities of limited foods even though "Your
cooking is delicious." A slim, vivacious ex-patient told
me, "I did a lot of talking, so nobody noticed how little
I ate."

98. Are low-calorie food substitutes healthful?

There is no evidence that sugar substitutes in moderate amounts are at all harmful, and removing fat from foods doesn't impair their nutrition, yet such foods save lots of calories. For instance compare a moderate 200-calorie portion of ice cream with a 10-calorie serving of sugar-free gelatin dessert.

99. How can I manage to eat and yet diet in restaurants?

Eat only the foods that are on your diet, and instruct the waiter to bring cocktail sauce instead of mayonnaise with shrimp, no butter sauce on your broiled steak, and so on.

100. Isn't it natural to eat as long as one sits at the table?

You avoid temptation if you get up from the table as soon as it's polite and go into another room or, better yet, take a walk if you have no guests.

101. When the food is right there, how can I resist second helpings?

At home you should bring to the table only the plateful you're permitted; when dining out you just have to be firm in refusing second helpings by saying, "No, thanks, I'm dieting."

102. I'm a non-stop eater, so how can I keep from gobbling up all the cookies and other such rich foods in sight?

Keep those tempting foods out of sight—if you're permitted 1 cookie on Stay-Slim Eating, then put only 1 cookie on your plate and place the rest back in the cupboard.

103. Does chewing gum and hard candy help relieve hunger?

Yes, but limit yourself to artificially sweetened chewing gum and hard candies, and only one such candy as a snack, no more than two sticks of gum a day.

104. Is skim milk as nutritious as regular milk?

Non-fat milk is just about as nutritious as regular milk, with only the fat removed, and saves you almost half the calories (90 calories instead of 165 per glass).

105. Isn't it true that I should "feed a cold"?

Positively not! You should neither feed a cold nor a fever nor any other illness if you're overweight, for if you stuff yourself you add further discomfort to your system.

106. When is the best time to start a reducing diet?

Now. The longer you delay, the greater the danger of overweight to your health and happiness (unless you're undergoing some exceptional mental or nervous pressures).

107. Are seasonings permitted on quick weight loss diets?

Yes, enjoy the flavorings of herbs and spices but use a minimum amount of salt (or use no-sodium salt substitutes), and no salt, of course, where specified, as on salt-free diets.

108. Is it necessary to have a "big, hot breakfast" for proper nutrition?

This is an old-fashioned, thoroughly fake myth promoted primarily by producers of foods for "big, hot breakfasts"—for overweights to pile in hot cereals soaking with butter or cream, syrup-drenched griddle cakes, sausages swimming in fat, and such calorie-heavy foods, is not only undesirable for nutrition but downright dangerous.

109. Is artificially sweetened canned fruit less nutritious than similar fruit packed in heavy syrup?

What you lose in the artificially sweetened fruits are fat-producing calories, not any needed nutritional elements. You don't need the sugar calories, since you get enough "energy" in other foods on my diets.

110. Are steam baths a valuable reducing aid?

Enjoy steam baths if you like but don't count on any lasting weight reduction, since all you lose is an outpouring of water from perspiring heavily.

111. I eat like a bird, so why do I keep putting on weight?

People who "eat like a bird" usually take a nibble here and a nibble there all day long, all the nibbles adding up to a load of excess calories that load on excess weight. *Total* calories, not just a few here and there, are what count.

112. Doesn't quick weight loss raise the blood pressure?

Exactly the opposite. Taking off pounds rapidly for overweights generally relieves high blood pressure.

113. Is it bad to go without food one day a week?

For overweights, going a day without food is healthful, relieves the system and generally decreases rather than raises the appetite for the next day. Drink plenty of sugar-free beverages and lots of water, and take a couple of vitamin tablets on "starvation" days.

114. When I lose rapidly and reach my ideal weight, isn't that a good time to lose more as insurance against getting overweight again?

Ideal weight is called "ideal" because that's healthiest for you, and neither much less nor much more is recommended.

115. I get fatigued when dieting—doesn't that mean I need something to eat right away?

Some moderate exercise and activity, such as a brisk walk, is probably what you need, as there's no reason to feel fatigued on any of my diets. Get in motion and get your blood flowing faster so you'll feel pepped-up.

116. How can I diet when I must lunch with business clients almost every day?

At your client luncheons, eat moderately from permitted foods and make lunch your one "big" meal of the day.

117. Doesn't dieting cause menstrual problems?

> No, overweight is more likely to cause problems, but if you have menstrual difficulties you should see a doctor at once.

118. What can I do about getting irritable and depressed from dieting?

> Recognize that your irritability probably comes not from dieting but from being overweight and unhappy about it—which will be relieved when you're slim and more attractive, less uncomfortable.

119. How can I avoid the pains I get—like having an ulcer—when I go on a diet?

> You either have an ulcer or are seeking a reason not to diet. See a doctor and have the ulcer treated (if you have one), then get that weight off quickly and you'll feel better in every way.

120. What can I do about getting bored with dieting?

> If fattening food is the only thing that keeps you from boredom, you'd better find some new interests instead of blaming the diet.

121. How can I keep from eating when I feel ill?

> If you're really sick, you're not likely to have an appetite, so you're probably using illness as an excuse to avoid dieting.

122. How can I stay on a diet when vacationing or traveling and enjoying the meals so much?

> Many people vacation, travel, enjoy themselves and stay slim—if you can't manage it, go on a quick weight loss diet as soon as you return until you reach ideal weight.

123. How can I make up for falling off a diet?

> Instead of wasting time scolding yourself, go right back on the diet. The quick weight loss should keep you dieting.

124. How can I get back to my former slimness after having a baby?

> As soon as your body has recovered completely from the birth, go on a quick weight loss diet until you're again at ideal weight, then go on my Inches-Off Diet if you want to thin down "problem spots" further.

125. What can I do when I get anemic from dieting?

> Have a blood test, which will undoubtedly prove that your "anemia" is in your imagination—then you'll go back on your diet without further worry.

126. How can I diet when I'm not psychologically fit for it?

> Don't depend on self-analysis as an excuse to avoid dieting—have a psychiatrist decide whether or not you're "psychologically fit."

127. Do birth-control pills bring on an increase in weight?

> There is no medical evidence that this is the case with most women; some may add 2 to 3 pounds of water.

128. Isn't it true that people who have always been overweight are better off that way, and that a few more pounds won't hurt?

> It's not true. Overweight for any length of time burdens the system and is unhealthy, and "a few more pounds" may be just enough to bring on serious problems, attacks and worse.

129. How can I diet when I can't fall asleep unless I have hot cocoa and a cookie at bedtime?

> You're fooling yourself that you can't fall asleep without rich food. If you must eat something, have a little cottage cheese, a small apple, or something else that is permitted on your diet.

130. How can I lose weight after an operation when I need plenty of food for rebuilding?

> If you're still overweight after an operation, the extra fat is worse than ever for you, and you should limit your

intake, then go on a quick weight loss diet as soon as you're recovered.

131. I can't resist sweet drinks all day long, so how can I lose weight?

Drink artificially sweetened sodas that satisfy your "sweet tooth." Only your mind detects a difference, your taste doesn't—as proved often.

132. Shouldn't I eat more if I get constipated on a diet?

No. If you're troubled, take a mild laxative, but don't pile in food.

133. Is there any way to diet without getting to look sickly and scrawny?

At ideal weight you'll look fit and attractive, neither like a balloon nor sickly and scrawny.

134. Why should I diet when people say I am "the picture of health"?

Science proves that a chubby look is invariably an unhealthy fact; don't pay attention to what people tell you but what your scale shows you—if you're overweight you're endangering your health.

135. Is there any proof that overweight shortens life?

According to statistics, on the average, life is shortened in years by about the same percentage as a man or woman is overweight: 10 percent overweight means 10 percent shorter lifespan, 20 percent overweight means 20 percent shorter lifespan, and so on. Thus, if a man's normal life expectancy is age seventy, and he's steadily 10 percent overweight, he's likely to die at age 63 by life-insurance expectancy figures.

136. Does overweight tend to bring on illness?

Yes, according to what I've seen in 45 years of medical practice, and statistics from the American Medical Association show the same: high blood pressure, hardening of the arteries, diabetes, arthritis, heart trouble and strokes are found much more often among overweights than those at ideal weight.

137. Should I be concerned about 5 pounds excess weight?

Even a few pounds overweight don't do you any good and may lead to harm by burdening your system; also, you generally add another pound or two until you're considerably overweight. Your best health rule is to reach and stay at your ideal weight.

138. Is there any relationship between overweight and sexual potency?

While there is no clear medical relationship, it's a fact that overweight makes a man or woman less attractive to the other sex and often leads to decrease in sexual activity and even potency, as well as dragging down one's health and vigor in general.

139. I'm ashamed of being a fatty, but how can I face long, tedious months of dieting?

Just try my quick weight loss dieting for one short week —you'll be so pleased with how easily the pounds drop and how the inches start to diminish that you'll probably find such reducing challenging and exhilarating rather than "tedious."

140. Isn't it true that some people die from stringent dieting?

I've never encountered any such result in decades of medical practice and research. Investigation shows that such deaths are not caused by dieting but by some serious mental or physical disorder.

141. Is there anything I can do about getting hunger headaches when dieting?

Such headaches are usually psychological in origin and go away in a few days. If headaches persist, have a doctor check you.

142. I enjoy gourmet eating so much, how can I give it up?

Take off your overweight quickly and then continue your gourmet meals, limiting your intake by calorie-count on Stay-Slim Eating. While on the diet, substitute the more uplifting enjoyment of fine books, music, art, instead of gourmet foods.

143. My husband is "a happy, fat man"—why should I urge him to slim down?

If you want him around for a long time, get him to slim down for the sake of his health and longer life—and for his increased happiness (and yours and your family's), since most "happy fatties" are basically concerned about their health and overweight appearance and put on a cover-up act. Happiness is definitely *not* a swollen stom-. ach.

144. How can I afford the costly steaks, seafoods and other expensive foods on a quick weight loss diet?

I've checked this point with my patients, who report that they *save* food money on a diet, since they avoid rich desserts and other expensive foods. Also, choose from the best buys instead of high-priced cuts—chicken and eggs on a high-protein diet, for example, instead of steaks every day.

145. Are packaged low-calorie foods desirable on a diet?

Most such foods are as wholesome and nutritious as their high-calorie counterparts and are a great boon that dieters didn't have not so many years ago. Artificial sweeteners used in moderation offer you a great new way to save calories.

146. What can I do if my overweight family won't eat packaged low-calorie foods?

Serve the food without letting them see the packages—chances are that they won't even know that they're saving calories with such foods as special imitation mayonnaise and artificially sweetened sodas unless you tell them so (proved in many taste tests).

147. *Is it better to buy low-calorie foods in "health-food stores"?*

Such stores usually charge high prices out of all proportion to the food values—for example, you can't buy better non-fat dry milk than at low cost in supermarkets, no matter what the "health-food" label promises. Also, most "health foods" aren't low-calorie foods. Always check the labels.

148. *Is artificially sweetened gum and candy bad for children?*

There's no evidence that there's anything "bad" about moderate intake of such sugar-free sweets for children (not infants) and adults—and just about every dentist will tell you that they're far preferable to sugary confections that promote tooth decay.

149. *Is there any difference in calorie content between white and dark meat of poultry?*

Dark meat is slightly higher in calories than white meat; always remove and discard the skin from poultry just as you remove the fat from meats.

150. *Do most fruits and vegetables have about the same calorie content?*

No, they vary widely—for example, a medium apple has about 70 calories while a medium pear has about 100 calories; a cup of cooked carrots has about 45 calories but a cup of lima beans has 150 calories. Always check the calorie tables.

151. *Is it all right to use herbs and spices in low-calorie cooking?*

Herbs and spices add flavor, not calories, but go easy on the salt, and on low-salt diets use only non-sodium salt substitutes.

152. Is there really much difference in calories in "low-calorie" foods?

Compare labels and tables on each type of food and you'll know exactly what the difference is; for example, an ounce of one brand of low-calorie salad dressing is only 15 calories, while an ounce of a similar "regular" salad dressing is about 150 calories—quite a saving!

153. Are dry-roasted nuts lower in calories than the "regular" packaged nuts?

Yes, but don't let that lead you astray—even dry-roasted nuts are a high-calorie food and not recommended when dieting.

154. Is "calories per portion" printed on a package a dependable guide?

This is a tricky problem that you must check with each package. If a package states "300 calories per portion" and "two portions in this package," you'll be consuming 600 calories if you eat the entire contents, which may not seem like (and may not really be) more than one portion in usual quantity.

155. Is "gourmet food" automatically high in calories?

Many rich, creamy recipes are considered "gourmet" by some and are very high in calories, but I consider a well-aged, lightly spiced, perfectly broiled rare filet mignon as an example, one of the finest of "gourmet foods"—and permitted on many of my quick weight loss diets.

156. Is overweight hereditary, since it seems to run in many families?

Overweight "runs in families" because the children indulge in the high-calorie meals and overweight eating habits that have made their parents heavy—and it's difficult to get teenagers to reduce when their bulky parents set a bad example right before their eyes.

157. Isn't it healthier for babies and children to be plump?

Not according to pediatricians, who state that this is an old-fashioned faulty concept, and that the fat baby and child is not a healthier one. Beware of well-meaning but misinformed people who urge you to stuff excess food into a baby or child—"Eat! Eat! Eat!"

158. Isn't losing weight rapidly dangerous for elderly people?

On the contrary, elderly overweights should take off excess pounds as quickly as possible, since time is shortened for them and the dangers of imminent sickness, disability and death from overweight is greater.

159. Should one eat less upon growing older?

Generally, yes, since elderly persons have a much lower metabolism, usually are less active and, as a result, less food is required; also, because burdensome overweight is even more of a menace to the organs and physique. Your body metabolism decreases 1 percent each year after age 25. By age 65, your body metabolism is about 40 percent lower, so you must lower your food intake a little each year or you'll gain weight.

160. Do you recommend that an overweight smoker give up cigarettes and go on a diet at the same time?

Do one or the other, but few people have the will power to cut down on smoking and eating at the same time without excess strain: I recommend that the heavy smoker get down to ideal weight, then give up cigarettes, since the person with the better chance for vigorous, lasting health is the slim non-smoker.

161. Why do people usually gain weight when they give up smoking?

The smoker usually seeks to satisfy his oral (mouth) desires, so that when he gives up cigarettes, he seeks a substitute in sweets and rich foods that he keeps stuffing into his mouth; also, heavy smoking tends to dull the sense of taste and has some fat-inhibiting effect on the system.

162. Is there any particular time when it's more undesirable to smoke in relation to putting on weight?

Don't smoke a cigarette directly after a meal or during the meal, as it induces increased absorption of fat and tends to increase weight.

163. Should I be concerned about high-cholesterol foods and those high in polyunsaturated fats?

Let your doctor check and advise whether you have a high-cholesterol or a low-cholesterol problem. My quick weight loss diets automatically reduce intake of animal fats and high-fat dairy products, usually much healthier eating for anyone.

164. Should I use "reducing drugs" when dieting?

Only use such drugs on the advice of your physician; he has available many worthy drugs and will prescribe them if he thinks they are indicated in your case.

165. Aren't "natural health foods" better for a person?

It bears repeating, since so many people are fooled, that "natural health foods" sold in stores and by mail are usually far more costly and have no superior qualities for sutaining health and life than the usual natural, processed or concentrated foods found on regular supermarket shelves.

166. Is there any way to reduce just by exercising more?

Some exercising is recommended when reducing and always, but no matter how much you exercise, if you're taking in more calories daily than your body is using up, you'll pile up fat deposits and gain weight—as an example, you'd have to run energetically for almost an hour to get rid of the calories piled on by eating an ‌age slice of chocolate layer cake.

A famous statesman said "Remember this also, and be well persuaded of its truth: The future is not in the hands of Fate, but in ours." Another advised, "The future is a world limited by ourselves." There is much in your future that you cannot control due to external circumstances and forces. But one part of the future that is in your own hands, nobody else's, is your better appearance, health and happiness as affected by your overweight.

On these pages you have the instructions that can work for you to help make you as slim and attractive as you can possibly be. You have the precise details on how to take off pounds and inches so that you need never be obese or "unpleasingly plump" again. Now you are fully aware of the terrible health hazards of overweight, the stupidity and emptiness of false fears about taking off fat, and knowledge of the wonderful benefits that you can achieve.

I know from 45 years of medical practice that inside most every unhappy fat person there is a slim, healthier, happier individual wanting to get out. You *can* reduce by my quick weight loss and inches-off methods, as hundreds of thousands have done successfully, no matter how many times you may have failed before. "Instant weight loss" right from the first dieting day, and lasting slimness, can be yours. It's up to you. I assure you that your loss in pounds and inches will be my gain in pleasure ... for helping to make overweights into slimmer, healthier, happier individuals is my personal lifelong crusade.

Your success will be my reward.

Dell Bestsellers